# Gray Phantoms of the Cape Fear

ALSO BY DAWSON CARR

*The Cape Hatteras Lighthouse: Sentinel of the Shoals*

# *Gray Phantoms* of the Cape Fear

RUNNING THE CIVIL WAR BLOCKADE

*Dawson Carr*

John F. Blair, Publisher Winston-Salem, North Carolina

Printed in the United States of America

Front cover photos:
**Top:** The *Ella and Annie.*
**Bottom:** The *Eolus* captures the blockade runner *Lady Sterling* as she attempts to leave Wilmington.
(Both photos courtesy of U. S. Naval Historical Center)

Design by Liza Langrall

The paper in this book meets the guidelines
for permanence and durability of the
Committee on Production Guidelines for
Book Longevity of the Council on Library Resources.

Library of Congress Cataloging-in-Publication Data:
Carr, Dawson.
Gray phantoms of the Cape Fear : running the
Civil War blockade / Dawson Carr.
p. cm.
Includes bibliographical references and index.
ISBN 0-89587-213-7 (alk. paper)
1. Blockade—North Carolina—Cape Fear River—History—
19th century. 2. Cape Fear River (N.C.)—History, Naval—
19th century. 3. Wilmington (N.C.)—History—19th century.
4. North Carolina—History—Civil War, 1861–1865—Naval operations.
5. United States—History—Civil War, 1861–1865—Naval operations.
I. Title.
F262.C2C37 1998
973.7'3'0975627—dc21 98-21315

*To my parents,*

Leo Dawson Carr *and* Carita Horne Carr

# CONTENTS

Acknowledgments —ix

Prologue —1

Chapter 1 *The Blockade* —5

Chapter 2 *Defending the Cape Fear* —41

Chapter 3 *Bermuda and Nassau: Friendly Ports* —67

Chapter 4 *The British Influence* —89

Chapter 5 *Wilmington: Center of the Storm* —125

Chapter 6 *North Carolina Takes a Role* —153

Chapter 7 *Closing the Gateway* —185

Epilogue —207

Appendix *Sample Cargo of a Confederate-Owned Blockade Runner* —214

Bibliography —216

Index —221

# ACKNOWLEDGMENTS

A BOOK IS almost never written single-handedly. Dozens of people contribute to bringing a story into print, and I want to thank those who gave generously of their time and knowledge to help me.

First of all, I thank the staff of the Sandhills Community College Library. Their help in obtaining rare books and manuscripts through the interlibrary-loan system was invaluable. I especially appreciate the patience and able assistance of Joy Mercer, who labored faithfully to help me find necessary sources and never chided me when I needed the material longer than expected.

Beverly Tetterton and Joe Shepard of the North Carolina Collection at the New Hanover County Library in Wilmington made my research productive and enjoyable. Their bookshelves and file cabinets hold a rich store of North Carolina history, especially of Wilmington and the coastal region.

John M. Coski and Terri Hudgins of the Museum of the Confederacy in Richmond, Virginia, provided photos of blockade runners and helped me locate rare copies of cargo lists for ships that docked at Wilmington during the Civil War.

Richard Lawrence, Mark Wilde-Ramsing, and Barbara Brooks of the Office of State Underwater Archaeology, North Carolina Division of Archives and History, took time from their busy schedules to help me locate details of the designs of blockade runners and their engines.

Connie Mason of the North Carolina Maritime Museum in Beaufort and Mary Strickland of the Southport Maritime Museum provided contacts for obtaining information on Cape Fear River pilots. Mary treated me to a view of rare, original copies of John Maffitt's charts of the Cape Fear region, drawn when he was a United States naval officer stationed there before the Civil War.

Gehrig Spencer, site specialist at Fort Fisher, generously stayed after working hours to share his knowledge of the fort and the battle to capture it. His descriptions of the locations and armaments of the other fortresses built near Cape Fear during the war provided details that would have been difficult to find elsewhere.

The Duke University Special Collections Library provided me considerable information; Elizabeth Dunn, women's studies reference archivist, was instrumental in helping me obtain facts on Rose O'Neal Greenhow.

The North Carolina Collection and the Southern Historical Collection, both housed in the Wilson Library at the University of North Carolina, are excellent sources of historical information on North Carolina and the Civil War. The staffs there were very helpful to me.

The staff of the North Carolina Division of Archives and History provided access to maps from the Civil War years and to the letters of Governor Vance from the same period.

I am indebted to Wesley Loy, who allowed me to draw information from his treatise, "10 Rumford Place: Doing Confederate Business in Liverpool," which he wrote following a visit to England while a student at the University of Mississippi.

A special note of thanks goes to Robert and Elsie Aycock, who allowed me to use an excerpt from one of the letters in their privately published book, *The Civil War Letters of W. D. Carr of Duplin County, North Carolina.*

I appreciate the help given me by the staffs of the Library of Congress and the Naval Historical Foundation in my quest for appropriate illustrations to include in the book. I especially thank E. C. Finney, Jr., and Janice Smith of the Naval Historical Foundation.

I had the honor of interviewing descendants of two of the Smithville-based Civil War pilots. Joseph "Joe Sam" Loughlin and his wife, Eleanor, allowed me into their Southport home to hear stories from their family's history. John Julius Swain and his wife, Pauline, also of Southport, shared their family background with me as well. Joe Sam is a descendant of Thomas Washington Brinkman, pilot of the *Condor,* and John is the great-grandson of John Julius Dosher, pilot of the *North Heath.*

I needed help to decipher the mysteries of computers. Diane Innes of the Computer Engineering Department at Sandhills Community College helped set up my computer for word processing, and Shari Smith of the college's Writing Center patiently tutored me on the commands and capabilities of the program. My son Larry helped me out of many computer tangles and listened faithfully, often into the wee hours, as I tried to explain by phone the problems I had created.

Stephen Smith, professor of English at Sandhills Community College and columnist for the Southern Pines newspaper, *The Pilot,* gave me advice when I first became interested in writing this book. He later loaned me a laptop computer for use at various libraries, saving me many hours of scratching out notes on three-by-five cards.

I thank my friend Wayne Burris for reading the early draft of the manuscript and for his perceptive suggestions.

I am indebted to the staff of John F. Blair, Publisher, for without their help, there would be no book. I owe a debt of gratitude to Andrew Waters, who read my sample chapter and outline. I also appreciate the work of Liza Langrall, who fashioned the cover and handled the layout and design work, and Anne Holcomb and Molly Yarbrough for their help in publicity and sales. Most of all, I thank Carolyn Sakowski, who gave me a contract, and Steve Kirk, who worked diligently to help me put the rough manuscript into better form and proper order.

Lastly, I thank my wife, Bobbi, who encouraged me when I was down and understood when my writing prevented me from assuming my full share of the responsibilities of home and family.

# Gray Phantoms of the Cape Fear

# PROLOGUE

THE MOST DEADLY war in United States history continues to fascinate readers and scholars almost a century and a half after it ended. Perhaps no story among the countless episodes of heroism, suffering, and sacrifice by both sides during the Civil War is more amazing than the contest that evolved between the ships of the United States Navy and the blockade runners that sought to deliver cotton to Europe and bring armaments and supplies to the Confederacy in return.

The South had few weapons and virtually no factories to produce them. It was obliged to fight a well-armed Northern foe whose population outnumbered the Confederacy's by more than two to one. Aware of the South's weakness, President Abraham Lincoln established a blockade of the Southern coastal states to prevent the delivery of arms from outside sources. The Rebels immediately set out to challenge that blockade, for without imported arms and supplies, the Southern armies would have had no chance.

When Union forces brought New Orleans, Mobile, and Charleston under their heel early in the war, the burden of supplying General Lee's army fell on Wilmington, North Carolina, a small port town on the banks of the Cape Fear River about twenty-five miles inland from the Atlantic Ocean. In hopes of defending this vital port against Union invasion, the Rebels built a vast system of earthen fortifications along the river and on the beaches that bracketed Cape Fear. This powerful network of fortresses helped provide a haven for the hundreds of blockade runners that slipped through the screen of Union vessels offshore.

By the final years of the conflict, Southern war production had grown with surprising rapidity, and the Confederacy was able to supply nearly half the needs of its increasingly desperate armies. But nearly all the remaining products that fed, clothed, and armed the thinly stretched Rebel forces had to be brought in from Europe, and Wilmington was the major supply link. North Carolina's largest town thus found itself second only to Richmond in its importance to the Southern war effort.

The North moved to shut off the Cape Fear River by increasing the size and capability of the North Atlantic Blockading Squadron. Yet the flow of goods through Wilmington grew to enormous proportions, reaching its peak when the Union forces were the most able. In spite of an increasing rate of losses among the illicit traffickers, new ship designs, the use of camouflage, and stealth tactics assured the continuing flow of goods through the Yankee warships that surrounded Cape Fear in a ring of iron.

The daring and ingenuity of the officers and men of the blockade runners—a contingent that included private citizens and Confederate sailors—proved vital to the success of the slippery steamers. Without any defensive weapons and greatly outnumbered, the sleek ships entered and left Wilmington with what must have seemed frustrating regularity to the sailors of the North Atlantic Blockading Squadron. Moving through the dangerous waters around Cape Fear with muffled sidewheels, their shadowy forms barely visible, the silent blockade runners must have seemed more like apparitions in the mist than real ships. But their cargoes were indeed real and vital, and the risk of death or sinking from enemy gunfire was a fact of life.

In this book, I tell the story of the blockade runners and crews who dared to challenge the United States Navy and the dangerous waters of Cape Fear to reach Wilmington with their desperately needed cargoes. The chapters cover such topics as the Cape Fear defenses; the scene in Bermuda and Nassau, which were the jumping-off points for the Cape Fear blockade runners; and life in Wilmington during the blockade. Interspersed among these are true-life tales of blockade runners, their captains, their pilots, their crewmen, and the exciting chases and unusual predicaments in which they sometimes found themselves. I also portray some of the difficulties faced by the men of the United States Navy, who suffered months of shattering boredom aboard their gunboats and were constantly demoralized by the saucy blockade runners, which seemed to race by almost at will in spite of diligent efforts to stop them.

Chapter I

# THE BLOCKADE

"There is but little rest for a blockader, night or day; he must be wide awake and always ready, for, independent of any desire he may have to serve his country, his reputation, life, interest and all are at stake—reasons sufficient, one would suppose, to make him vigilant."

A. Ludlow Case,
*captain of the USS* Iroquois,
*North Atlantic Blockading Squadron*

# THE BLOCKADE

WIND WHISTLED THROUGH the rigging of the United States sloop of war *Jamestown,* causing the ship to roll and tug at her anchors just off New Inlet on the turbulent Cape Fear coast. A storm had begun the previous evening, and now, on Thursday morning, April 24, 1862, it was blowing with gale force from the northeast quadrant. Fearful that his ship would drag her anchors and be blown onto the sand bars of Frying Pan Shoals or forced aground near the bar at New Inlet, Captain Charles Green weighed anchor and headed into deeper water, leaving his station unguarded.

The *Jamestown,* one of four ships assigned to blockade the inlets to the Cape Fear River near Wilmington, North Carolina, was the only sailing craft in the group, which included the *Mount Vernon,* the *Monticello,* and the *Victoria.* In fact, the *Jamestown* was the only ship stationed at New Inlet as the second year of the Civil War began.

When the storm finally moderated, Captain Green ordered his ship back toward New Inlet. While still several miles from her station, she passed the *Mount Vernon,* whose crew indicated that they were low on coal and were headed to Beaufort, North Carolina, for resupply.

As Federal Point came into view, the crew of the *Jamestown* spotted a large sidewheeler in the inlet, surrounded by what appeared to be several smaller steamers. Suspecting that they were waiting to run the blockade, Captain Green moved his ship in as close as he dared, not wanting to get into the shallows or come within range of the Rebel batteries on shore.

Upon looking closer, he discovered that the largest vessel was grounded and that the others were tugs engaged in removing her cargo. Realizing the stranded ship had slipped into the inlet while the *Jamestown* was at sea, Captain Green believed he might still prevent the cargo from reaching Wilmington if he could destroy the vessel. Aware of the difficulty of attempting an assault from his slow-moving, deep-draft ship, Green tried to alert the steamers at Old Inlet by firing rockets and even a cannon, but he failed to get their attention. Since the wind had dropped to three knots, the officers of the *Jamestown* lowered their small cutter into the water and headed out across Frying Pan Shoals to bring the *Monticello* and the *Victoria* over to lead the attack.

It was Saturday morning before the *Monticello* finally reached the *Jamestown*, and she came alone, the *Victoria* having been sent to check a suspicious schooner she had spotted as she rounded the shoals. A full day had elapsed since the blockade runner had first been sighted, but the *Monticello* took the *Jamestown* in tow, and they headed for the inlet prepared to do battle. Unfortunately, the capricious northeast wind had risen again, straining the hawser linking the two ships and preventing the *Monticello* from making headway while towing the heavy *Jamestown*. Seeing the futility of their joint effort, Green signaled the *Monticello*'s captain, Lieutenant D. L. Braine, to cut his tow and carry out the attack alone.

Leaving the *Jamestown* to battle the wind on her own, the steamer headed toward the inlet. But as Captain Green watched the *Monticello*'s progress through his glass, he was surprised to see the ship turn around and head back in his direction. As the *Monticello* drew near, Lieutenant Braine informed Green that the grounded ship had been freed and had moved out of range into the river.

By this time, the *Victoria* had returned from her own unproductive chase, and Green had to request that she relieve the *Jamestown* temporarily, since he judged he must move out to sea again to escape the rising winds. The *Monticello* headed back to her station at Old Inlet, which had already been left open to enemy traffic for several hours.

Thus ended another frustrating attempt by the ships of the North

Atlantic Blockading Squadron to stop the hemorrhage of blockade runners through their thin line of defense during the early part of the Civil War. Equipped with insufficient numbers of vessels, most of them ill-designed for the mission, the men of the early blockade managed to capture only one of every fourteen runners at Cape Fear, in spite of their best efforts. Adding salt to their wounds, their vigilance was constantly questioned by officials in Washington, and courts of inquiry were demanded when the escape of blockade runners caught the public eye.

The navy's unpreparedness for war was partly the fault of President Abraham Lincoln, who believed until the very last moment that armed conflict with the rebelling states could be avoided. Only when Fort Sumter was attacked did he become determined to defeat the secessionists at all costs and return the Southern states to what he regarded as their proper place in the Union. He refused to recognize the Confederacy as a separate country and declared the rebellious states to be in insurrection. He then issued a call for troops to put down the revolt and set in motion a massive program to purchase and build what would become the world's largest navy.

Most Northerners felt the war would be short-lived. The agricultural center of the nation, the South had developed almost none of the heavy industry required to sustain armies in the field. The population of the Confederacy was less than half that of the North, and the South had no military schools of the caliber of West Point and Annapolis. It had practically no warships and owned just a handful of merchant vessels, mostly small craft suited only for use on rivers or sounds.

What troops might be conscripted from the farms of the Southern states would have few effective weapons except those that could be purchased from abroad. It seemed likely that the Federal army—reinforced by seventy-five thousand recruits—could subdue the rebellion with little trouble if the Rebels could be prevented from acquiring armaments. As a government faced with an internal uprising, the United States had the legal right to close the Southern ports and inhibit the shipment of arms to the insurrectionists, a move that would have been understood by Europeans in spite of their great need for imported cotton.

Lincoln met with his cabinet to discuss a way to choke off the South from the outside assistance it would need to survive. The plan involved separating the Western states from the South to keep food and supplies from reaching the Confederacy across the Mississippi River. It also involved cutting off the Southern ports from outside trade by blocking the entry and exit of ships. Called the "Anaconda Plan" by some, the scheme eventually led to the defeat of the South through its isolation and ultimate suffocation by the Union army and navy.

As part of his design for victory, on April 17, 1861, Lincoln proclaimed a blockade of the Southern ports, a move that confused just about everyone but delighted the Rebels immensely. England and France were unable to fathom Lincoln's purpose, since, under international maritime law, it was customary for a nation to *close* its own ports when attempting to put down an insurrection but to *blockade* those of a separate nation at war; it appeared, then, that Lincoln had erred in his use of the term *blockade.*

The Declaration of Paris had spelled out the criteria for coastal blockades in 1856, and most Europeans relied on this as a guide to the legality of attempts of one nation to block the ports of another. Although the United States had not signed the declaration, many on both sides of the Atlantic still deemed it the ultimate prescription for acceptable conduct among ships on the high seas. Lincoln's proclamation thus allowed the Europeans an opportunity to recognize the Confederate States of America as a nation separate from the United States and to trade with it as a neutral party.

Lincoln's action further bewildered the Europeans since, according to the declaration, a blockade was legal only if it could be effectively maintained. In April 1861, the United States had only about thirty ships to guard three thousand miles of shoreline, giving each vessel the impossible task of patrolling a hundred miles of enemy coast. On April 27, the president extended the blockade to include North Carolina and Virginia, adding another five hundred miles of inlet-riddled shoreline to the blockaders' chore.

The United States bent the rules further by not adhering uniformly to the policies for notifying ports and neutral ships of the existence of the blockade. It made questionable captures of vessels merely suspected

## *Wilkinson's Ruse Saves the* Giraffe

In addition to depleting the active fleet, the constant flow of traffic from the duty station at Cape Fear to the depot at Beaufort, North Carolina, aided the Rebels in ways the Yankees did not consider. The escape of the *Giraffe* early in the war shows the ingenuity that often allowed blockade runners to elude capture.

Three days out of Nassau, the *Giraffe* churned her way through the telltale ripples that revealed the edge of the northerly flowing Gulf Stream. The giant sidewheeler was wrapped in curtains of rain and mist and covered by low-hanging clouds as gray as the blockade runner herself. But the overcast also concealed the morning sun, preventing any possibility of taking a reading to confirm the ship's location. Lieutenant John Wilkinson, delivering the ship to Wilmington for the Confederate government, would have to rely on dead reckoning for much of the remainder of the voyage.

Wilkinson understood that his inability to confirm the *Giraffe*'s location might put her far off course. The strong flow of the Gulf Stream had the power to push a ship miles off track.

Gale-force winds buffeted the steamer and choppy waters slammed against her hull, causing the *Giraffe* to shudder from stem to stern. By midday, she emerged on the landward side of the Gulf Stream just as the weather began to clear. Hastening to put his sextant into action, Wilkinson took a quick sighting. As he had feared, the *Giraffe* had strayed from her course—by almost fifty miles!

Once across the Gulf Stream, the *Giraffe* left the outer ring of blockaders behind, the ones Wilkinson feared the most. She then moved into the territory patrolled by the coastal gunboats, which lacked the speed of the deepwater cruisers but whose numbers made detection more likely. Despite the *Giraffe*'s precarious position so far from her intended landfall, Wilkinson dreaded turning back to face the fast Union ships plying the open seas more than trying his luck against the coastal gunboats.

The *Giraffe* was so far north that she found herself on the edge of the dangerous Lookout Shoals. And she was also near the shipping lanes that the vessels of the blockading squadron traveled between Beaufort and Cape Fear. The Wilmington blockaders kept up a steady flow of traffic in the region, as ships came to replenish their coal at Beaufort and supply vessels maintained a relay between the base and vessels on patrol. It would be nearly impossible for the blockade runner to move toward Cape Fear without being spotted. It looked as if the Confederacy's new ship would never reach port to begin a career of running the blockade.

Wilkinson considered his dilemma and decided that his best shot would be in pretending to be just another Union supply vessel. It was a ruse with some justification, for the Yankees usually turned captured blockade runners into ships of the squadron. The best and fastest were assigned to blockading duty, but even slower vessels were utilized as mailboats and supply ships. A significant part of the Union fleet consisted of recently confiscated blockade runners, many still in their original paint and with only their flags showing them to be part of the United States Navy.

Wilkinson ordered the Stars and Stripes hoisted at the mast, and the *Giraffe* turned toward Beaufort to join the broken line of vessels headed in the same direction. The crew slowed her speed to less than that of her unsuspecting companions, since Wilkinson did not really want to get to Beaufort. Thus, the *Giraffe* gradually fell far behind the others. When a warship came within a couple of miles of her, the crew of the blockade runner saluted the enemy with a dip of their flag and received a similar courtesy in response.

Before long, the sea was empty except for the *Giraffe*, and the crew pointed her prow toward New Inlet. Steam whistled from her pipes, and her wheels began to spin rapidly, thrashing the water into froth. The bow lifted and the stern settled, sending the blockade runner surging forward in the manner a civilian passenger once likened to "a horse preparing for a great leap."

From that point, no other blockader got close to the *Giraffe*, although Lieutenant Edward Hooker of the USS *Victoria*, patrolling off Cape Fear, reported sighting a strange steamer at about that time on the day in question, Sunday afternoon, December 28, 1862. Hooker described the vessel as a dark-colored, two-masted steamer with two rakish stacks. He said she was moving very fast and quickly left his own vessel astern. Hooker surmised that she must have been one of the squadron's own ships. Within a short time, all he could see was a faint wisp of smoke. He was probably the last Yankee to see the *Giraffe*, which docked unscathed in Wilmington on Monday, December 29. She was turned over to Confederate authorities and rechristened the *Robert E. Lee*.

Lieutenant Wilkinson would go on to command the *Robert E. Lee* on a number of successful runs to and from Wilmington. The ruse he employed in making his vessel a temporary Union supply ship was only one of the many he used to avoid the Federal ships that sought to lay hands on one of the Confederacy's most popular blockade runners.

of violating the blockade, though some of these were later released and damages paid to the owners.

Secretary of the Navy Gideon Welles realized the United States fleet would have difficulty stopping shipments into and out of Southern ports if his ships were to adhere precisely to Lincoln's proclamation. He therefore asked the president to issue an additional proclamation closing the ports. Congress enacted legislation in August 1861 giving the president the authority to close the ports.

Even then, some actions taken by ships of the blockading squadron were of questionable legality. The requirement to warn suspicious ships—mandated by the Declaration of Paris—was frequently ignored except by some captains who, if close enough, would command, "Heave to, or I'll sink you," more to save the ship for the prize courts than in strict obedience of the rules. Medicines that should have been exempt from control were treated as contraband, forcing many Rebel soldiers to suffer the fevers of malaria without quinine and, worse, the pain of amputation without anesthesia.

As a nonsignatory of the Declaration of Paris, the United States made its own decisions regarding the actions of the blockading squadron, rather than adhering to laws laid down by Europeans. Still, the Americans wanted European support for their actions, and they operated as closely as possible within the framework of international maritime law in dealing with ships of neutral countries. The principal objection the United States had to the Declaration of Paris was the rule that eliminated privateering, a right the Americans wanted to continue. However, when Jefferson Davis encouraged Southern privateers to attack the Northern merchant fleet, Union officials accused the Rebel raiders of piracy and were ready to accept the Declaration of Paris.

Leaders in Washington realized that naval warfare was changing and that winning the war would require new strategies to meet unprecedented challenges. The Civil War brought new technologies that would forever alter war at sea, mandating revised policies. The rights of ships at sea were open to new interpretations.

Within two weeks of Lincoln's proclamations, Secretary of the Navy Welles authorized the formation of two blockading squadrons, one to guard the Gulf coast and the other the Atlantic shore from Key West to Chesapeake Bay. Rather than sending his ships cruising ineffectively up and down the coast, Welles concentrated his fleet at the major Southern ports. Of these, New Orleans was the largest and busiest, but there were a handful of others along the Gulf of Mexico and a few along the coasts of Georgia, South Carolina, and North Carolina. It was these few points that he would surround with his blockading ships. The Atlantic Blockading Squadron was ordered to seal the ports of Savannah, Georgia; Port Royal and Charleston in South Carolina; Wilmington, Beaufort, and Morehead City in North Carolina; and Norfolk, Virginia.

Admiral David Farragut captured New Orleans in April 1862, costing the South its best site for running the blockade. Although it would be two more years before he moved his fleet against Mobile, Alabama, attempts at running the blockade from ports in the Gulf were hampered by the loss of New Orleans.

Norfolk had the railroad links and the deep harbor to make it an ideal center of commerce for the Confederacy, and its proximity to General Lee's army meant it was well suited for transporting goods through the blockade. Unfortunately, its only access to the Atlantic passed through the Hampton Roads area, the United States Navy's own backyard, and there was little chance that ships could elude the formidable gathering of Federal ships anchored in Chesapeake Bay.

The capture of Forts Hatteras and Clark on North Carolina's Outer Banks in August 1861, followed by the loss of Fort Macon in April 1862, gave the Federals control of the only two inlets to Morehead City, eliminating it from any role in running the blockade.

Union control of Port Royal and the South's failure to develop Savannah's potential as a blockade-running port meant no trade of any consequence would take place through Georgia.

Until the middle of 1863, Charleston was the dominant seaport for trade between the Confederacy and Europe. The main offices of John Fraser and Company, a powerful and well-respected firm with strong European connections, were located in Charleston and contributed mightily to import and export traffic through that city. But by the end of 1863, the increasing strength of Union naval forces around Charleston and the capture of some strategic land-based defenses gave the Federals control over the entrances to Charleston Harbor. The shuttling of goods through the blockade slowed to a trickle.

After Charleston was eliminated as a major blockade-running port, Wilmington fell heir to the task of maintaining the flow of goods that would keep the Confederacy in the war. Fortunately for the South, although the small town had been a port of secondary importance before the war, it had all the requisites for growing into a larger role.

The town had a prewar population of fewer than ten thousand residents, including slaves. It was located on the banks of the Cape Fear River, whose brown, muddy waters emptied into the Atlantic about twenty-five miles downstream. The silt-laden river widened threefold after passing Wilmington and had been dumping its sediment over a large area around its mouth for centuries, forming several square miles of treacherous reefs. These sand bars were known as Frying Pan Shoals, the deadly southern tip of the "Graveyard of the Atlantic." The dread they inspired gave Cape Fear its name.

Wilmington's proximity to Bermuda and Nassau added to its geographical advantage; those two intermediate stop-offs for ships bringing contraband to the South from England were less than seven hundred miles away. Fast runners could reach Wilmington in just three days from Nassau and four days from Bermuda. Both locations were under British rule, making exchange of cotton for munitions possible without interference.

Wilmington was served by two major roads and three railroads, which radiated outward like a fan across the state. Distribution routes were a prime necessity for a port, since goods brought to the South were of little value unless they could be quickly transported to areas of need. Likewise, cotton raised in the South had to be carried to the docks for shipment if it was to be a valid medium of exchange for European goods. The Wilmington and Weldon Railroad led almost directly north from Wilmington to Virginia, making it an effective conduit to Lee's army. And the Cape Fear River was navigable by small riverboats as far north as Fayetteville, offering another route to the interior of the state.

All of these features combined to make Wilmington a haven for blockade runners throughout the war and the key Southern port during the last year and a half of the conflict. By the waning months, Wilmington was virtually the only port receiving the foreign supplies needed by the increasingly desperate South. The successful runs of blockade runners into and out of the Cape Fear River kept the Confederate armies in provisions long after hope for victory had faded.

The early years of the blockade saw many failures. Secretary of the Navy Welles appointed Silas S. Stringham to command the Atlantic Blockading Squadron. The demands on Stringham were exacting, and the support he received from his superiors was negligible. The Atlantic Blockading Squadron suffered frequent humiliation as a result of the ridiculously small number of vessels and the unreasonable expectations of government officials. Officers were assigned a motley collection of improvised gunboats to stop the flood of blockade runners, then ended up scapegoats for the poor planning and lack of understanding of men like Secretary of State William Seward.

Welles had informed Stringham that there would be "some irregularity" with his ships because of the "hasty manner" in which men and vessels had been assembled. But Stringham could hardly have expected the situation to be as bad as it was. Even on his flagship, the USS *Minnesota,* Stringham complained of an inadequate crew, including a fleet surgeon who had been seasick throughout his ten years of service and an assistant surgeon who had never been to sea.

Lack of enough men to serve on the blockading ships would plague the squadron until the last stages of the war, when the navy grew to nearly sixty thousand men aboard more than six hundred ships. Draftees were given an opportunity to serve in the branch of the military they preferred, and many chose the navy as the least hazardous and easiest way to meet their obligation. Still, most of those inducted in this fashion were farmers and non-nautical types who had no training at sea and little aptitude for the occupation. Such men did not adapt well to the boring isolation of months on the water and were prone to jump ship when in port, even though minie balls sometimes whizzed by their ears as they ran. Crews were occasionally reinforced by escaped slaves who were persuaded to enlist.

On the rare occasions when a blockade runner was captured, it was necessary to place a skeleton crew on board to guard the original crew and to sail the ship back to a Northern port for adjudication by the prize courts. This left the undermanned blockaders that remained on station in an even more deficient condition. Sickness further reduced manpower.

When ordered to take the USS *Iron Age* to blockading duty, Lieutenant Commander Edward E. Stone complained of the many problems he faced in trying to run his ship. One fireman, two seamen, two coal heavers, and three landsmen had been sent to the hospital; two firemen, one seaman, one coal heaver, and six landsmen had jumped ship; one fireman had been discharged; and one landsman was awaiting court-martial.

Almost three months of war passed before the navy finally sent a force to blockade Wilmington. Even then, in July 1861, it sent only one small steamer, the *Daylight,* to guard two inlets that were fifty miles apart by sea. The *Daylight* was sneered at by local residents,

## *A Dark Passage for the* Don

After the lighthouses along the North Carolina coast were extinguished by order of the governor, the difficulty of finding one's bearings around Cape Fear intensified for both runners and blockaders. Even the excellent Wilmington and Smithville pilots had trouble finding the inlets on dark nights, for there were few landmarks of sufficient height to give crews any certainty about their location as their fast-moving ships wove their way through the shallow waters. The mound battery at Fort Fisher, sixty feet tall, was almost like a lighthouse. Its huge hulk could be discerned against the skyline even on moonless nights. Eventually, a signal light for incoming blockade runners was placed at the apex of the mound battery. It then became much easier to find New Inlet.

After the loss of the Union vessel *Peterhoff* in a collision in the darkened waters of Cape Fear, followed by a collision between the USS *Mystic* and the USS *State of Georgia*, Admiral Samuel Phillips Lee ordered the blockading squadron's flagship anchored at a fixed location two miles from the river. Lee wanted a light hung from the foremast, which would serve as the squadron's guide to navigation.

Pleased to have this additional marker, blockade runners quickly took advantage of the known location of the flagship to help them find their way to the inlet. When the Yankees discovered the misuse of their light station, they hurriedly revised their scheme and began to change the location of the flagship every night. At that point, the crews of the blockade runners were left again to rely on the mound light.

The following is an account of one blockade runner lucky enough to be able to use both Confederate and Union aids to navigation.

The *Don* was fresh off the slips of noted shipbuilders John and William Dudgeon of London and under the command of Captain Augustus Charles Hobart-Hampden. A man of many aliases,

Hobart-Hampden was perhaps best known as "Captain Roberts." He was on leave from the Royal Navy and wanted to try his luck at running the blockade, both for profit and for fun. He and his hand-selected officers and crew, also on furlough from the Royal Navy, were eager to challenge the United States Navy.

By the time she sat rocking gently under the rhythmic swells in the snug harbor at St. George's, Bermuda, in anticipation of her upcoming voyage to Wilmington, the twin-screw, four-hundred-ton steamer had undergone a major transformation. Her two masts had been removed and replaced by short, slender poles without cross spars; these were barely visible except for the small crow's-nest on the foremast, where a lone lookout would stand. The lifeboats, lowered almost to the deck, were concealed by the slight gunwales, which also served to shield the forecastle and quarterdeck. The single telescoping smokestack was compressed to its lowest reach, and the hull was covered with a coat of light gray paint.

The men had received half their generous pay in advance, as was customary. Smokeless coal was stored below, and the cargo was placed on board and secured for fast running. By the third week of August 1863, the *Don* was primed and ready to go. She weighed anchor at daybreak and steamed slowly out of the harbor, leaving the blue waters of the subtropical island for the deeper-hued depths of the Atlantic.

Daylight of the second day revealed a large United States cruiser lurking nearby. She spotted the *Don* at once and turned in her direction. At a distance of a half-mile, well within range of her big guns, the ship commenced firing at the blockade runner. The *Don* was aided by the wind and the futile efforts of the enemy captain to veer his ship from side to side to bring more guns to bear. She soon pulled away from the erratically falling shells. Within four hours, only a faint haze of smoke on the horizon marked the position of the blockader. Soon, even that faded from view.

By late afternoon, other ships began to pop into view. The frequent calls from the *Don*'s crow's-nest kept the crew hopping to avoid further detection. By now, they had traveled nearly two-thirds of the seven-hundred-mile route to Wilmington, and they anticipated frequent contact with blockaders the rest of the way.

Nightfall brought welcome relief from the constant fear of being spotted. The crew aimed their ship westward in the hope of being near New Inlet by the next night.

Relaxing confidently and contemplating a pleasant stay in Wilmington, where he would spend a week celebrating and resting before heading back into danger, Captain Roberts was jolted from his reverie by the sounds of shouting from close off the port side. To his dismay, he saw an enemy ship riding just yards from his own vessel. The shouts were from the blockader's commander, who demanded that the *Don* surrender or be sunk. Shocked that an enemy gunboat had approached without being seen and had her guns aimed at the *Don* from point-blank range, Captain Roberts sang out that he was indeed stopping.

His mind raced as the blockader's boats moved toward the *Don*, the men aboard the small cutters laughing about the easy capture. As soon as he heard the sound of the wooden skiffs striking the metal hull of the *Don*, he called down the tube to the engine room for full speed ahead. Before the rattled men on the skiffs and the enemy steamer could collect their wits, the *Don* zipped away into the darkness. The move was so sudden and unexpected that not a shot was fired in her wake.

Humiliated by the trickery, the Union blockaders decided that in the future, they would shoot first and hail later.

Another day of watching and evasive maneuvers brought the blockade runner within a few dozen miles of New Inlet. As dusk faded into night, Captain Roberts slowed the *Don* to consider the situation. A beehive of enemy ships awaited him ahead in the darkness. The shallows would offer an additional challenge. He decided that the best tactic would be to wait until complete darkness, then to plow right through the blockaders at full speed.

Every light on board was extinguished, and the masts were lowered all the way to the deck. No one was allowed to smoke, for fear that the slight glow of the ashes would give away the ship's position. The darkness was so complete that a sailor could barely see his hand in front of his face. On the other hand, the thick gloom also concealed the landmarks the men aboard the *Don* needed to help them make safe passage into the inlet. Feeling their way at high speed in the blackness soon had their adrenalin flowing. Everyone peered anxiously ahead, their eyes straining to penetrate the night.

The light wind and choppy seas covered the slight sounds of the *Don*'s engines and screws, and she passed right by several blockaders at top speed without being detected. Just when it seemed she might make it, the bare outline of a steamer moved into view directly in her path. Hurriedly reversing one engine, the captain was able to slue his vessel around 180 degrees and come to a complete halt almost within a ship's length of the enemy. He and his crew waited for the Federals to move on. They had been within seconds of plowing headlong into a blockader.

The blockader glided slowly by and was swallowed by the darkness, leaving Captain Roberts to turn once more and head toward where he believed New Inlet lay. A few casts of the lead warned him that the *Don* was close to shore, so he directed that she move ahead at almost dead slow until he could determine the exact bearing.

Suddenly, the men on the *Don* spotted the dim glow of a mast lantern and the faint outline of the stationary Union flagship. They had been informed of the enemy's practice of anchoring this ship as a beacon, and they were soon able to use her to determine their course.

Other blockading ships were in the vicinity of the anchored flagship. As soon as the crew of the *Don* saw a gap widen between the motionless vessel and the closest gunboat, the captain ordered full speed ahead, and the blockade runner darted through the narrow passage without being spotted.

Though they were now inside the inner ring of blockaders, the men of the *Don* were still not safe, for they were unable to see the inlet. Within minutes, though, the pilot made out the dark image of the mound battery of Fort Fisher. The *Don*'s crew flashed a small light toward land, carefully concealing its glow from the enemy. A light flickered to life at the top of the mound, and another pair of lights flashed from the beach. By steering a course that brought those two lights into alignment, the crew found their way into the inlet.

The *Don* glided smoothly into the river and under the guns of Fort Fisher. Safe at last, the men lit their lanterns and raised a toast to melt the tension that had held them in its grip for four days and nights. If the English officers and crew sought adventure and excitement, they had found plenty waiting for them at Cape Fear.

who threatened to "put daylight through her" with gunfire.

Taking their station off New Inlet on July 13, the crew of the *Daylight* noticed a ship moving swiftly out of Old Inlet. They headed the *Daylight* around Frying Pan Shoals to make an interception and possible capture. As they rounded the shoals, they saw they were too slow to catch the small steamer. As they happened to glance back toward Federal Point, they saw several vessels dashing brazenly out to sea through the now-unguarded New Inlet. The frustrated men of the blockader recognized the impossibility of blocking two such widely spaced inlets with just one vessel, a lesson that their superiors would be slow to learn. Within two weeks, the *Daylight* developed mechanical difficulties and was forced to return to Hampton Roads, leaving Wilmington completely open again.

The frequent gales and rough seas in the Cape Fear region and the demands made on the engines by constant patrolling and chasing placed great stress on the blockading ships, making breakdowns common. A list of problems among the vessels at Wilmington during just one month later in the war included a broken pump aboard the *Maratanza,* leaking boilers on the *Chocura* that almost extinguished her fires, and worn-out boilers, broken stay bolts, and a leaking hull on the *Dacotah.* The *Cambridge* was forced back to Hampton Roads in such a serious state of deterioration that she could barely remain afloat in bad weather because of the poor condition of her boilers and machinery.

Sailing ships were not exempt, as boards in their decks and sides were sprung by the force of the sea. Hulls needed frequent scraping, and vessels lost anchors with alarming regularity.

On one occasion, Lieutenant Commander Joseph E. De Haven of

USS *Daylight*
The first Union ship sent to blockade Wilmington was ridiculed by the Rebels but remained on duty with the North Atlantic Blockading Squadron until the end of the war.

WATERCOLOR BY ERIK HEYL. COURTESY OF THE U. S. NAVAL HISTORICAL CENTER.

the USS *Penobscot* begged the senior officer of the Wilmington group, Captain B. F. Sands, for permission to return his ship to port for repairs. He said her eleven-inch Dahlgren gun was completely disabled. Among the *Penobscot*'s other ailments were open cracks in the deck. The gaps were so large that when it rained, deck-scrubbing sand caught in the cracks mixed with rainwater and poured in a gritty stream onto the men sleeping below, collecting in deep pools on the floor beneath their hammocks. The galley had been condemned for three months, leaving the cooks without proper means for preparing food. A collision with another blockader had damaged the head, making the toilet facilities insufficient for the crew. And the ship's timbers had buckled and split in a grounding accident eight months earlier, causing the *Penobscot* to become unseaworthy in bad weather.

The ships' need to make frequent returns to port for rations and supplies kept them away from their stations for significant periods. Steamers burned coal at a rate of at least ten tons per day, which quickly depleted their maximum load of about a hundred tons. Until supply ships began delivering provisions and fuel to the blockaders, the problem of resupplying the squadron significantly reduced the number of vessels actively blockading the inlets. And since steam engineering was a new science, mechanical breakdowns were routine. Until Beaufort was captured in April 1862, ships needing repairs or resupply were forced to travel to Hampton Roads or even farther north, which required at least a week's round trip from Cape Fear. This kept the blockading fleet continually depleted.

When the Union gained possession of Beaufort and converted it into a logistics depot, it reduced the time vessels had to be away from Cape Fear by half, which dramatically increased the number of ships on hand to guard the inlets. Yet as late as 1864, between 30 and 40 percent of the ships in the blockading squadron were away for repairs or resupply at any given time.

As runners eluded the blockade at Cape Fear in the early stages of the war, Secretary Welles received reports from individuals loyal to the Union who were concerned over the number of vessels seen at Wilmington's docks. He contacted Stringham on August 10, 1861, about the embarrassment this brought on the Department of the Navy.

Although the fault lay more with the government for setting a blockade without the ships to carry it out than with any dereliction of duty by Stringham, the blame fell on Stringham as commander.

Only a week later, Welles cautioned Stringham to warn ships rather than capture them, since the ports were blockaded and not closed. This frustrated the flag officer even more. In September, Stringham complained that eight of the twenty-three ships available to the Atlantic Blockading Squadron were either in repair docks or were loading provisions. Only the *Cumberland*, the sailing bark *Gemsbok*, and the auxiliary cruiser *Young Rover*—reportedly so weak that she couldn't steam against the wind—were assigned to Wilmington. On September 18, as a result of continual complaints about the laxity of the blockade, Stringham resigned.

Upon Stringham's departure, Welles decided to split the Atlantic Blockading Squadron into two groups. After October 1861, the ships guarding the ports of Virginia and North Carolina were called the North Atlantic Blockading Squadron, and the vessels on blockade duty from South Carolina to Florida were called the South Atlantic Blockading Squadron. Welles appointed Captain Louis M. Goldsborough to command the northern squadron and Captain Samuel F. DuPont to head the southern squadron.

Goldsborough immediately requested a loosening of the guidelines for capture. He wanted to grab any vessels with contraband goods headed for any blockaded port. He also wanted to take any ships that cleared any of those ports if their papers showed they had been warned by another blockading vessel. Goldsborough attempted to organize supply operations for his ships and ordered that no more than one ship at a time could leave for coaling.

In March 1862, the *Thomas L. Wragg* (formerly the *Nashville*) entered and left Beaufort, sailing casually through a cordon of Union gunboats. In April, the former commerce raider entered Wilmington through the blockade. In spite of great vigilance, she then escaped Wilmington, all of which created considerable dismay in the Department of the Navy. Inquiries were held, but little blame could be placed except on the general inadequacy of the blockade. Three months later, the *Kate* eluded the blockade to enter Wilmington. A few weeks after that, she slipped back out to sea, still untouched. Courts of inquiry followed, but no one on the blockading ships could even admit to having seen the *Kate* on her entry or exit.

A disagreement with Secretary Welles led Goldsborough to submit a request to be relieved of command as flag officer of the North Atlantic Blockading Squadron on July 15, 1862. He was replaced by Acting Rear Admiral Samuel Phillips Lee in September.

At the time of the *Thomas L. Wragg*'s foray into and out of Wilmington, only five ships were stationed at Cape Fear. By July, when the *Kate* eluded the blockade, ten ships were assigned to guard the Cape Fear River inlets. In August, Commander William A. Parker of the USS *Cambridge* at New Inlet still bemoaned the lack of a sufficient force to blockade Wilmington, stating that some of the steamers were slow, that others needed repairs, and that at least one was unseaworthy. He made an insightful suggestion by recommending the assignment of a coaling ship to the region.

Shortly after taking command, Lee confirmed Parker's assessment, stating that there were actually only seven serviceable vessels off Wilmington. In October, he wrote his commanders that he had heard that Wilmington was being referred to as an "open port," a rumor he denounced as "a reproach to the blockade."

Late in 1862, United States consuls in England reported that several steamers were under construction there for the apparent purpose of running the blockade, which caused Lee to press for additional ships to strengthen the forces around Cape Fear and to call for increased vigilance from the blockaders.

Though he expressed mortification at the enemy's success, Captain B. F. Sands of the USS *Dacotah* did not think the crews could be any more vigilant. He reported that officers were always on the bridge and that lookouts stood constantly alert on the bows, the gangways, and every high point on the blockaders, day and night. The officers never went to bed at night and remained fully dressed and ready for action even when napping during daylight. After remaining at anchor and sleeping in the day, the crews pushed their ships as close as possible toward the inlets at night, each with an assigned area to watch. Still, there were not enough ships to close the gaps between them to less than a mile,

# *The* Little Hattie *Humbles the Yankees*

An increasing capture rate and a growing fleet of new and faster vessels gave Union sailors confidence that they would at last be able to stem the tide of ships bringing supplies to the Rebel armies. But they soon learned that this was not the case. The speed and stealth of the blockade runners and the fact that their crews could choose the time and place of entry gave them an edge. Even the weather seemed to favor the Rebels in the stormy waters off Cape Fear. The chase of the *Little Hattie* by the USS *Pequot* is but one example of the amazing escapes that continued to stymie the best efforts of the blockaders.

The *Pequot* encountered a cold headwind as she cruised along the calm, glassy Atlantic just off Masonboro Inlet. During the last hours before daybreak, Lieutenant Daniel L. Braine had tried to be especially vigilant, since many blockade runners liked to slip through in the wee hours before dawn, when there was no moon and lookouts might be dozing. His new commander, David Porter, who had replaced Admiral Lee as head of the North Atlantic Blockading Squadron just the month before, was a no-nonsense leader who expected action and had little tolerance for excuses when ships escaped the blockade of Wilmington.

Now that night had faded, the chance of encountering a blockade runner was less likely. It was November 1864, and eleven ships—including the *Pequot*—were assigned to New Inlet at Cape Fear. Another sixteen encircled the Western Bar. The Union navy finally stood a good chance of screening the area from the persistent blockade runners.

It was almost eight o'clock and full daylight when the exhausted commander began to think of breakfast. He made one last scrutiny of the shoreline, where the beaches were a slender, wavering strand in the hazy distance. Suddenly, Braine thought he detected a patch of white moving across the nearly white background. Although the *Pequot* was only a little more than a mile from land, he could not be sure of what he had seen. He decided to take a closer look and ordered the ship into action.

Close inshore, the blockade runner *Little Hattie* was slipping quickly through the waters near the surf line. Pilot Ron Grissom probed the shallow water with careful eyes, attempting to avoid hidden reefs that might ground his ship and cost him his bonus as well as his freedom. The crew had misjudged their time of arrival from Nassau, reaching the coast thirty miles above New Inlet too late for a nighttime entry. To compensate, they were running their engines at high revolutions. The sidewheels propelled the ship through the shallows at almost fifteen knots.

Captain Henry S. Leffy of the *Little Hattie* gazed eastward and was alarmed to see a thick pall of smoke. A closer look showed it to be emanating from a steamer headed his way. Because of the heavy smoke and the ship's course, Leffy did not think it was another blockade runner. He calmly urged the pilot to move the *Little Hattie* as quickly as possible toward the inlet.

Grissom did not need a second look to know they were being trailed by a blockader of the United States Navy. The crewmen of the *Little Hattie* were encouraged to extract every possible knot from the straining engines. The streamlined vessel sprinted ahead, her bow lifting with the added speed.

On board the *Pequot*, Braine could now clearly see a long, low-slung steamship with two stacks, painted nearly white from bow to stern. He ordered a shot fired across the bow of the speeding vessel. When the only response from the target was a further burst of acceleration, he knew he was in pursuit of a blockade runner. It was unusual that a runner would be brazen enough to try and sneak by in the daytime.

Braine knew that the cruisers of the New Inlet blockading flotilla waited ahead and felt there was no way the prey could escape. He called for full canvas. With steam engines running wide open, he hoped to close on the blockade runner or to force her into the waiting ring of gunboats. He ordered the production of black smoke from the boilers and fired several rockets to alert the other blockading ships of the enemy's approach. He also fired several rounds at the *Little Hattie*, not so much expecting to hit her as to further warn his comrades aboard the blockaders.

The commanders of the other ships understood at once that the warnings signaled the approach of a blockade runner, but try as they might, they were unable to discern a ship in the direction indicated by the rockets. The crews of the blockaders had been preparing to discontinue their patrols and head back to their anchorage far from the guns of Fort Fisher, but they now focused their attention on New Inlet, gazing intently along the track an incoming ship would follow to enter the Cape Fear River. They saw nothing in the misty air.

Braine watched the other ships through his glass but saw no efforts by any of them to intercept the speeding blockade runner. Frustrated at their lack of cooperation, he fired additional rockets and continued to discharge his cannon. In the meantime, the *Little Hattie* had almost reached Fort Fisher, and the pursuing *Pequot* had come within range of the batteries located north of the main fortress. The weapons at those sand ramparts opened fire on Braine's ship, the shells splashing into the sea close about the *Pequot* or whining overhead and ripping through the sails.

By now, the other blockaders knew something was definitely headed their way. They began to move toward what seemed to be the prey but unfortunately mistook the *Pequot* for the blockade runner. Moving to head off a fast-approaching steamer that was under full sail, they were mystified when the Rebel batteries started firing at her.

When Braine saw the blockaders approaching him aggressively while the runner was making good her escape within plain sight, he quickly displayed the United States flag to prevent being fired on by his own ships.

At long last—and before Braine could open fire on his fellow blockaders, which he was probably contemplating—a crewman aboard the USS *Howquah* spotted the *Little Hattie* just as she entered New Inlet. While he and his mates watched helplessly, she scooted into the inlet. Within minutes, only her stacks and rigging could be seen above the dunes.

To the mortified sailors of the New Inlet blockading fleet, it seemed impossible that a ship could have passed them unseen and unscathed less than a mile away in broad daylight when they had been fully warned of her coming. To Braine, it was a lesson in the value of boldness and a notification that the blockade of Wilmington was far from airtight.

and it was almost impossible to see or hear a steamer passing at much less than half that distance.

In a risky maneuver designed to slow the escape of blockade runners, captains started ordering their small boats to be launched at night, manned by squads of men who sailed or rowed almost into the inlets, where they waited in the darkness for vessels to appear. If they spotted a blockade runner, they were to fire rockets in the direction of her course to alert their ship of her movement, in hopes of heading her off.

On one such venture, Acting Master William Earle and a small crew of men from the *Dacotah* anchored their picket boat in eight feet of water just off the Western Bar at Old Inlet around nine o'clock on a moonless February night in 1863. After an hour of fruitless waiting, they steered their craft across the channel and anchored again, still in shallow water. High tide came around midnight. They moved back across the channel and dropped anchor to sit in wait just a quarter-mile from Fort Caswell, which was only vaguely visible in the gloom.

After almost seven hours of crouching and shivering in the cramped confines of the narrow boat, they saw a small light twinkling on the eastern horizon. As the faint glimmer grew brighter, they realized it must be a steamer—one that was moving rapidly in their direction.

Suddenly aware that they were in danger of being run down, they raised anchor and rowed urgently toward shore. They were barely out of the steamer's path when she glided swiftly past, a gray giant measuring at least 250 feet from bow to stern, eerie in her silence as she swept by mere yards away. Except for the rocking of their boat from the speeding ship's wake, she might have been a shadow.

Remembering their mission, they hurriedly fired a rocket across the stern of the vessel, but the runner was moving so quickly that she was over the bar and into the river before their ship could take any measures to prevent it. The disgusted crew of the picket boat then signaled the *Dacotah* to cancel the call for action. The blockade runner, a low sidewheeler with two swept stacks, signaled to Fort Caswell, received a blinked message in return, and was gone. From first appearance to disappearance had taken less than five minutes.

Daybreak was near by the time the cold, exhausted sailors climbed back aboard the *Dacotah*. The blockade runner, probably the *Robert E. Lee* out of Bermuda, continued up the river to Wilmington and safety.

Rear Admiral Lee believed the use of small boats in the inlets was ineffective. In a communication to Captain Sands of the *Dacotah,* he stated that not only were the lightweight craft incapable of stopping a ship, but that there was considerable danger of their being run down as well. He also believed that sending in picket boats would tempt the men on the blockaders to lower their guard. He ordered Sands to continue maintaining a close-in presence at night, but to use picket steamers rather than dories.

Lee also complained to Captain A. Ludlow Case of the USS *Iroquois* regarding the spacing of the three vessels blockading the area east of New Inlet. Rather than having them stationed at one-mile intervals, he ordered that one steamer be used to watch the bar and the other two move in as close to the beach as possible.

At the end of March 1863, Lee reported that only one blockade runner of the eleven known to have attempted to reach Wilmington since December had been captured. It was clear to him that in order to avoid detection, the ships were approaching shore a few miles from the inlets, then running right along the beach, their gray camouflage blending perfectly into the shoreline, the noisy surf disguising the sound of their engines. In short order, they were under the guns of the Rebel batteries, where they were relatively immune from attack.

By placing steamers at the bar and as near the beach as possible along both sides of the inlet, he felt the blockaders were sure to catch the ships before they could reach safety. He ordered that each blockading vessel keep a tide table on deck, since runners were likely to choose high tide for their attempt to get over the bar at the inlet. Grouping the blockaders far from shore had been permitting the enemy to slip between them and the beach or to pass unseen among the widely spaced vessels. Lee hoped his new plan would eliminate many of the evasions.

He wrote Welles to request speedier vessels for his blockading force, stating that vigilance without speed was not enough to keep the enemy out of Wilmington. He expressed his conviction that only swift and well-armed steamers could hope to capture the fast, slippery blockade runners, and he advised Welles that unless he had more and better vessels, the blockade was doomed to failure.

When involved in a chase, steamers of both sides resorted to desperate measures to increase their speed. Blockade runners with cotton on board sometimes cast bales overboard not only to lighten their loads but also to impede the progress of the pursuing vessels. If the chasing ships were using sails as well as steam, the captains of the blockade runners turned into the wind; using steam alone, they were often capable of superior speed and were thus able to escape. When blockading ships seemed to be gaining, the crews of the runners sometimes threw turpentine-soaked cotton into the boiler fires, which provided the Rebel vessels sudden bursts of acceleration.

On March 1, 1863, the *Mount Vernon*, the *Cambridge*, and the *Daylight* joined in chasing a steamer in the vicinity of New Inlet. The long, low, pale gray sidewheeler with two rakishly swept stacks was first spotted around nine in the morning bearing northeast. Before the blockaders could close in, fog obscured the prey from view.

Anticipating that the ship would move shoreward, the three blockaders tried to position themselves to intercept her. When the sun burned the fog away, they spotted her a couple of miles distant. Raising all sails and pouring on full steam, they attempted to overtake their streamlined quarry. In a couple of hours, they thought they might be within

Confederate blockade runner *Armstrong*
Captured near Cape Fear in December 1864, she was one of the last ships to be taken before the fall of Fort Fisher.

COURTESY OF THE U. S. NAVAL HISTORICAL CENTER.

range. But firing their rifled cannon, they saw the shots plunge into the sea at least a half-mile shy of the target.

Around noon, the blockade runner turned into the wind, forcing the chasers to bring in their canvas. But the runner still could not elude their pursuit. After another hour and a half, during which neither side gained an advantage, the enemy suddenly seemed to pull away. As the blockaders followed, they saw several hundred barrels bobbing in the wake of the enemy. As the crew of the runner tossed more cargo overboard during the next hour, the distance between the ships continued to widen.

Aboard the closest ship, the crew of the *Mount Vernon* heaved half a barrel of pitch into their fires, causing dense, black smoke to gush from their stacks as the ship surged forward. When the flames subsided, they tossed in several barrels of condemned pork in a last-ditch attempt to overhaul their quarry, but in spite of their efforts, they gradually fell farther behind. By dark, they lost sight of the speeding blockade runner. Their only consolation was that the escape had cost that vessel half her cargo.

It had been a long, fruitless chase, and the engine of the *Mount Vernon* was groaning from the strain of the past hours. Raising the sails, the crew headed back for New Inlet, disappointed at the escape and frustrated with the inferiority of their ship.

But gradually, Rear Admiral Lee's efforts began to make a difference. With additional ships—some of them very fast—he was able to mount three layers of defense around the Cape Fear inlets. Small, fast steamers patrolled the shoreline after sundown; though within range of the Rebel guns, they were safe under the cover of darkness. Other ships ringed the inlets a few miles out. The really fast vessels were kept far outside to roam the Gulf Stream, some even roving as far as Bermuda, when the fleet grew large enough to spare them.

The crews of the blockaders learned to darken their ships at night, though it heightened the risk of collision and the danger of firing on their own vessels. On one occasion, the *Monticello* and the *Peterhoff* were both darkened when the *Monticello* saw the other steamer crossing her bow within a few feet. Before Captain Braine could even utter an order to change course, his ship plowed into the *Peterhoff*, rending the unfortunate vessel's hull severely. The damaged steamer sank so quickly that the crew barely had time to escape with their lives.

To prevent such accidents and to help the blockading ships maneuver in the dark, the Federals started placing one ship at anchor during the night, so a light placed on her mast could be used for navigational purposes. However, when Union officers discovered that blockade runners were using the ship for the same purpose, it became necessary to move the vessel to a new location each night.

By October 1863, the United States Navy was finally waking up to the difficulty of blockading Wilmington. Lee expressed a need for at least twenty steamers to effectively block Old Inlet and another ten for New Inlet. Of the twelve vessels under his command, he listed four as fast, four as having fair speed, and four as suitable only for watching. Five more ships soon arrived, four of which had very good speed. It was still not enough, but it marked a drastic improvement over the earlier blockading fleet.

As more ships continued to join Lee's squadron, the blockade began to have a telling effect on the runners. Between September 15 and October 21, 1863, the *Arabian* was chased ashore at New Inlet; the *Hebe,* the *Phantom,* the *Duoro,* and the *Venus* were all forced onto the beach above Fort Fisher; the *Elizabeth* grounded at Lockwoods Folly; and the *Juno* was captured. Although the *Venus* was reputed to be one of the fastest runners, the USS *Nansemond* proved too much for her and would have caught her if her captain had not run the harried vessel onto the beach.

Pleased with the quality of the *Niphon* and the *Nansemond* and their aggressive commanders, Captain Sands of the *Dacotah* said that if the blockade had a few more men and ships like those, it could put an end to the "nefarious British trade" and finally close Wilmington. Although an overly optimistic appraisal, it was a good indication of increasing morale among the blockaders.

During late October and early November, the North Atlantic Blockading Squadron made further inroads by snagging some of the Cape Fear's most notorious and capable blockade runners, including the heavily loaded *Ella and Annie.* Assistant Secretary of the Navy G. V. Cox congratulated Lee and his blockaders for their success and promised to send even more ships to help bottle up Wilmington.

The crews of blockading ships were anxious to acquire the precious cargo carried aboard the runners, for they could share in the enormous profits awarded by Northern prize courts. Because the faster chase ships stood to collect the most prize money, men on the slower vessels had to hope they could at least remain within signal distance of the capture in order to be eligible to share the rewards. Rivalry and bitterness sometimes resulted from the desire to take a Rebel ship.

On the night of November 4, 1863, the *Niphon* spotted a blockade runner approaching New Inlet and started chasing and firing at her. The *Howquah* also saw the ship and fired her guns, forcing the runner out to sea. After chasing the vessel all night, the *Niphon* and the *Howquah* were joined the next morning by the *Keystone State* and the *Nansemond.* While the chase was in progress, the *Fulton,* a troop ship from New Orleans, lumbered into the fray and fired her cannon at the retreating ship. With five armed blockaders on her tail, the harried runner *Margaret and Jessie* hove to and surrendered.

USS *Monticello*
Commanded by Lieutenant Daniel L. Braine, she was one of the first three blockade ships sent to guard Cape Fear and would still be on station at the war's end with a new captain, Lieutenant William B. Cushing. It was from the *Monticello* that Cushing made his abortive atempt to capture a Confederate general in Smithville.

DRAWING BY CLARY RAY. COURTESY OF THE U. S. NAVAL HISTORICAL CENTER.

The *Nansemond* approached the vessel, sent a boat over, raised her flag, and claimed the prize. An hour and a half later, the *Keystone State* arrived on the scene, and her commander demanded the right to take possession, since he was the senior officer within signal distance of the capture. The captain of the *Fulton* then came forward to claim that since his shot was the one that had caused the surrender, he had the right to take the prize. The reward was eventually awarded to the *Keystone State,* and the others only shared in the money received from the sale of the vessel and her cargo. The *Niphon* and the *Howquah* had been left so far behind in the chase that they were not in sight when the capture was made, so their men got nothing.

The monotony of shipboard life was lessened by dreams of receiving large prizes. Many of the blockade runners were valued as high as

$150,000, and their cargoes could be worth that much or more. Even though sales often brought figures much below the assessed value, men of the capturing vessels could still reap significant awards. Half the return from the sale of a confiscated ship and her cargo went to the Naval Pension Fund, but the other half was divided among the crews who made the capture or were within sight when the ship was taken. The captains and officers got the largest cuts, since the award was proportional to the regular pay scale. Still, even lowly deck hands sometimes earned more than they could make in five years at regular salary. During the conflict, almost $12 million was divided among the lucky crews of the blockading squadrons.

The captains of blockade runners frequently chose to ground their vessels if they could reach shore before being taken. This kept the Federals from converting the ships for use against other blockade runners, and it also eliminated the chance for prize money for the crews of the blockaders. No items were supposed to be taken by sailors who boarded stranded runners, but most captains turned a blind eye as their men confiscated whatever they wanted. As a result, there was often chaos among the boarders, who grabbed what they could before firing the vessel.

The loss of the grog ration was a serious blow to crewmen of the blockading ships. The boredom of cleaning decks, scraping metal, and training continuously was broken only by meals and a few hours of idle time. Fishing, reading, and playing cards were among the few enjoyments available. Alcohol was an avenue of release that many sailors sought. But once independent sources were added to the daily ration, drinking began to interfere with the performance of duties, so the official ration was eliminated by the navy. Private sources, however, continued to flourish, including the booty from blockade runners, most of which carried excellent brandy and wine among their cargo.

Mail always generated excitement, but delivery was intermittent and infrequent. Some of the men hoped for their ships to break down, because it meant a chance to go to port for a short leave or to receive mail from home. Although supply ships out of Beaufort brought mail on their sporadic visits, sailors joked that they would rather have their mail delivered out of Nassau or Bermuda by blockade runners, because they ran with greater regularity.

Long periods of blockading duty induced homesickness and a longing to get to shore. In a few cases, they inspired adventure. One enterprising officer, William B. Cushing, initiated forays that carried him and some of his men ashore, where they captured a few Rebels and returned them to their ship. In fact, Cushing tried to capture a Confederate general—and probably would have succeeded except that the officer was not at home. He later attacked several saltworks on the beaches, destroying the pans and scattering the workers. A trip up the Cape Fear in a small boat landed him on shore, where he cut the telegraph cable to Wilmington. Cushing's shore leaves were short but stimulating to both sides.

Interrupting the monotonous cruises were hits and occasional near misses from cannon fire from the Rebels on shore. Even when anchored more than four miles offshore, men on the Union gunboats were frequently startled by the sudden whistle of a shell fired from the highly accurate Whitworth rifles and even larger Blakely rifles. Since the projectiles traveled faster than sound, the roar of the cannon was not heard until the rifled bolts had already arrived. Sometimes, the first round hit the water within a hundred feet of a blockader, and others quickly followed, the distance between splash and ship decreasing at an alarming pace, leaving the vessel little time to move out of range. Several sailors were wounded or killed by the long-distance weapons. Union cruisers had to stay more than five miles from the Confederate strongholds on shore to avoid danger. The Parrot guns and Dahlgrens of the blockading ships could barely shoot farther than two miles, and even that depended on skipping the round shells across the water like rocks across a pond.

Bad weather added to the tribulations of the men of the North Atlantic Blockading Squadron. In winter, constant nor'easters battered the ships and their crews, and the cold air was made more penetrating by the strong winds that seemed to blow eternally across the choppy seas. In summer, there was no way to escape the heat, although the breezes did help. The men often wore straw hats to shield them from the sun, only to see the purpose of their headgear defeated by rays bouncing off the sea.

Of course, their suffering was nothing compared to that endured by army troops, who faced death daily on dusty or muddy fields, where grapeshot cut troops to ribbons and rifle fire and sword slashes left dead and wounded men scattered across the landscape. Yet the men on the blockaders fought a battle as important as that on land. Their sacrifices were real, and when death found them, it was no less final than for men on shore.

Chapter 2

# DEFENDING THE CAPE FEAR

"Every day this strong place is becoming stronger."

SAMUEL PHILLIPS LEE
*to Gideon Welles, May 10, 1863*

# DEFENDING THE CAPE FEAR

THE LATE-AFTERNOON SUN glinted off the Cape Fear River as Sergeant Frederick Dardingkiller scanned the waters of Old Inlet. Several times each day, he climbed to the top of the high masonry wall at the apex of the pentagon-shaped Fort Caswell to survey the choppy waters where the river met the Atlantic Ocean, more to assess the prospects of good fishing than to search for enemies.

It was April 16, 1861, and the United States was not yet at war with North Carolina, since the state had not decided to join the seven members of the Confederacy. The thirty-six-year-old fort was maintained by a skeleton crew of Sergeant Dardingkiller and two other soldiers. Dardingkiller's caretaker assignment was not difficult duty except for the boredom. He frequently sought relief from the monotony by fishing in the swirling surf in front of the fort, where he also collected fees from local fishermen who came over from nearby Smithville.

The only military action the fort had seen in years had come in January, when several members of the local militia had suddenly appeared wielding muskets and pistols, demanding that the fort be turned over to them. Fort Johnston, just across the river from Fort Caswell, had also been a target of the overly enthusiastic militia, whose minds had been clouded by the fiery rhetoric of secessionism. When North Carolina governor John Ellis heard of the illegal takeover, he worried about the dim view the United States government would take of the seizure and sent word for the volunteers to return the forts to their legal caretakers at once. Yielding to the governor's authority, the militiamen had released their prisoners and returned to their homes, leaving the slightly ruffled United States soldiers once more in control of the two forts.

Today, Dardingkiller was uneasy. Just three days earlier, South Carolina militiamen had fired on Fort Sumter and overwhelmed its small contingent of soldiers. Now, with the prospect of war close at hand, doubts about the future loomed large in the thoughts of North Carolinians. In nearby Wilmington and the small town of Smithville, located just two miles from the fort, heated debates were raging between those who wanted to join the rebellion and those loyal to the Union.

On April 15, President Lincoln had asked North Carolina to contribute two regiments in his call-up of seventy-five thousand troops to defeat the Confederate States, a request the governor had refused. Ellis knew his action was defiant, if not mutinous. Although North Carolina would not secede for another month, he decided to prepare the state for the conflict he knew would follow if North Carolina cast its lot with the Confederacy.

The forts that protected the state's few deepwater ports would be critical to North Carolina if war should come. With Fort Caswell and Fort Johnston practically unguarded, it seemed prudent to move on them before the United States could reinforce them with additional troops and weapons. If strengthened while still in Union hands, they could dominate Wilmington—the state's largest port city—and prevent North Carolina from bringing in the supplies needed to survive the war. In a preemptive move, Ellis ordered Colonel John N. Cantwell, commander of the Thirtieth North Carolina Regiment in Wilmington, to seize Fort Caswell and Fort Johnston at once.

Around four o'clock in the afternoon, as Sergeant Dardingkiller looked northward toward the Cape Fear River, he saw a steamer headed his way. Upon reaching Fort Johnston, it slowed to a halt and lowered several boats filled with armed men, who promptly rowed to shore and rushed into the fort. Some of the men soon returned to the small ship and, confirming the ordnance sergeant's fears, headed in his direction.

The vessel chugged across the narrow channel and dropped anchor near the rear of Fort Caswell. Several dozen men—who proved to be members of the Wilmington Light Infantry, the Wilmington Rifle Guards, and the German Volunteers—disembarked, charged into the fort, and demanded its surrender. Outnumbered, outgunned, and with no other recourse, the fort's keeper capitulated, bringing an abrupt end to his monotonous duty as well as his fishing.

The capture also ended the Union's possession of Fort Caswell and Fort Johnston for nearly the entire Civil War. It would be almost four years before United States soldiers again entered their ramparts.

Clearly, the United States had missed a golden opportunity, for the mouth of the Cape Fear River later became the most critical gateway of the Confederacy. Governor Ellis and the local militia had exercised a bloodless coup whose significance would equal or surpass many of the South's battlefield victories.

Even so, the potential of the forts was not obvious at the time of their confiscation. Fort Caswell was in a serious state of disrepair, its moats filled with sand and debris, the heavy barrels of its only two mounted cannon hanging precariously by rust-weakened iron bolts from crumbling wooden mounts. The weapons—if they could be called such—could not have been fired even had there been an available squad of trained men with the daring to try.

Fort Johnston was even worse. A dilapidated walled enclosure, it had been authorized by the North Carolina assembly in 1745 to protect the local colonists against Spanish incursions. It was designed to hold up to twenty cannon. Named after Governor Gabriel Johnston, a member of the commission appointed by the Lords Proprietors to oversee its construction, it was built of tapia, a concrete-like material made by mixing burnt oyster shells, crushed shells, and sand with water. Tapia was not known for its strength, and whenever one of the fort's cannon was fired, the concussion filled the air with choking clouds of dust, obscuring any view of the target. Muzzle blasts frequently caused chunks of the fort—and probably the confidence of its soldiers—to crumble away.

By the time Fort Johnston was finished around 1764, it was too late to serve against the Spanish but was just in time for the Revolutionary War. When the fort was about to be taken over by the colonists, the outgoing British spiked the guns, which led the disgruntled patriots to burn all the wooden buildings, leaving an empty shell of a fort.

North Carolina, in possession of the remains, tried to give them to the United States in 1794 under the condition that a new fort be constructed on the site, but the federal government showed little enthusiasm. Finally, in 1809, with a new threat from the British on the horizon, the fort was restored by Joseph Garner Swift, who, taking advantage of the abundance of oyster shells and sand, used more tapia to resurrect the disintegrating walls. The state, keeping its promise, ceded the fort to the United States.

Now, fifty years later, it was in the hands of North Carolina again.

Fort Caswell was more imposing, its masonry bulwarks rising like the walls of a medieval castle above its deep moat. Gloomy and massive, its empty gunports glaring out to sea, it dominated the eastern point of Oak Island. Built to protect the entrance to the Western Bar in the mouth of the Cape Fear River, it sat on a well-chosen site that ships had to pass to reach the port of Wilmington. Its high parapets made it easy for sentinels to spot an enemy from afar.

The fort had been authorized by the United States Congress in 1825. Construction had started in 1827 and continued for eleven years. When finally completed, the fort was named Fort Caswell in honor of Richard Caswell, the man elected as North Carolina's first governor after the Revolutionary War. The giant fortress cost nearly half a million dollars. It was built to house more than sixty guns capable of targeting ships, as well as an array of lesser weapons to repel assault by land. Its thick ramparts had ports designed to facilitate small-arms fire while offering maximum protection.

During the Civil War, Fort Caswell would prove a cornerstone of the defensive shield of forts and lesser batteries protecting Wilmington from naval assault and providing a sanctuary for blockade runners. But before it could hope to battle the ships of the United States Navy, it needed major renovations.

Other than Forts Johnston and Caswell and Fort Macon near Beaufort, there were virtually no significant fortifications along the North Carolina coast at the outbreak of the Civil War. Although the state moved hastily to develop Fort Hatteras and Fort Clark to protect the inlet between Hatteras and Ocracoke Islands on the Outer Banks, the Confederate government in Richmond ignored pleas for troops and weapons, and the small forts were attacked while construction was still incomplete. In August 1861, a combined naval and land operation led by Admiral Silas S. Stringham and General Benjamin Butler overwhelmed the small squads of poorly armed defenders, making Forts Hatteras and Clark the first two military installations in the state to fall to the Union. The defeat was a serious loss for North Carolina and the Confederacy. Fort Macon fell to Union forces within months, putting most of the state's northern coast under Federal control after only a year of war.

The failure to fortify and defend that region was a serious blunder by Confederate officials, for the Union conquests stymied blockade running from Beaufort and Morehead City, put a halt to the small steamers of the "Mosquito Fleet," which had used Pamlico Sound to attack United States commercial vessels, and gave land forces a foothold for harassing rail traffic between North Carolina and Virginia. Even more significant for the Union navy was the subsequent development of a coaling and supply station at Beaufort, which increased the time that ships of the blockading squadron were able to remain at Cape Fear.

After witnessing these disastrous losses, General William Henry Chase Whiting, who had been placed in command of the defenses of the Wilmington area in the spring of 1861, grew determined that his region would not suffer the same fate. He ordered a major buildup of fortifications throughout the Cape Fear.

Though the South at first had almost no large cannon suitable for coastal defense, more than a thousand excellent guns were left behind by Federal forces in their evacuation of Norfolk, and many found their way to North Carolina. Other guns—some of them the latest breechloaders with rifled barrels—were brought in from Europe through the blockade.

Early engagements in the war showed brick-and-mortar walls like those at Fort Caswell to be inadequate against the high-velocity shells of modern guns. Tapia walls like those of Fort Johnston were no better than eggshells. On the other hand, earthen ramparts like those erected

## *The* Venus *Provides a Show*

Blockade runners were sometimes spotted as they tried to slip through the inner ring of blockaders. A desperate attempt at escape almost always ensued. When that happened, the guns along the sea face of Fort Fisher, the two rifled cannon mounted atop the sixty-foot mound emplacement, and the Whitworth guns that could be shifted along the beach often meant the difference between capture and salvation.

On a warm September morning in 1863, the crew of a blockade runner that had arrived from Nassau during the night witnessed the effectiveness of the fort's firepower. As the ship lay at anchor just inside New Inlet and the crew relaxed in the shadow of Fort Fisher, the Sunday calm was shattered by the sound of cannon fire. Looking to the east, the men saw a blockade runner sprinting toward the inlet, pursued closely by a Federal gunboat. Other blockaders were converging on the racing ship to try to cut her off, firing wildly in her direction.

The iron sidewheeler *Venus* was one of the fastest ships trying the blockade, and all her speed was called for in her present plight. The ship had arrived too late for a nighttime entry, and when the crew found themselves in the midst of the blockaders in broad daylight, there was little alternative but to charge through at full throttle.

The crew of the anchored runner had a ringside view. They watched in amazement as Captain Charles Murray of the *Venus* stood atop a sidewheel box directing the ship as shells whistled all about him, some landing so close that spray from their impact with the ocean drenched him with water. Other near misses passed so close that crewmen ducked.

Aboard the USS *Nansemond*, following within a half-mile, Commander Roswell H. Lamsen felt sure he would either capture the ship or drive her ashore. His guns bracketed the runner as she swerved to reach the inlet, and there seemed little chance she could escape. Soon, it appeared that the captain of the *Venus* intended to drive his vessel ashore on Smith Island, just south of Fort Fisher. Lamsen watched as a boat was lowered over the side of the blockade runner in preparation for the crew's getaway. At that moment, either by fantastic marksmanship or pure luck, a shell from the *Nansemond*'s bow cannon struck the wooden dory and smashed it to splinters.

If the crew of the *Venus* had meant to ground their ship, the loss of their lifeboat destroyed any such hope and spurred them to even greater efforts to reach the river. Plowing ahead at nearly sixteen knots, the ship aimed straight for New Inlet regardless of the hot, accurate fire of the pursuers. Captain Murray continued to bare himself to the enemy fire, never flinching as the shells ripped through the rigging and raised geysers on all sides of his vessel.

Alerted by the cannon fire, the lookouts at Fort Fisher spotted the pursuit. Within minutes, the fort's gunners found the range of the *Nansemond*, peppering the sea around the fast-approaching blockader and forcing her to fall back in the chase. That was all the *Venus* needed. The slender steamer flashed across the rip and into the sanctuary of the Cape Fear River, her stacks still pouring smoke and her engine popping and groaning from the strain of the run.

The captain's bravery and the accurate fire from the fort's gun crews had saved the day for the blockade runner and her men. As the waves created by the *Venus*'s breakneck entry rocked the other blockade runner, the spectators aboard that vessel and the soldiers at the fort cheered the men for their narrow escape.

The *Venus*'s cargo of salt pork, bacon, coffee, sugar, and armaments was soon in the hands of Lee's Army of Northern Virginia.

On her very next trip into Wilmington, the *Venus* was destroyed by the enemy. The men of the *Nansemond* tasted sweet revenge, participating in that attack. But for one day in September 1863, at least, the blockade runner showed her heels to the best the Union navy had to offer, and the Yankees learned new respect for the weapons of Fort Fisher.

hastily by Rebels at Sewell's Point, Virginia, proved surprisingly resistant to projectiles. At Sewell's Point, the softly packed earth had absorbed much of the force of the projectiles thrown by the USS *Monticello.* And damaged ramparts at such fortifications were easily restored with bags and baskets of earth.

Thanks to these early experiences and an almost unlimited supply of sand along the North Carolina beaches, earthworks became the standard fortifications constructed near Wilmington and the Cape Fear River inlets.

General Whiting's determination to develop an effective defense for the Cape Fear led him to constantly badger leaders in Richmond for more troops, largely to no avail. He pleaded with local plantation owners to volunteer the services of some of their slaves to help with the preparation of defenses. Hundreds of slaves were eventually sent to Wilmington to work on the fortifications. Neither did Whiting spare his own troops from the backbreaking labor; when they were not engaged in military training, they spent much of their time hauling sand, leveling dunes, felling trees, and building ramparts. Whiting's force of more than two thousand workers gradually strengthened the existing fortifications and built dozens of additional batteries and small forts to augment the region's defenses.

Sand fortifications soon lined the beaches and both banks of the Cape Fear River, and the black snouts of cannon peered over almost every knoll between Wilmington and the sea. The old walls of Fort Johnston were torn down and replaced by earthen walls. Fort Caswell was reinforced with a deep layer of sand that added several feet to its height and thickness. Logs placed side by side against the inside walls held the sand in place and afforded additional strength, while a mat of saw-grass turf covered the outer walls for the same purpose. Bombproofs—thick earthen walls encased in a layer of large timbers and armored with iron rails—were raised to protect men and ammunition inside the forts. Cannon were placed between high earthen mounds that could defend against anything but a direct hit.

At Fort Johnston, half a dozen large guns overlooked the anchorage just inside the Western Bar. Fort Caswell's two sea walls were armed with an array of large-caliber weapons, including an Armstrong 150-

pounder and several Columbiads capable of hurling a nine- or ten-inch shell more than two miles. Both forts also had smaller weapons that could be used against land or sea assault.

Oak Island's firepower was increased by the guns of a small fort built a mile down the beach west of Fort Caswell. The angled wall of the little fort—named Fort Campbell—paralleled the ocean for about a hundred yards, then zigzagged across the dunes for another two hundred yards. The fort's Atlantic face held four ten-inch Columbiads and a hundred-pounder Brooke rifle. Each could fling heavy shells for two miles at any threatening ship. Halfway between Fort Campbell and Fort Caswell, a low revetment of sand called Battery Shaw was raised to screen a single nine-inch Columbiad. Its weapon brought the total number of large coastal defense guns along a one-mile stretch of Oak Island to almost two dozen.

When the first vessel of the Union blockade appeared off Oak Island in July 1861, the men aboard it saw the Rebel flag flying over Fort Caswell and counted at least fourteen mounted cannon and several field pieces available for action. It was enough firepower to keep them cautiously at a distance. Additional Rebel batteries under construction were visible a couple of miles away.

In the spring of 1863, a battery was placed on Smith Island, located on the eastern edge of the river's mouth a couple of miles south of Fort Caswell. The small triangle of sand and marsh was an ideal site for the emplacement of additional guns, since it bordered the river and the Atlantic at their juncture near Old Inlet.

The first battery of large weapons there was named Battery Holmes in honor of General Theophilus Holmes; in 1861, Holmes had been named to head the North Carolina Department of the Confederate army by President Jefferson Davis. When the walls continued to grow as more batteries were created, the structure was renamed Fort Holmes. Like other large fortifications at Cape Fear, Fort Holmes consisted of walls of packed sand, their interior faces reinforced by a layer of palmetto and oak logs. One wall ran parallel to the Atlantic and another stretched along the river, the two meeting in a point overlooking Old Inlet. A third wall joined these two in the rear, forming a large triangle.

Most of the fort's heavy guns were aimed toward the Atlantic, with the largest concentration near Old Inlet, where they could lay down a heavy cross fire with the weapons of Fort Caswell. Most of the cannon on Fort Holmes's Atlantic side were large coastal defense guns, including Columbiads and Brooke rifles. The rear wall held twenty-four- and thirty-two-pounders that could be fired toward land or sea.

Until they finally fell in 1865, Fort Caswell, Fort Johnston, Fort Campbell, and Fort Holmes kept the Union fleet at bay and provided safe haven to the blockade runners that crossed the Western Bar at Old Inlet.

Before 1761, Old Inlet was the only route between Wilmington and the sea. That year, the powerful winds and scouring seas of a major storm pounded the coast of southeastern North Carolina mercilessly for four days. Before the tempest was finally over, it ripped through the long, narrow peninsula that separated the Cape Fear River from the Atlantic, gouging a deep, wide trench that stretched from the river to the sea. The resulting trough divided the southern part of the isthmus, isolating Smith Island and forming a new, prominent tip on the truncated

Blockade runner *Fanny and Jenny*
Grounded near Masonboro Inlet in attempt to enter New Inlet
in February 1864, her famous captain, Louis Coxetter,
was drowned as the officers and crew made for shore.
The ship was left to be fired and destroyed by men of the USS *Florida.*

WATERCOLOR BY ERIK HEYL. COURTESY OF THE U. S. NAVAL HISTORICAL CENTER.

# *Whitworths Can't Save the* Fanny and Jenny

The attack on the *Fanny and Jenny* was typical of the battles waged between Rebel land forces and Yankee vessels when blockade runners were the stakes in the vital contest played out along North Carolina's shores.

On a cold night in February 1864, the storm-tossed Atlantic forced the notorious blockade runner *Fanny and Jenny* off course. Using only the ship's compass and dead reckoning, the pilot had hoped to approach New Inlet at a point two miles north of Fort Fisher. But now, as the vessel neared the beach, he was uncertain of the location and could barely distinguish the shoreline.

Luckily, the *Fanny and Jenny* had avoided contact with the ring of ships blockading the inlet, but now it was necessary to drop anchor in toward the rolling surf until the pilot could determine the proper heading. The crew would have to rely on the heavy darkness to hide them, just as it had on so many other trips during the past year when Captain Louis M. Coxetter brought in vital cargo for the Confederacy.

Before the pilot could get his bearings, the high waves forced the *Fanny and Jenny* nearer the beach and caused her iron hull to scrape noisily along the bottom, which startled the crew into action. Fearing the worst, the men worked frantically to get their vessel into deeper water, raising her anchor and pushing her powerful steam engine to its design limits in an attempt to get free of the sand bar. But although the engine could propel the streamlined ship at nearly fifteen knots in the open sea, it was no match for the power of the breakers, and the blockade runner continued to be forced toward shore. In spite of the sailors' desperate efforts to bring her about, the *Fanny and Jenny* bucked and rolled, thumping violently against the sea floor, her paddle wheels churning rapidly in the shallows. With a final shudder that shook the slender ship from stem to stern, she ground to a stop. All efforts to free her were unsuccessful.

The gray light of dawn left her naked to the ships of the Federal blockade. The crew of the USS *Florida* spotted her at once and approached to take possession of the unexpected windfall. Thrilled at the prospect of capturing the loaded ship intact, Captain Pierce Crosby ordered a towrope attached to the *Fanny and Jenny*.

It was not to be so easy, for before the exuberant sailors of the *Florida* could recover the beached blockade runner, a gun crew from Fort Fisher arrived on the shore, bringing a long-range, rifled Whitworth cannon with them. Their first shots ripped into the enemy ship, crashing through a paddle-wheel housing, smashing two of the arms of one of the wheels, and slicing through one of its rims. As other shells hit the *Florida*, threatening to sink her, the crew of the blockader finally managed to return fire to suppress the attack.

The sudden barrage alarmed the men aboard the *Fanny and Jenny*, who quickly lowered their boats in an attempt to escape to shore. The rough seas that had taken their ship now caught the lightweight boats and tossed them around like toys, drowning the famed Captain Coxetter. Called a pirate by Abraham Lincoln, Coxetter was one of the most outstanding blockade-running officers. His record included an amazing list of successful trips through the blockade and a victorious cruise on a Confederate commerce raider. It was a tragic loss. One other man was lost in the swirling waters, but about half the crew made it to shore. The rest were captured when the men of the *Florida* later boarded the grounded blockade runner.

Though the gun crew from Fort Fisher did not succeed in saving the *Fanny and Jenny*, they did enable some of the runner's sailors to make good their escape. And the damage they inflicted on the *Florida* prevented that vessel from towing the *Fanny and Jenny* away as a prize, perhaps to be used against other blockade runners in the future.

The *Fanny and Jenny* was abandoned, but a portion of her cargo was salvaged by the Rebels. She was left permanently grounded on the beach a few miles north of New Inlet.

peninsula. This tip became known as Federal Point. The channel between Smith Island and Federal Point constituted a new entrance to the Cape Fear River almost nine miles closer to Wilmington than the old inlet. It was wide and deep enough to allow the passage of medium-draft ships.

Surprisingly, the new inlet was boon to neither ships nor port. Since it was only deep enough to permit the entry of vessels drafting less than twelve feet, large schooners could not use it to reach Wilmington. Of greater concern was the impact it had on the depth of the original channel. Formerly, the swiftly flowing Cape Fear River had transported sand and debris well beyond the bar and out to sea, which kept the channel deep and clean. But the new opening slowed the river's flow, resulting in detritus being deposited in the river itself. By 1800, silting in the old channel made it difficult for ships of deep draft to cross the Western Bar.

Attempts to close New Inlet were in progress when the Civil War began, but the hostilities ended those efforts. Both sides made plans to dump stones in the inlet at the beginning of the war, but the schemes were meant to impede the movement of ships, not stop the flow of water. Nothing came of either attempt. That New Inlet remained open to ships throughout the war was fortunate for the Confederates, as the existence of two navigable inlets to Wilmington significantly increased the problems facing the blockading ships and greatly enhanced the success of runners carrying contraband goods to and from the state.

Although New Inlet and Old Inlet are only about nine miles apart as the crow flies, Smith Island projects into the Atlantic for several miles between them, and the vast web of sandy reefs that forms Frying Pan Shoals sprawls outward for another twelve miles. This large protrusion of land and shoals forced Civil War ships to travel a fifty-mile circuitous route to pass safely from one inlet to the other. And since a typical blockading ship could barely eke out ten knots, at least five hours were required for transit between the inlets. The problems presented to blockaders trying to close the port of Wilmington were considerable, especially in the early days, when there was frequently only one ship on picket duty at Cape Fear.

The availability of two inlets gave the blockade runners an edge in the competition with the Federal squadron, but obtaining full benefit from the second inlet would require fortifications as powerful as those emerging at Old Inlet.

At the beginning of the war, there were no fortifications at Federal Point. Only a lighthouse stood along the lonely, isolated beaches to mark the inlet. After North Carolina joined the Confederate States of America, locals began referring to Federal Point as Confederate Point.

In 1861, a few small batteries were constructed to protect the inlet. The largest structures were Battery Bolles and a rectangular enclosure known as Fort Fisher, which had emplacements for a few cannon.

Early that same year, William Lamb, a former newspaper editor and now a major in the Confederate army, was transferred from Virginia to Wilmington and assigned as chief quartermaster of the Cape Fear District. A native of Norfolk, Major Lamb had grown up in a sheltered environment, and his law-school and newspaper background belied an avid interest in military affairs. He was bright and energetic and had spent a great deal of time studying military fortifications. In fact, Lamb had seen firsthand how the earthen mounds at Sewell's Point had withstood the worst the enemy could produce.

When he was promoted from quartermaster to commander of Fort St. Phillip, a small fort midway between Wilmington and the Atlantic, Lamb saw a chance to explore his theories on the building of forts that could resist the fire of modern weapons.

He soon had dozens of men expanding the little fort by using sand and logs and adding gun emplacements. Sitting on the west bank of the Cape Fear River approximately fifteen miles north of Old Inlet, the fort overlooked a narrow point in the river, an excellent location for controlling the flow of ships up the channel. The improved installation, renamed Fort Anderson, grew into one of the most important fortifications in the Cape Fear region. Thanks to river obstructions lining the narrows and the stationing of a river gunboat across the stream, it could challenge any enemy vessel attempting to reach Wilmington.

Lamb's accomplishment in transforming the small earthen fortress into a major defensive work caught the attention of General Whiting and of General Samuel French, who had recently been assigned the responsibility for defending the Cape Fear region. Both men were looking for someone to reinforce the inadequate defenses at New Inlet. The scattered collection of revetments and guns there was too weak to pose a threat to ships of the blockading squadron, and blockade runners needed an umbrella of protection that would allow them to enter the inlet safely.

Major Lamb looked like the ideal officer to take charge of the project. He was promoted to the rank of colonel of the Thirty-sixth North Carolina Artillery and reassigned to Confederate Point.

When Colonel Lamb arrived at his new assignment on July 4, 1862, he found a smattering of batteries reinforced by sandbags and palmetto logs spaced at intervals of a hundred yards or more near the inlet and along the beach. Each battery contained only one or two guns, most of them obsolete. On Confederate Point itself, there was only one long-range gun that he judged fit for service—and it later exploded when fired at a blockading ship.

After a brief survey of the defenses at Confederate Point, Lamb concluded that the few guns and batteries lying scattered about the sand dunes were useless for protecting the inlet. So on the second day of his new duty, he began a series of improvements that would continue unabated until the end of the war. Long before the final assault brought it down, Fort Fisher had been turned into the largest and mightiest coastal fortress of the Confederacy. It was called "the Gibraltar of the South" by many who knew it.

As Lamb was directing work parties one day, he noticed a blockading ship anchored hardly more than a mile away, her sailors calmly watching the crews at work at Confederate Point. When Lamb asked if it was unusual for the enemy to come so close, his men responded negatively, saying the ship often harassed them by firing on them while they worked. He could hardly believe his ears when the soldiers stated they never fired at the ship unless the enemy fired first. He stated flatly that it would never happen again as long as he was in command. Lamb immediately ordered the crew of the best available cannon to open fire on the audacious Yankees. When the first shells whistled close across the bow of the blockader, her surprised crew hastily hoisted their anchor and moved out to sea.

As long as Fort Fisher stood, the ships of the blockading squadron never again approached within four miles except after dark or in hot pursuit of a blockade runner racing for the inlet.

Colonel Lamb knew the power of the guns of the United States Navy. He had all his men and several hundred slaves prepare sand walls with sloped faces covered with grass; he knew these could stand up to any assault. He discovered that logs of palmetto, known locally as cabbage trees, rotted quickly, so he eliminated them from the fort. He wanted only the strongest and most durable materials for his walls.

The Confederates built two lines of fortifications, one skirting the edge of the sea for a mile, the other extending a half-mile across the dunes from the river to the north end of the Atlantic wall, where they met at a right angle. Resembling a slender arm bent at the elbow, the fort had plenty of muscle in the numerous heavy cannon soon placed along the parapets of both walls. The revetments lining the beach held two dozen weapons, their muzzles barely visible over the top of the high sand wall. Comprised of large-bore Columbiads, several Brooke rifles, an Armstrong 130-pounder, and a superb 170-pounder Blakely rifle, the guns that eventually lined the Atlantic wall of Fort Fisher formed an iron gauntlet no individual blockade vessel was likely to challenge. The land face mounted an equal number of weapons, and there were a few large mortar emplacements in the interior.

The most prominent feature of the fort was the mound battery at the southern tip of the sea face. Connected to the rest of the fort by a protective wall called a "curtain," the mound was sixty feet high. Aboard the Union blockaders more than four miles at sea, men with telescopes watched in wonder as steam engines transported tons of sand to the top of the mound until it grew into a small mountain. Two guns were placed on top of the conical sand structure, where the unusual height gave the gun crews an excellent view of targets at sea—and stirred cautious respect among the sailors of the Union ships, who worried about the battery's ability to deliver fire downward onto their decks.

The mound was so prominent that blockade runners could spot it in the dark. A light was eventually placed at the top to flash coded signals to runners and to serve as a range light to help them find the inlet in misty conditions and darkness. The mound became a reassuring landmark to pilots and crews of blockade runners as they struggled to feel their way along the ragged shoreline, hoping to find New Inlet on moonless nights. They felt that once they could see the mound light, they were safely under Fort Fisher's guns.

Fort Fisher was manned by around sixteen hundred troops. Though this was twice the number of men stationed at Fort Caswell, it was not

Whitworth cannon
The British-made, rifled breechloader was pulled by horses to fixed positions along the beach. Its accurate fire and five-mile range kept the Union blockade ships wary of approaching shore, even when in pursuit of a blockade runner.

COURTESY OF THE LIBRARY OF CONGRESS.

## *The Destruction of the* Hebe

It was common practice for both sides to try to salvage the cargoes of stranded blockade runners even while under enemy fire. The shallow-draft steamers usually grounded so close to shore that Rebel soldiers were able to wade through the surf to reach them. And blockading ships launched small boats to carry out their own recovery efforts.

If Rebels retrieved armaments and drugs, the salvaged goods were turned over to the government. Likewise, if Yankees recovered military items, the spoils were sent to Northern prize courts for adjudication. But if expensive liquors or exotic foods were aboard a stranded vessel, it was every man for himself. Life at the fort or aboard the blockading ships waxed more zestful for days or weeks following such windfalls.

With each side trying to prevent the other's success, it was not uncommon for a ship to be utterly destroyed in the contest, at which time she joined the growing fleet of derelicts lying abandoned near the inlets to the Cape Fear River. If neither side was able to lay claim to the freight, the doomed vessel was bombarded with cannon fire until she burned or her hull was sufficiently pierced to allow seawater in to destroy the contents.

Such was the lot of the blockade runner *Hebe*, which was forced ashore ten miles north of Fort Fisher by the USS *Niphon* one night. The *Niphon* followed her in with the idea of towing the *Hebe* back to sea and then to Beaufort. But when the Federals' intent was discovered by the men at Fort Fisher, a Whitworth squad and a salvage crew were sent racing up the beach to fend off the enemy.

By the time the *Niphon*'s boats were dispatched toward the stranded runner, Rebel soldiers were already scrambling to bring cargo ashore. The Rebel gun crew aimed at the *Niphon* and opened fire, but sharpshooters from the Yankee gunboat managed to force a halt to the recovery efforts.

As the dories from the *Niphon* approached the *Hebe* in an attempt to secure a hawser for towing, two of the small boats sank in the heavy surf. Before the sailors could escape, fifteen of them were captured by Rebel soldiers, who rushed out through the surf and grabbed them.

A group of armed men from the *Niphon* then landed on the beach and rushed the Whitworth cannon. The Confederate artillerymen, overwhelmed by superior numbers, beat a hasty retreat to Fort Fisher, losing their priceless weapon to the enemy.

At that point, ready to call the battle a draw, the *Niphon* also withdrew. Fearing the arrival of reinforcements from Fort Fisher, and having already lost a large number of men, the captain thought discretion the best option.

Unable to take the *Hebe* as a prize or to recover any of her cargo, the frustrated crew of the *Niphon* opened fire on the hapless ship after moving farther offshore. With the Whitworth silenced, they were able to remain at close range. The *Niphon* was then joined by several other blockaders. Within a short period, the *Hebe* was punctured numerous times by fire. The deserted vessel was soon left a burning derelict.

enough to protect the fort from a major assault by land troops. When the fort was finally conquered, it was its lack of men that led to its downfall, not the vulnerability of its weapons or its structure.

Colonel Lamb organized a specially trained squad of soldiers armed with breechloading, rifled Whitworth cannon that had been brought from England and salvaged from the grounded blockade runner *Modern Greece.* Lamb maintained a cordial relationship with officers of the blockade runners, and he received other rifled weapons as gifts from the companies engaged in running the blockade. It was a small investment in the protection that Fort Fisher provided for ships that came under attack by Union gunboats.

When blockade runners grounded in the shallows and were attacked by blockading ships, or when they were hounded so closely that capture appeared imminent, the Whitworth gun crews, called "flying brigades," would hook their weapons to teams of horses and go wheeling across the dunes to predetermined sites, where they opened fire on the enemy from behind crescent-shaped walls of sand. They could slip quickly from one firing site to another to thwart any return fire from the Federal ships. Extremely accurate up to five miles, the British-built weapons generated respect and caution among Union sailors, who watched in alarm as the three-inch hexagonal shells unerringly found their mark. When Union vessels were driven from their blockade-running victims, it was usually the persistent fire of the Whitworth crews that forced them to withdraw.

Additional batteries were placed along the beaches to extend the radius of defense beyond the reaches of the fort. Battery Gatlin was located a few miles north of Fort Fisher, and Battery Buchanan was constructed at the edge of the inlet on the side near the river. The fort itself was defended by scattered rows of buried land mines designed to be fired from the fort in the event of land attack.

Although the United States discussed carrying out an attack against Fort Caswell and Smith Island, it was clear by late 1864 that the dominant power protecting Wilmington was at Fort Fisher. If Fort Fisher fell, the others would quickly follow.

Gunboats were stationed at various locations along the Cape Fear River to add their firepower to the river's defenses. The schooner *Arctic,* brought to North Carolina a few years before the war, was converted into a lightship and renamed *Frying Pan Shoals Lightship #8.* She was anchored on the outer edge of the shoals as a warning to ships until 1861. Once war commenced, Governor Ellis ordered all of North Carolina's lighthouses extinguished in an attempt to strike a blow at

*Opposite:* Civil War fortifications of the Cape Fear Coast. The multitude of earthwork fortresses and batteries that lined the Cape Fear River and its inlets shows why blockade runners were able to use this route until the Union captured Wilmington.

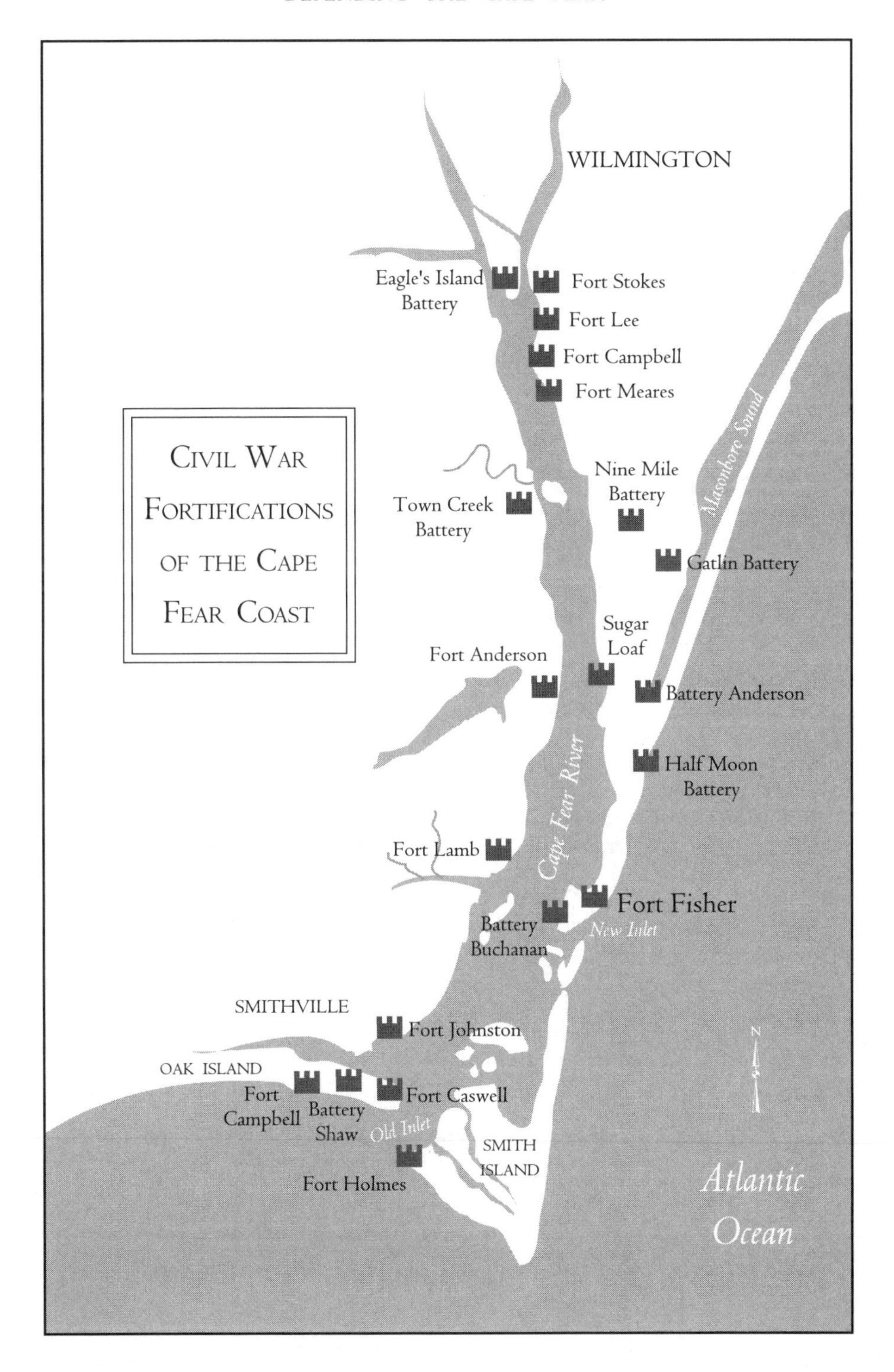
CIVIL WAR FORTIFICATIONS OF THE CAPE FEAR COAST
WILMINGTON
Eagle's Island Battery
Fort Stokes
Fort Lee
Fort Campbell
Fort Meares
Masonboro Sound
Nine Mile Battery
Town Creek Battery
Gatlin Battery
Sugar Loaf
Fort Anderson
Battery Anderson
Cape Fear River
Half Moon Battery
Fort Lamb
Fort Fisher
New Inlet
Battery Buchanan
SMITHVILLE
Fort Johnston
OAK ISLAND
Fort Campbell
Battery Shaw
Fort Caswell
Old Inlet
SMITH ISLAND
Fort Holmes
N
Atlantic Ocean

the United States Navy while imparting a negligible threat to the meager Southern fleet. As part of this exercise, *Frying Pan Shoals Lightship #8* was brought in over the Western Bar, armed with four cannon, and anchored at the narrows just across from Fort Anderson.

A large ironclad christened the CSS *North Carolina* was built in Wilmington and launched in 1864. The South did not have the means to produce enough steam engines for even its small number of vessels, so the new ironclad was fitted with an engine salvaged from the captured tugboat *Uncle Ben.*

Although underpowered, the ship was armored with iron rails all the way to the water line, much like the vaunted *Virginia.* She represented a dangerous threat to wooden-hulled ships, and men aboard the blockaders around Cape Fear followed her progress with trepidation. But when the *North Carolina* reached Old Inlet on her maiden voyage, her draft of fifteen feet was too great to allow her to pass over the bar, and the proud ship completed her service as a lowly river gunboat.

Ill-fated from the start, the *North Carolina* was soon denied even the role of a gunboat, for the armor plating that had been applied so diligently could not protect her against what proved to be her true enemy. As she lay at anchor in the salty water at the river's mouth, her wooden hull was penetrated not by the iron shells of the Union but by the small, soft bodies of teredo worms. In a short time, they chewed the pine bottom of the vessel into a wooden sieve, leaving her powerful coat of armor to settle harmlessly beneath the waves. But while she was afloat, the *North Carolina* was a force to be reckoned with and added to the ring of defenses that General Whiting forged around Cape Fear.

Another scheme designed to thwart Union invasion of the Cape Fear region was the placement of obstacles in the river. In a channel that was already narrow, winding, and shallow, the laying of mines, "torpedoes," and other obstructions would seriously hamper the progress of United States ships should they attempt to reach Wilmington. Sunken pilings, cribs of stone, and floating explosives were all used by Rebel forces to prevent the movement of enemy ships up the Cape Fear River. Metal cylinders filled with powder were anchored to float just beneath the surface, where they could be fired from crude electric batteries located on shore. Smaller powder charges called "torpedoes" were placed on the ends of poles ingeniously designed to be automatically raised or lowered with the tide; the charges would explode on contact if struck by a passing vessel.

Many of the obstructions were placed at curves and narrows in the river. The constricted passageway near Fort Anderson was heavily barricaded with obstructions, and a chain was stretched across the river to limit passage through the bottleneck. Ships stalled by the barricade would lie exposed to the fire of Fort Anderson and the guns of *Frying Pan Shoals Lightship #8*.

Uncertainty about the nature and extent of river obstructions kept Union naval leaders hesitant to invade throughout the war.

When hostilities began between the South and the North, neither was prepared to defend the Cape Fear. But by the end of the war, the Cape Fear coast and the river route to Wilmington were incredibly well defended. Although the South moved slowly, it also worked tirelessly in readying an array of fortifications unparalleled in the Confederacy.

The North continually failed to recognize the importance of Wilmington, allowing General Whiting and his men to proceed almost unimpeded in their efforts. Leaders in Washington did not appreciate the critical role the port city played in prolonging the conflict until the war supplies brought in by blockade runners finally caught their attention. Even when the Union did begin to understand the necessity of blockading the Cape Fear, it was slow to comprehend the magnitude of the force required to close the port. By the time the United States Blockade Strategy Board finally got around to sending enough ships to make a reasonable attempt at halting the movement of contraband into and out of North Carolina, its squadron was met by such an array of fortifications that it was unable to stanch the flow of elusive gray steamers slipping quietly in the dark of night.

Yet in the end, it was the Confederacy that failed to see that the course of the war hinged on the fate of Wilmington. Few troops were sent to protect the fortresses when many were needed.

# Chapter 3

# BERMUDA AND NASSAU: FRIENDLY PORTS

"I have undoubted information that
ten steamers are waiting at Nassau
to run into Wilmington, N.C.,
as soon as the nights are dark."

MAJOR GENERAL JOHN A. DIXON
*to Gideon Welles, December 2, 1863*

# BERMUDA AND NASSAU: FRIENDLY PORTS

THE RUGGEDLY HANDSOME Charles Wilkes had a talent for insolence. When the Civil War was barely six months old, he single-handedly offended the British almost to the point of their declaring war against the United States.

On a sunny November day in 1861, he boarded the inoffensive mail packet *Trent* in international waters in the Bahamas Channel. His contingent of marines held the crew and officers of the British vessel at gunpoint as he examined the passengers on board. Having been advised that two Confederate agents were on the small ship, he was quite pleased when they admitted their identity under his questioning.

Although the boarding fell within the rights of a belligerent nation to inspect neutral ships, Wilkes went farther. He removed the two Confederate emissaries and their secretaries virtually by the scruffs of their necks, without proof that they or the ship carried any illegal Southern contraband or dispatches. He then released the *Trent* to continue her voyage but transported the Southern representatives triumphantly to New York. There, he was hailed as a hero, for among his captives were James Murray Mason and John Slidell, hated men in the North. Wilkes had intercepted them on a mission to secure recognition of the Confederate States of America in Britain and France. Although there was little reason to expect they could do any better than the agents already striving to acquire recognition from Europe, their diplomatic skills were respected and feared.

The British were outraged. Ironically, this event placed the United States and Great Britain in a strange reversal of roles, since the Americans had long defended the rights of men on the high seas to be safe from impressment by foreign powers, an action freely engaged in by the English against American seamen until the War of 1812.

Secretary of State William Seward and the United States Congress praised Wilkes, but Gideon Welles was less impressed with the bold action. If incriminating documents had been found on the men or aboard the *Trent*, the arrest of Mason and Slidell might have been justifiable, but without evidence, there was no recourse but to release them.

Appeasing the English would require more than freeing the captives. On the other hand, the British were not anxious to fight the United States, having tried twice before. When they were informed that Wilkes had acted entirely on his own, it provided a subtle means of lessening tensions between the two countries. Although the United States assumed a belligerent attitude toward England throughout the war, the Union was not seeking another combatant, since the fight with the South occupied its full attention.

Wilkes was given a mild rebuke by Welles but was not reined in sufficiently to prevent his further adventures in international relations. In September 1862, he was assigned to command a roving armada of ships in the Gulf Blockading Squadron. His West India Squadron immediately began to pursue any and all ships that looked suspicious, capturing several and sending them to New York for disposition by the prize courts. His men also harassed a number of innocent British vessels, apparently determined to put a halt to blockade running at all costs.

Wilkes's aggressive and ruthless methods also got him in trouble with the British colonies in the Atlantic. Given the assignment to pursue and capture the Confederate raiders *Alabama* and *Florida* (formerly the *Oreto*), Wilkes seemed unable to find them. Although the two enemy ships were known to be operating in his region, he never saw either and spent a good portion of his time steaming around scouting for blockade runners instead. When he received word from Edward

Throwbridge, the United States consul in Barbados, that the *Florida* had been allowed to take on coal there after less than the legal ninety-day waiting period since coaling in Bermuda, he steamed into the harbor at Bridgetown, Barbados, stormed into Governor James Walker's office, and confronted him for his alleged violation of Britain's neutrality guidelines. Wilkes later admitted to Gideon Welles that he had "quite a row" with the governor. He also reported his suspicion that the governor of Barbados and the governor of the Bahamas were working in collusion with Captain John Maffitt of the *Florida* to "afford him [Maffitt] all facilities," in contradiction to the queen's rules.

Bitter about what he considered the unequal treatment of Southern and Northern ships in the harbors of Nassau on the island of New Providence in the Bahamas and St. George's on the island of Bermuda, he decided to show the island upstarts that they couldn't fool around with the United States Navy, and in particular with Charles Wilkes. He attempted to intimidate both the crews of blockade runners and colonial government officials by sending his ships into the harbors and keeping them there in spite of the "Twenty-four Hour Rule," which was designed to prevent belligerent vessels from remaining in port for more than a day. Wilkes also encouraged his ships to loiter in the channels around the islands, waiting for vessels carrying contraband for the South to emerge.

At the end of September, he cruised to Bermuda, where he ordered the *Tioga* into the harbor at St. George's for coal while he anchored there in the USS *Wachusett*. British regulations stipulated that no warship of either North or South could receive coal more often than every three months, and then only in sufficient quantity to reach the nearest port. Since the *Tioga* was eligible, she was granted permission to receive fuel by the island's governor, H. St. George Ord. Wilkes then asked the governor to allow the *Sonoma* in for repairs, although that vessel had been illegally anchored in the channel outside the harbor and had refused to leave even when ordered to do so by the British ship *Desperate*. The governor agreed, but only on the condition that the ship receive no coal and that she leave as soon as repairs were completed. Wilkes, his own twenty-four-hour limit expired, was also ordered to leave, but he claimed his ship had developed mechanical problems that would not allow him to go. In the meantime, he ordered that coal be placed on board the *Sonoma,* in spite of the governor's directive.

The governor immediately contacted Wilkes about the coaling violations but said that he would not apply the rules strictly at that point. However, he stated that he must "instruct" Wilkes that since the *Tioga* had received her limit of coal, she would not be permitted to return to the harbor.

Upon receiving the note, Wilkes became enraged. He fired off a lengthy response in which he questioned the governor's good sense and his veracity and pointed out what he called "peculiar expressions" in the governor's note. He was especially incensed by the use of the word *instruct,* saying that only his own government could instruct him, and that he could not permit the governor to instruct him about where the *Tioga* could or could not go. He closed his letter on an incongruous note ("With great consideration, I have the honor to be, sir, your most obedient servant") and signed it Charles Wilkes, acting rear admiral, United States West India Squadron.

Secretary of the Navy Welles received notification of the incident and tried to assuage the insult suffered by the governor, hoping to prevent further damage to relations between the United States and Bermuda. About two months later, Wilkes received a message from Welles indicating it would be "very desirable" if the rear admiral would keep his vessels out of British ports and if he would advise his officers to abide by the established regulations. Welles also suggested that if Wilkes had complaints about the treatment of his squadron in Bermuda or Nassau, such comments should be "communicated to the Department."

But Wilkes still had the independent spirit and dogged determination that had made him a noted explorer before the war. He continued to harass shipping in the region. Some of his vessels were accused of firing on suspected blockade runners within the territorial waters of the British island colonies. Stray shells reportedly damaged houses on shore and endangered the local population.

As the ships of the West India Squadron continued to hang around Nassau and St. George's just outside (and occasionally inside) the three-mile limit, ready to pounce on ships seeking to run the Northern blockade, it gave the islanders the feeling that the United States was blockading their ports as well as those of the Confederacy. In the early years of the war, when the majority of ships attempting to run the blockade embarked from Nassau, Union ships could be spotted at both ends of the Bahamas Channel, which stirred resentment among the residents. If there had not already been strong support for the Southern cause at Nassau and St. George's, the heavy-handed treatment by Wilkes and his subordinates would have generated it. But in fact, there was plenty of bias on behalf of the Confederacy.

For several years before the Civil War, England had been gradually slipping its bonds to the Bahamas. The cost of defending its wide-spread empire had forced Britain to make hard choices regarding the relative importance of its different colonies. Bermuda merited a few thousand troops, but Nassau did not. Along with these relaxed military ties came a decrease in commerce between England and the Bahamas, leaving the thirty thousand residents of New Providence Island in a financially depressed state.

Although they enjoyed some ongoing trade with the United States, the islanders received only minimal income from it. The Bahamians did not grow sugarcane, and the thin topsoil of their coral islands would not support other major agricultural products for export, which meant that they had to survive any way they could. That often meant fishing and salvaging in the clear blue water surrounding the coral reefs, where sea life and wrecks were plentiful.

Located just five hundred miles off the coast of the Confederacy, Nassau provided an excellent harbor for the transshipment of supplies between the Southern states and Europe. When the contraband trade began to flourish, Nassau was at the center of activity. The abundance of wealth that followed gave the residents even more reason to support the South.

Bermuda was hardly better off financially. Though it, too, was regarded as a stronghold of the South, Bermuda was a little slower to get involved in running the blockade. From the coast of North or South Carolina, it took at least a day longer to reach St. George's than it did to reach Nassau. This offered Union vessels more time to intercept blockade runners. It also meant that more coal—a scarce commodity—had to be burned to complete the trip.

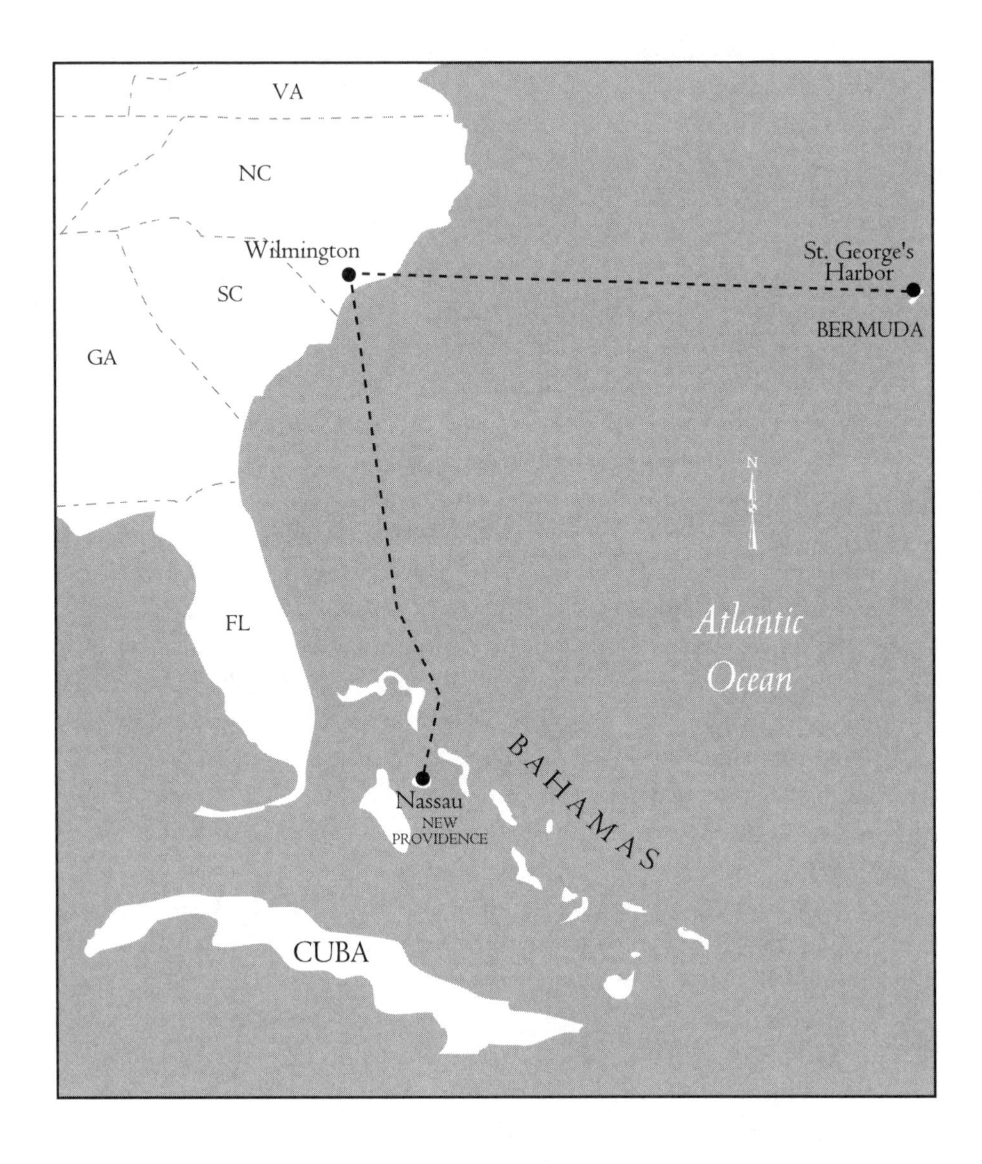


Paths followed by ships as they traveled between St. George's Harbor, Bermuda, or Nassau, New Providence, and Wilmington, North Carolina

The intermediate shipping points between Europe and North Carolina made transfer of supplies easier aboard the shallow-drafted small steamers that ran the blockade.

By 1862, ships from England were sailing to New York loaded with goods for the South, then departing New York Harbor ostensibly for Nassau. This permitted them to get supplies to the South by subterfuge, either sailing directly through the blockade or transferring their cargo to steamers at Nassau for a short hop to the coast.

When military officials in the United States realized the quantity of munitions and other war contraband being transported through their own ports to reach the Rebels, Secretary of State Samuel P. Chase took measures to halt the practice. Henceforth, any ship traveling from New York to Nassau would be required to post bond equal in value to its cargo and would have the bond refunded only upon reaching Nassau. Chase also forbade ships traveling the New York–Nassau route from transporting anthracite coal, the smokeless fuel so eagerly sought by blockade runners.

These regulations, which applied only to shipping between New York and Nassau, further alienated the Bahamians. It also stymied some of the legal Nassau trade. Those seeking to run the blockade merely changed their entry port to Boston or Philadelphia and began listing St. George's rather than Nassau as their destination. Thus, traffic to Bermuda increased. St. George's became an intermediate stopover for voyages destined for Nassau or a phony destination for ships intending to pass directly through the blockade into a Southern port.

Welsh coal, though not as good as that from the United States, was brought in and stockpiled at the island ports to fuel the blockade runners. Ships leaving Nassau or St. George's were loaded with coal by wheelbarrows at the wharves and sometimes even by lighters outside the dock areas, confounding the American consuls and the crews of United States cruisers. Classified as merchant vessels, the runners were considered exempt from the ninety-day regulation that applied to warships, a distinction that grated on the already raw nerves of the officers of the Union blockade.

Vessels arriving in Wilmington were not so blessed with an abundance of good fuel. On their return trips to Nassau or St. George's, they sometimes had to resort to burning wood or low-quality coal mined in North Carolina. After using their good coal to escape pursuit, the

# *Bad Coal Endangers the* Robert E. Lee

The *Robert E. Lee* was one of the most successful runners operated by the Confederate government. Her twenty-one successful trips through the Wilmington blockade, many of them involving exhilarating chases and narrow escapes, were attributable in large part to the intelligence of her commander as well as to the quality of the workmanship in her hull and engines.

According to her captain, the scariest episode came in mid-August 1863 and resulted from a shortage of fuel at Bermuda. Captain John Wilkinson faced a dilemma as he prepared the long, gray sidewheeler for a run to Wilmington. The moon was right for the trip, but there was no coal to fuel his steamer. It appeared he would have to wait a fortnight for the voyage unless fuel could be found at once.

Not content to sit idly while Rebel forces needed the supplies stashed in the *Robert E. Lee*'s holds, Wilkinson scoured the wharves looking for fuel. He discovered a pile of old coal lying abandoned near the waterfront, where it had been pulverized under the feet of countless workers. Raking off the surface coating, he found to his immense satisfaction that the layers underneath were still more or less intact. Wilkinson ordered his men to shovel the chunks and powder into the ship's bins. When the firemen fed the powdery, black mixture into the furnaces, it burned fiercely and gave the engines a full head of steam. Pleased at the intense heat produced by the newly discovered fuel, the captain ordered the ship under way. Within an hour, Bermuda was just a green mound in the distance.

Although the crew had placed a large quantity of the granulated coal on board, it burned so rapidly that the pile soon became alarmingly low, which caused Wilkinson to wonder whether he would have enough for the return voyage to the islands.

The trip to Wilmington was uneventful. The *Robert E. Lee* arrived on Friday, August 28, without being chased or having to make unusual detours, either of which would have eaten fuel. But her supply was meager indeed. Readying for the return to St. George's, Wilkinson was forced to supplement his fuel with the slate- and dirt-impregnated coal brought in from mines in Chatham County, located in the center of North Carolina.

When the *Robert E. Lee* slipped from the Cape Fear River into the Atlantic, she was exposed to brief fire from the inner cordon of blockaders. Lieutenant John MacDiarmid, commander of the *Victoria*, was the first to spot the *Robert E. Lee*. He signaled his discovery to the rest of the squadron as he took up pursuit. The *Florida* joined the *Victoria* in the chase, but neither could rival the sidewheeler's speed, and they soon dropped from the race. When the sun rose two hours later, the speeding blockade runner was already thirty miles offshore.

The high-speed breakout had exhausted the last of the runner's good coal, and the engineers were thus forced to dig into the North Carolina store. The inferior fuel caused the ship's speed to drop noticeably and produced heavy smoke from the twin stacks. The towering smoke hung in the clear sky, pointing the way of the ship's passage to all concerned.

Lookouts on the USS *Iroquois* saw the smoke and turned in its direction. By eight o'clock that morning, the blockader was in full pursuit and gaining on the *Robert E. Lee*, which appeared to be a half-dozen miles away. For the next two hours, the Federal cruiser continued to narrow the gap. Captain A. Ludlow Case of the *Iroquois* considered capture a good possibility.

When lookouts on the *Robert E. Lee* announced that an enemy vessel was moving up on their stern, Wilkinson ordered all of the cotton that was stacked on deck thrown overboard. About 125 bales—each weighing five hundred pounds and worth several hundred dollars—were cast off, which lightened the ship by over thirty tons. The captain also asked for more speed, but the bad coal refused to produce a single additional knot. He then steered a course that brought the wind to the advantage of his schooner rigging, forcing the square-rigged pursuer to haul in her canvas. But still the enemy gained.

When Captain Case saw the cotton bales floating in the wake of the blockade runner, he must have thought about stopping to recover them as booty. The expensive fiber could have brought thousands of dollars in prize awards, to be shared by officers and crew. But he steamed on through the valuable flotsam, never slowing. He had richer rewards in mind.

Wilkinson met with his chief engineer to discuss the *Robert E. Lee*'s plight. As they talked, the captain noticed that three dozen barrels of turpentine were still tied on deck. He hit on a plan to use the volatile liquid to boost the heat of the ship's boilers. It was a risky move, for the residue from burning the sticky resin could foul the boiler tubes. But Wilkinson decided that desperate straits called for desperate measures.

He ordered the crew to rip open one of the remaining cotton bales and dip large wads of the absorbent fiber into a barrel of turpentine. Once the cotton was saturated, it was tossed into the furnace, where it ignited with a roar and produced a blaze of such intense heat that the men were forced to jump backward to avoid being burned. Even heavier smoke billowed from the stacks, but it mattered little, since the ship's whereabouts were already well known to the enemy.

The effect on the *Robert E. Lee*'s speed was instantaneous and even greater than Wilkinson had expected. The ship fairly bounded through the waves, her bow lifting from the increased thrust of the wheels. The *Iroquois* began to slip farther behind. Both Wilkinson and the chief engineer were excited at the increased pace. Out of curiosity, they tossed a log overboard to determine their actual rate. They were amazed to find that the ship's speed had jumped from nine knots to thirteen knots—an increase of almost 50 percent in just five minutes! It was as fast as the ship would ever move, which was fortuitous, for the dogged enemy was still trailing.

The good luck did not last. Late in the afternoon, the chief engineer reported that burning the turpentine-impregnated cotton had indeed clogged the tubes. The ship was losing steam pressure and slowing down. As Wilkinson looked back, he could see the white bow wave of the oncoming blockader.

He ordered several kegs of gold he was secretly carrying for the Confederate government brought on deck from their hiding place. If the *Robert E. Lee* was to be captured, he planned to distribute some of the gold among the crew and passengers and to drop the rest into the ocean, which would be better than letting the Yankees get it. But Wilkinson was no quitter. He asked the engineers to try to keep the ship going until dark, which was approaching a little faster than the *Iroquois*.

When the sun settled below the horizon, the enemy was within four miles. It was going to be a close race. As the sky gradually darkened, Wilkinson ordered the engineers to generate as much smoke as possible. By the time darkness finally covered the *Robert E. Lee*, she was leaving a heavy trail for the Yankees to follow.

The minute his lookouts announced that the chasing vessel had been lost in the murky distance, Wilkinson ordered the dampers closed, which completely cut off the flow of smoke. He then told the helmsman to make a hard right turn. Proceeding on a new course ninety degrees from the one last shown to the enemy, the *Robert E. Lee* was soon out of danger. Within an hour, Wilkinson felt safe enough to remove his shoes and lie down.

The runner's deck, which had grown almost unbearably hot from the overheated boilers, popped and cracked as it cooled and began to contract. It was music to the ears of the crew. The nervous passengers, some of whom were women, congratulated Wilkinson and thanked him for their miraculous escape.

By the time the *Iroquois* returned to her station, Captain Case's pursuit of the blockade runner had involved a round trip of nearly three hundred miles. During the chase, the *Iroquois*, too, had suffered problems with poor coal. Case felt that the impurities in his fuel, which was laced with streaks of slate, had prevented him from maintaining sufficient steam pressure in the boilers, one of which leaked seriously.

His inability to capture the *Robert E. Lee* before dark had cost him a great prize. Although he had guessed correctly about the maneuver Wilkinson used to elude him, there had been little chance of continuing the pursuit after the enemy's disappearance.

crew of one ship was forced to rip the woodwork from the vessel's interior cabins to keep the boilers going until they reached port.

Ships departing Nassau usually cited Bermuda or Halifax, Nova Scotia, as their destination, intending to divert to the Carolina coast once they reached the open sea. Those leaving Bermuda typically listed Nassau as their destination but also aimed for the Confederacy after clearing the harbor. This pretext was meant to conceal their purpose from enemy agents and to make their voyages appear legitimate if they were stopped by United States cruisers, although hardly anyone was fooled. Cases of armaments were sometimes marked with misleading labels such as "General Merchandise," "Hardware," or "Combustible Material." This deceived no one but left the exact contents uncertain.

Though Nassau remained the main port for illicit commerce, outbreaks of yellow fever during the summer months of 1862, 1863, and 1864 slowed the blockade-running trade there. From June to August, ships increasingly brought their business to Bermuda. The steamy days of summer saw the docks at St. George's piled high with munitions and cotton intended for Southern or European ports. After Charleston was virtually closed by blockaders in the summer of 1863, almost all the ships leaving for the South headed for Wilmington.

American consuls at the island ports were dismayed by the flagrant disregard shippers and local officials showed toward the blockade. There were some feeble attempts to conceal the contents and destination of the cargoes, but local merchants generally participated openly in violations of the blockade, contrary to Britain's declaration of neutrality and its stated intent to respect Lincoln's proclamations.

During 1861 and 1862, it was clear to British agents working in Southern port cities that the blockade was a farce, an opinion shared by American consuls in Europe, the Bahamas, and Bermuda. Yet Lord John Russell, the British foreign secretary, declared early in 1862 that the blockade must be considered effective if it merely created a "danger" to ships, rather than actually prevented their passage to or from the South. It was a generous interpretation by a man who obviously wished to maintain peaceful relations with the United States.

Aggravated by the outrageous behavior of blockade runners moving freely into and out of Nassau and St. George's, the American consuls complained bitterly to island officials, who gave them a cool reception or simply ignored them. The best the consuls could do was report their observations of suspicious ships and cargoes to Secretary of State Seward and sometimes to Federal ships hanging around the harbor. Though hardly a foolproof method, these attempts did help, for the consuls sent accurate, detailed descriptions of the vessels and approximations of their likely times of arrival at the Southern coast, improving the odds of interception.

The American consuls also employed spies among the dockworkers and paid them generously for information. On islands where United States officials were continually harassed in the performance of their duties, acquiring spies was not easy. But it proved worth the effort, as the spies kept the consuls informed of much of the illegal freight loading daily at the docks. Already unpopular, the consuls became even more despised because of their attempts to interfere with the lucrative trade, which was benefiting local merchants and residents alike. It was not uncommon for residents and sailors to threaten or rebuke the consuls even in broad daylight.

Samuel Whiting, the United States consul at Nassau during 1862, claimed he knew of only one merchant in the entire port who was friendly toward the Union. Whiting was frequently insulted as he moved about town, and he was fearful of going out into the streets. On one occasion, a group stood beneath his balcony chanting, taunting him with insults about the American flag, and daring him to come down to the street. When he did so, he was arrested and fined.

Early in the war, it was understood that large, deep-draft steamers and sailing ships were not appropriate for running the blockade. What was needed were swift steamers with a shallow draft that could outrun the cumbersome Yankee cruisers and skim over the sand bars of the Southern coast. But such craft lacked the stability and the coal capacity for ocean voyages. Since they were best suited for short trips of a few days at most, it seemed that the ideal solution would be to use large ships to deliver goods from Europe to Bermuda and the Bahamas, then divide the cargoes among smaller steamers for transport through the blockade.

Once British-built steamers began to show up among the blockade runners, the South had seemingly found its solution for evading the Union blockade. Although the runners' tonnage was slight compared to that of ocean ships with large hulls, their swiftness and low profile made them elusive.

Managing the transfer of goods between ships from Europe and the blockade runners at the island harbors was a formidable task that required the cooperation of a multitude of operatives. It was not desirable to transfer cargo directly from one ship to another, since it made the goods liable to seizure under the "continuous voyage" concept; goods could be considered contraband and were open to confiscation if it could be demonstrated that the intended termination of the voyage was the South. Therefore, when freight was unloaded from an oceangoing vessel, it was moved to a storage facility, then later loaded onto blockade-running steamers. This was a transparent ruse that caused delays in shipment, but it introduced a technicality that lowered the risk of capture for ships traveling from England to the islands.

Even had blockade-running steamers been capable of transporting larger cargoes, it still would have been desirable to separate the payload into smaller parcels to reduce the risk of capture. Rather than sending an entire shipment of rifles on a single ship, for example, it was customary to distribute the precious weapons among several ships, so the loss of one or more vessels would not mean the loss of the entire consignment.

The process of transshipment called for people with knowledge of

The blockade runner *Lady Sterling* is captured by the *Eolus* as she attempts to leave Wilmington. A few ships like the *Condor* and the *Lady Sterling* used Halifax, Nova Scotia, as an intermediate stopover, rather than St. George's or Nassau.

COURTESY OF THE U. S. NAVAL HISTORICAL CENTER.

the islands' commerce and the shipping business, people who were also aware of the Confederacy's specific requirements. Fortunately for the South, such men were available.

One of the principal members of the team was Major Caleb Huse of the Confederate army. Sent to Europe by the Confederate secretary of war, Josiah Gorgas, to purchase munitions and weapons early in the conflict, Huse met with great success in securing rifles, cannon, powder, percussion caps, and a variety of other armaments. Although hampered by uncertain funding and by rumors spread by other agents jealous of his success, Huse is credited with furnishing more than half of the six hundred thousand small arms—most of them excellent Enfield rifles—shipped from Europe for use by Rebel soldiers.

Food, armaments, drugs, and industrial equipment procured in

Europe by Huse and other agents or shipped through the efforts of private companies were sufficient to supply the Southern armies throughout the war. The problem of meeting the wartime needs of the Confederacy was not one of availability, but of delivery. All the materials except those that could be produced by Southern factories had to be shipped into blockaded Southern ports and delivered by rail or wagon to the front.

There is no doubt that the support of the Bahamas and Bermuda was responsible for the South's success in keeping its troops armed and fed. Except for a few voyages from Halifax, Havana, and assorted locations in the West Indies, almost all the ships entering Wilmington during the last years of the war embarked from either St. George's or Nassau.

The Confederacy was blessed with the support of several major mercantile companies that embraced the Southern cause openly and worked throughout the war to assist in the delivery of munitions and supplies. One of the most effective companies engaged in getting goods through the blockade was John Fraser and Company of Charleston. Its Liverpool branch was Fraser, Trenholm and Company, a firm with years of successful shipping experience. Such companies provided a crucial mechanism for obtaining goods in Europe and delivering them by way of the Bahamas and Bermuda. And the Confederacy's association with Henry Adderly and Company of Nassau proved a reliable vehicle for bringing armaments to the South. These businesses owned fleets of ships used for running the Union blockade. They were instrumental in helping the South translate cotton wealth into weapons.

The Confederacy had military agents in Nassau and St. George's who worked with merchants in acquiring storage space for the cargoes. It was their job to see that the most urgently needed materials—such as lead, saltpeter, and rifles—received top priority for shipment. Louis Heyliger was the South's man in Nassau, and Major Smith Stansbury and Major Norman S. Walker were assigned to St. George's. All worked diligently to coordinate the delivery of armaments to the South and the shipment of cotton to Europe.

John Tory Bourne, a strongly pro-Southern commission merchant at St. George's, played a major role in getting cargo transferred from large ships to small steamers in the harbor at Bermuda. Bourne owned or rented warehouse space for storing goods. He was paid a sum based on a small percentage of the value of the cargo. He also traded some merchandise of his own.

With the help of Bourne and Henry Adderly and Company, Confederate agents worked to gain the cooperation of private owners of blockade runners and to supervise the movement of vessels to assure that needed supplies reached the Confederacy. It was the job of J. M. Seixas, the War Department's agent in Wilmington, to see that the supplies that got through the blockade were delivered to General Lee in Virginia and to see to the loading of cotton for return trips to the islands.

All in all, it was a well-developed team that worked to synchronize the movement of goods through the islands.

The Civil War was a golden age for Nassau and St. George's. Even with the occasional loss of ships and cargoes, most businesses involved in running the blockade reaped enormous profits, and the resultant wealth filtered down through all levels of the local economy. From small schooners that carried only salt and brought back less than a dozen bales of cotton to large steamers that could deliver hundreds of bales in one trip, dividends were prodigious for investors.

Such lowly cargo as salt could bring a profit of several thousand dollars on a hundred-dollar investment. Since there was no refrigeration for the vast quantities of meat required by the Confederate armies, thousands of tons of salt were needed to keep beef and pork from becoming tainted. Although several saltworks were developed along the North Carolina coast during the war, production at such small factories was too limited to meet even the state's own needs, and the price of salt rose enormously.

A much better source was the salt mines in the Bahamas. Many schooners that were barely seaworthy left the islands loaded with salt and set a course for the Confederacy. The captains of these leaky, ancient vessels were prepared to beach them if necessary to save the cargo, sacrificing their ships for the salt. If the salt could be salvaged, the loss of the almost worthless ships would be negligible. Because of Gideon Welles's policy of concentrating his blockading fleets around the major ports, many small inlets along the coast of the Carolinas were open to the passage of these small salt schooners. Their greatest risks were on the open sea, where they chanced encountering the North's roving cruisers or tempestuous weather.

The crews of blockade runners also stood to gain financially for the chances they took in bringing supplies into the blockaded ports. It took only a few days to reach Wilmington from Nassau or St. George's. Before quarantine periods were initiated later in the war, ships were sometimes unloaded, reloaded, and out of the harbor in three days, making a ten-day round trip possible. Since a voyage paid as much as $250 per seaman, each man could receive $25 a day, compared to the usual rate of $.50 per day for common sailors.

Officers received much more, captains and pilots getting the highest pay. A captain could get $5,000 and a pilot between $3,000 and $4,000, at least half of which was paid in gold. Captains and officers were usually allowed to transport a few items of their own to sell, and they thus subsidized their standard pay with profits from their small cargoes. An officer might purchase four or five five-hundred-pound bales of cotton in Wilmington at less than $.10 per pound, then sell them in Nassau or Bermuda for five times that amount, giving him nearly $1,000 in profit—which he could shrewdly invest in items that would pay even greater dividends in Wilmington, due to their scarcity.

The wealth produced by running the blockade greatly affected life in Nassau and St. George's. The price of goods, the value of property, and the pay for dockworkers rose rapidly. The large number of sailors and officers from the blockade runners nearly overwhelmed the available rooms and houses, adding to the pressures on living quarters already crowded by islanders flocking to town to share in the easy money. Building projects boomed—both those designed to provide shelter and those meant to create warehouse space for the large quantities of cotton, armaments, and other goods awaiting delivery.

Money that could be had so readily could be spent just as easily. Sailors waiting in port for the next trip spread their wealth freely, living for the day. It is said that street children who were used to dancing and singing for pennies were showered with silver and gold coins by the appreciative visitors. Rum, a specialty on both islands, was plentiful and added to the lack of restraint exhibited by outsiders. Parties honoring the officers of blockade runners upon their successful arrival were given by merchants, island officials, and Confederate agents. Sailors spent much of their time drinking and carousing in bars on the rough side of town.

Augustus Charles Hobart-Hampden, alias "Captain Roberts," one of the most successful captains of blockade-running ships, described Nassau as a town where everyone seemed prosperous and happy, where "rollicking captains and officers" and "drunken, swaggering crews" filled the streets. He talked disdainfully of the presence of Yankee spies and said there was so much wealth that dollars were spent as freely as pennies had been before the war.

John Wilkinson, famed captain of the blockade runner *Robert E. Lee*, spoke of the hospitality he and his crewmen were afforded at St. George's and of the civil treatment they were given by the island's residents.

In an attempt to persuade privately owned blockade runners to carry those goods most needed by the Confederate government, the Bermuda homes of John Bourne and Major Walker became active social centers. In Nassau, the Royal Victoria Hotel was a center of Confederate activity, where captains of blockade runners gathered to mix with Confederate officers and island officials. Dinners and social gatherings were used to entertain merchants in an attempt to cajole them into loading war goods on their ships. Still, beef awaiting transport to hungry Rebel troops rotted in the warehouses while expensive liquor and other extravagant items occupied much of the cargo space of the runners.

There were additional problems. Inadequate supplies of coal sometimes held ships in the harbor for lengthy periods. And swift Federal steamers waited around the harbor entrances to ambush any blockade runners trying to leave. But the main obstacle to transporting the South's goods from Nassau and St. George's remained the lack of cooperation of private owners.

The cargo that the blockade runner *Minho* carried when she departed St. George's in September 1862 exemplifies the disproportionate amount of space allowed for luxury items. Although there were a few kegs of gunpowder and several hundred cases of "Hardware" and "Merchandise"—which likely were armaments—the bulk of the cargo was whiskey, candles, thread, tea, stationery, sugar, sardines, mustard, starch, soap, coffee, and cigars. There were also more than a hundred barrels of brandy and nearly a thousand cases of wine, hardly wartime essentials.

It was early 1864 before the Confederate government instituted blockade statutes and took control of the business.

Nassau and St. George's remained active until the very end of the four-year conflict. When Fort Fisher fell in January 1865, there were still several ships in the island harbors, filled with armaments and food destined for Wilmington.

Long before then, Acting Rear Admiral Charles Wilkes had been eliminated as a bother to the island ports. Wilkes had made the mistake of commandeering a couple of ships from the powerful and famous Admiral Farragut, and he had also defied Secretary of the Navy Welles once too often. He was ultimately relieved of command. It is unlikely that his minimal success against blockade runners outweighed the effects of his alienation of the British colonies, for the contribution of Nassau and Bermuda to the continuation of traffic to and from Wilmington is unquestionable. The islands' role in the struggles of the Confederate States of America was invaluable, and the rewards they received in return were no less valuable to their welfare—and no less fleeting.

When the war ended, those living in the two island ports were returned to the sharp edge of poverty from whence they had been so suddenly and miraculously delivered. But while the good times lasted, island residents enjoyed a glorious life of international commerce, intrigue, and adventure as their small towns served as vital gateways for ships successfully challenging the mightiest navy in the world.

# Chapter 4

# THE BRITISH INFLUENCE

"We shall by blockade invite a common union on the part of the whole world, certainly the whole commercial world, with the insurgents, and a common enmity toward ourselves."

GIDEON WELLES
*to Abraham Lincoln,*
*August 5, 1861*

# THE BRITISH INFLUENCE

THE DISTANT SIGNALS of the USS *Mystic* were barely visible to D. L. Braine of the USS *Monticello* as he slowly read the routine message through his telescope. The night's lingering mist hung in remnants over the warm waters of Frying Pan Shoals, but the October sun was already burning the fog away on this bright Saturday morning, promising a clear day ahead. It was nearly eight o'clock, well beyond the usual time that steamers chose to make their brazen forays through his sparse group of ships. For the first time in more than twelve hours, Braine began to relax.

His reverie was interrupted by the sudden cry of his lookout, who had spotted a sail off the port bow. Excitement ran through the ship as crewmen jogged to their stations and the *Monticello* swung toward the southwest to intercept the suspicious craft. The vessel's boiler fires were still hot from a night of patrolling, and the ship soon had a bone in her teeth as she headed after what appeared to be a large schooner.

The *Monticello*, a 655-ton screw steamer, was not particularly fast. Most of the blockade runners could easily outdistance her, but a sailing ship was another matter. Frustrated with the continued lack of success in preventing blockade-running steamers from entering Wilmington more than a year after the blockade had been imposed, Braine was anxious to capture an enemy ship of any class.

The *Monticello* steamed rapidly toward the distant ship, which appeared to be under full canvas. At the mercy of a headwind, the sailing ship began to loom larger as the *Monticello* narrowed the gap. After less than two hours, the Federals were within hailing distance of their prey, which proved to be the English schooner *Revere*. Braine shouted out a demand for the ship to heave to. The *Monticello*'s three mounted guns were ready to fire, but when the captain of the other vessel ordered the sails dropped and the anchor lowered, the gun crews stood down.

Braine and a small group of his officers and crew rowed over to the schooner. A check of the ship's papers showed Baltimore to be her intended destination, but when the Union boarders discovered that the vessel had sailed from Nassau with a cargo shipped by Henry Adderly and Company, they were suspicious. That feeling grew when neither captain nor crew claimed to know what was in the cargo, or to have seen it loaded. Adding to the blockaders' doubts were these considerations: the vessel was nowhere near the track for a voyage from Nassau to Baltimore; the bill of lading carried no official signature and did not agree with the manifest; the muster roll did not describe the actual crew; and statements by the men and officers were contradictory.

Braine ordered the ship's officers to open some of the cargo packages marked "Harness" and found that they in fact contained soldiers' haversacks. He then asked the captain, Henry Gage, why he was heading westward when the wind was blowing favorably to carry him to the northeast, the direction he should have been taking for Baltimore. Braine did not receive a satisfactory answer.

Feeling he possessed adequate evidence that the ship had intended to run the blockade into Wilmington, Braine declared the *Revere* a capture and placed a prize crew on board to deliver the ship and her cargo of salt, pork, leather, and "Harness" to New York. Captain Gage, who admitted he had already spent seven months in jail for violating the blockade, was sent along for further incarceration.

Although the capture rate had slowly increased during the Union navy's year of residency along the Cape Fear shores, this seizure was one of the limited number made during the early stages of the blockade. Most of the catches, like this one, were sailing ships, vessels unable to compete with the independence of movement enjoyed by steam-powered blockaders. When faced with other steamers whose designs were equal to or better than their own, the thinly spread blockaders could do little more than fire occasional shots at swiftly retreating runners. One captain of a Union gunboat reported his consternation at having to watch helplessly as two runners whisked past his ship, tooting their whistles with impudence.

Until the blockading squadron grew to a sizable force and acquired ships suited to its purpose, virtually any type of vessel could be used to bypass the impotent Federals. Before the war, a network of small river steamers had maintained lively commerce between Wilmington and towns as far inland as Fayetteville. These small craft continued to make almost daily runs during the first few months after the blockade was imposed. Some sailing craft passed into and out of Wilmington's harbor untouched on their way to Europe and the Indies. Union spies in Wilmington reported with disgust the number of ships that lined the town's docks in the summer of 1861.

Initially, sailing vessels, sternwheelers, and small river steamers—some barely seaworthy—carried turpentine, pitch, lumber, and tobacco from Wilmington through the blockade to overseas markets. Using the two Cape Fear River inlets to advantage, they kept the skimpy fleet of Union gunboats shuttling inefficiently from one side of Frying Pan Shoals to the other.

Little cotton was transported until the South finally realized that its self-imposed embargo was not only ineffective in forcing Europe to enter the fray but was also counterproductive to the war effort. Eventually, cotton became the primary export from Wilmington. The blockade caused the price of cotton to grow tremendously in Europe. Even small boats could make a profit by delivering a few bales to Bermuda or the Bahamas.

The many inlets along the coast allowed small barks and schooners to continue some blockade running throughout the war; many such vessels carried fewer than half a dozen bales of cotton and brought small cargoes of salt or war supplies in return. But at the large ports where Secretary Welles concentrated his ships, sailing vessels of all sizes were almost completely eliminated from the contest by the end of 1862. Large, deepwater steamers were also of little use, for they were either too large to get across the shallow bars into Southern harbors or were so slow and visible that they made easy targets for blockading gunboats.

By 1863, many suspected that the Civil War would be a much longer conflict than had first been believed, for the men on both sides fought with the courage, tenacity, and bitterness that only a family dispute can produce. If those involved in running the blockade were to continue their success, they would have to adapt their ships to meet the new challenges created by the growing fleet of powerful, well-armed steamers surrounding the harbors of the Confederacy.

It was clear to merchants and investment companies seeking to make profits from running the blockade that success would depend on having ships with the right characteristics to survive a run through the Northern gauntlet. Because the inlets were shallow, the ships would need a draft of no more than twelve feet. They would require steam propulsion to free them from the vagaries of the wind. And their engines must have enough power to compete with the United States steamers waiting at the inlets. Speed was essential for escape should they be spotted on their way through the Union fleet.

As badly needed as were such technologically advanced ships, they could not be produced within the Confederacy. Southern shipyards were scattered and ill-equipped, and they lacked the labor and materials to produce more than a few ironclads, many of which never made it to sea. The few boilermakers capable of producing steam engines could not even meet the desperate needs of the Confederate railways.

It was therefore the British who inherited the task of producing the dozens of blockade runners sought by private companies and the Confederate government. Their shipyards would reap the benefits of a construction boom between 1863 and 1865. Every firm that could produce a steamer had willing customers ready to pay exorbitant prices for ships that could keep them in the lucrative trade of transporting armaments and cotton. The South needed the war supplies, England needed the cotton, and profits were to be had by those with adequate ships and the daring to risk the blockade.

The shipbuilding trade was but one aspect of the complex ties that developed between the Confederacy and Britain. In November 1861, the Southern government appointed Henry Hotze to travel to England and rally British support. An experienced journalist, Hotze paid half a

# *The* Banshee *Shows the Way*

The first blockade runner to employ an all-steel hull was the *Banshee*. The forerunner of a new class of ships that would challenge the best of the United States Navy, she made her first appearance at Cape Fear at almost exactly the halfway point of the war.

She was owned by the Anglo-Confederate Trading Company, a private English firm organized by several members of Edward Lawrence and Company, a Liverpool shipping establishment. The new company was organized for the purpose of running the Union blockade for profit.

The company made its first attempt at penetrating the blockade with the decrepit steamer *Despatch*, whose mission to deliver munitions to the Confederacy ended in disaster when it was discovered that her draft was too great and her speed too slow to give her any chance of reaching a Southern port. After unloading her goods in Nassau, the company attempted to recoup some of its losses by having her tow another ship to New York, but the unlucky *Despatch* had to drop off the other ship in a storm and proceed alone to port, where she was seized by the owners of the towed vessel. Only through the intercession of a friendly business acquaintance was the *Despatch* allowed to return to England—and then in humiliation.

It was clear to the partners of the Anglo-Confederate Trading Company that if they were to run the blockade successfully, they would need a ship of superior qualities. The company contracted with a shipyard in Liverpool to construct a vessel designed specifically for penetrating the blockade.

Upon completion, the new ship was christened the *Banshee*. She had a narrow, 20-foot beam and measured 214 feet from bow to stern. Powered by steam engines and twin sidewheels, the steel ship was capable of speeds in excess of 10 knots. Thanks to her draft of just 8 feet, the sleek steamer could easily cross the sand bars at the inlets to the Cape Fear River. To make the *Banshee* harder to see, she was constructed so that her deck rose just 4 feet above the water line when she was fully loaded. Her stacks were swept back at a rakish angle; even her masts and lifeboats could be lowered almost to deck level. The entire vessel was covered with a coat of light gray paint that would make her virtually invisible in darkness or fog.

Jonathan W. Steele, an experienced captain, was named master, and Thomas Taylor was sent aboard to take charge of the *Banshee*'s cargo, a load of munitions and supplies for the Confederate army. Despite a few minor problems with buckled deck plates, the ship reached Nassau in May 1863. After a brief wait for a moonless night, the *Banshee* left for Wilmington and her first chance to challenge the ships of the blockade.

Three uneventful days out of Nassau, she neared Cape Fear on a warm night in the middle of the month. A light fog hung over the low shoreline, masking the moss-covered oaks and scattered pines and obscuring the pale gray steamer. The misty air was a blessing, for it had grown increasingly difficult to elude the blockade at Wilmington.

Steele's plan was to steam several miles north of New Inlet, then travel down the coast under cover of darkness and slip in undetected. As the vessel turned southward in her run for the river entrance, the helm was taken over by Tom Burruss, the pilot. Burruss had lived and worked around Cape Fear before the war and had been recruited by Steele in Nassau. His knowledge of the maze of shifting reefs and inlets scattered along the North Carolina shore would be an invaluable resource if the *Banshee* was to steer safely through the narrow, elusive passage to Wilmington.

As she cruised slowly southward, all lights on board were extinguished except the compass light, which was shielded lest a glimmer betray the runner's presence to nearby Union gunboats. The only sound was the steady thrashing of the paddle wheels, and even that was masked by the roar of the surf. All forward motion ceased as the pilot called for a sounding to check the *Banshee*'s course. A sailor dressed in light gray clothing stole softly forward along the foredeck and cast a lead to gauge the depth and the type of sand on the sea floor.

On hearing the depth report and examining the sand recovered from the lead, Burruss realized the vessel was too far to the east, a location that could put her within the inner ring of blockaders. He changed at once to a more westerly course, hoping to bring the *Banshee* under the protection of the guns of Fort Fisher before she came within range of Yankee cannon.

As the engines resumed their slow, steady beat, the sailors spoke in whispers or not at all as they sat hunched together in the narrow confines left them by the tightly packed cargo. The masts had been dropped to the deck except for a crosstree on the foremast, where a lookout was perched to watch for enemy ships. But it was the alert Burruss who first spotted a ship lying off the starboard bow. The captain ordered a quick change of course. As the *Banshee* passed within two hundred yards of the other ship, it hardly seemed possible that she could escape detection. The crew could hear the sound of voices—but fortunately no command to open fire—across the water.

After leaving the other ship in their wake, the crew of the *Banshee* detected another blockader just west of their course. A turn of the wheel avoided that threat. Then a third Union ship emerged from the darkness directly in their path. Captain Steele called softly down the tube to stop all engines. As the ship paused, the men had to endure the fear that steam might blow off suddenly from the stopped engines, which would alert everyone within a one-mile radius.

The blockader gradually pulled away and vanished in the distance, leaving the *Banshee* to resume her course. By then, the crew realized they were sailing right through the midst of the Union patrols. The captain urged that they make a run in the general direction of Fort Fisher. Still uncertain of their exact position, they steamed directly toward the breaking surf, then turned to skirt the coastline in hopes of using its bare features both for concealment and as a means of determining their location.

As first light, the shoreline became more distinct. Burruss soon recognized the mound battery straight ahead. But as the *Banshee* aimed for Fort Fisher, her men spotted at least a half-dozen enemy ships steaming in their direction. The Yankees opened fire. Shells whined overhead, while others raised geysers of water high over the deck. The *Banshee*'s engines were located well below the water line and were relatively safe from gunfire, but a direct hit on the sidewheels could disable them.

Often, blockaders elected to fire grapeshot to try to eliminate an enemy crew rather than sink their ship, for the primary goal was generally to capture the vessel and gain her cargo as spoils of war. But the *Banshee*'s quarter-inch steel plates could resist grapeshot. And if larger shells penetrated her hull, her four watertight compartments had enough flotation capacity to keep her above the waves. Still, there was danger that a shell or sparks from an exploding projectile might ignite the tons of gunpowder in the holds, detonating the ship like a bomb.

The *Banshee*'s speed was her main hope for eluding the slower enemy ships. Unfortunately, it was necessary for her to move into deeper water to bypass North Breaker Shoal. This brought her closer to the Yankee gunboats, which suddenly saw a chance to overtake their target.

Burruss maneuvered desperately, twisting and turning the ship to avoid the heavy fire from the converging attackers. Underwater explosions from near misses reverberated through the ship, causing her steel hull to ring like a bell and numbing the ears of the crew. No thought was given now to the sounds of the drumming engines and hammering wheels.

Captain Steele had spent time in a Northern jail after being caught trying to run the blockade while commanding the *Tubal*

*Cain*, and he had no intention of surrendering as long as his ship would move. The *Banshee* carried no defensive weapons, for if her crew returned fire, they ran the risk of being hanged as pirates if they were captured. It was better to face grapeshot than a hangman's noose.

The trim ship sped around the shoal and aimed directly for New Inlet, which now lay dead ahead. Daylight had laid bare the *Banshee* to the enemy, but it had also exposed the Yankee gunboats to the men of Fort Fisher. As the blockade runner closed on the narrow opening to the river, shells from the guns along the fort's sea wall whistled toward the blockaders. Veering away sharply at the heavy rain of shells from the fort, the Union vessels sent one last, frustrated volley at their lost prize. The Federal ships then steamed to their daytime anchorages several miles at sea to await the next target.

As the *Banshee* anchored safely in the river, her crew gave a cheer for the gunners of Fort Fisher. After raising a few toasts of champagne in honor of their successful voyage, they steered the blockade runner up the Cape Fear River and within hours tied up at Wilmington.

The *Banshee*'s first run proved the value of recent breakthroughs in marine architecture. She was destined to complete seven two-way forays through the blockade at Cape Fear, bringing thousands of tons of munitions and supplies to the Confederacy before she was finally caught.

dozen local reporters to put a Southern lean to their writings. He also wrote and printed the *Index*, a propaganda sheet distributed to members of Parliament and on the streets. It was a unique leaflet, for Hotze reported truthfully on the successes and failures of the South. The veracity of his writing and the Confederate victories at that point in the war gradually brought many around to favor the South.

The North was quick to deliver its own agents to England in an effort to discourage help for the Confederacy. Fortunately for the South, many of these men assumed an arrogant stance and tried to bully the English. United States Consul Thomas H. Dudley also took a high-handed role, attempting to tell the English government what it should do.

Southerners, perhaps guided by the failed techniques of their United States counterparts, used a courtly, genteel approach to win over people and businesses in Britain, including formerly unfriendly newspapers. Many in England already identified with the South more than with the North, for a large percentage of those who had settled the Southern states were immigrants from England, Scotland, and Ireland. Southerners had British surnames, and the kinship was felt across the Atlantic. Yet at the beginning of the war, almost everyone in England was repulsed by the concept of slavery and was slow to rise to the Southern banner. Only after hearing arguments by Confederates that theirs was a war for independence did the majority of the populace begin to change their views. A further point in the South's favor was the abhorrence most in Britain felt for the blockade.

Southern agents and supporters focused on the common interests of the two nations. The enticement of the South's vast stores of cotton only added to the favor the mother country developed for the Southern half of her offspring. Once the British sanctioned the Confederacy's struggle—even if that support remained unofficial—it became possible for Southern purchasing agents to procure almost anything they needed.

In England, there were few spots as sensitive to—or as important to—the Southern cause as the busy shipping town that sits on the banks of the winding Mersey River. Brightly colored Rebel flags waved from the tops of several businesses lining the east bank of the river, adding color to the drab, water-stained buildings. Feelings for the South were intense among merchants and residents. It was here that much of the South's commerce was conducted and where Confederate agents and commercial traders met to plan the purchase and transport of supplies. The town was Liverpool, and some would claim it was home to the "Confederate Embassy" in England.

The location of the "embassy" was 10 Mumford Place, where a twenty-year-old, solidly built structure of brick and stone crowned by slate shingles housed the offices of a major firm. The three-story edifice was a crossroads for intrigue, a place where crucial negotiations took place between Confederate arms dealers and local manufacturers. Just a short hop from the river, it was within strolling distance of several well-established shipbuilding companies, including William C. Miller and Sons, builders of the *Oreto,* better known as the feared Confederate commerce raider *Florida.* Just across the river in Birkenhead rose the gigantic cranes and scaffolding of John Laird and Sons, world-renowned shipbuilders, who produced at least a half-dozen blockade runners during the war. Jones, Quiggin and Company built almost twenty vessels, including the innovative *Banshee,* the modernistic *Colonel Lamb,* the *Bat,* the *Owl,* and the *Wild Dayrell;* the firm still had eight vessels under construction when the war ended.

With its long history as a center of trade and shipping, Liverpool empathized with the South when the blockade was imposed. Its residents and companies were opposed to any policy that threatened trade on the oceans, for the town's prosperity hinged on freedom of movement on the seas. No establishment would engender more sympathy for the Southern effort or take greater interest in helping the Confederacy meet its substantial needs than the resident company at 10 Mumford Place, for these were the offices of Fraser, Trenholm and Company, a branch of the notably patriotic John Fraser and Company of Charleston.

Rumored to contain the offices of such notorious Southern agents as Caleb Huse of the Confederate army and James Bulloch, purchaser for the Confederate navy, the location was kept under scrutiny by United States Consul Dudley, whose own offices were less than a mile away. Dudley was confounded by the openness the company exhibited in helping the South gain credit among European companies and delivering supplies in direct violation of the blockade.

Dudley organized his own espionage network to check on the activities of Fraser, Trenholm and Company. When he turned up evidence of the company's complicity in the South's efforts to buy armaments and war supplies and ship them to blockaded Southern ports, the United States agreed to subsidize his spying. Between 1861 and 1865, he would spend thousands of dollars attempting to thwart

Confederate efforts to purchase and move supplies from England.

George Alfred Trenholm had made his fortune the hard way. He had joined John Fraser and Company as a youth and worked his way to the top through talent and dedication. By the Civil War, he was one of the richest men in the South. He was the principal owner of John Fraser and Company in Charleston, as well as other branches of the firm, including the one in Liverpool. Trenholm supervised operations in Charleston, overseeing the company's fleet of ships. When Union forces captured strategic military positions in Charleston Harbor and the navy closed in to seal the entrance, the center of Trenholm's operations shifted to Liverpool. There, his manager, Charles Kuhn Prioleau, worked closely with Confederate brokers to procure and ship supplies to the South.

Prioleau was born in South Carolina. He became a British citizen in 1863, after nearly ten years in Liverpool. His loyalties still ran strong for his Southern homeland, but his income was directly related to company profits, and he was first and foremost a businessman. Although Prioleau was instrumental in securing credit for Huse and Bulloch and even permitted them to charge arms and supplies to the company's accounts, he never wavered from his goal of assuring income for his company.

When Major Edward C. Anderson joined Huse and Bulloch in England, he sought the advice and support of Prioleau. With Prioleau's help, the three Confederate purchasing agents succeeded in acquiring a large quantity of war supplies after only three months in Britain. However, they had no way to ship them to the South. Prioleau then offered to transport the goods aboard a company steamer, the *Bermuda,* which was preparing for a trial run against the blockade. The agents were delighted until they heard the outrageous shipping charges they would have to pay. In fact, they would have backed out of the deal if there had been an alternate solution.

The *Bermuda* made it safely to Savannah with a large shipment of company goods and Confederate supplies, traveling the last fifty miles along the coast without passing a single blockading ship. It then picked up two thousand bales of cotton and delivered them to England, passing through the blockade once again without incident.

Income from the sale of cargo in Georgia, the compensation for hauling Southern freight, and the resale of scarce cotton produced a financial windfall for Fraser, Trenholm and Company. The *Bermuda*'s venture was the first of many trips to the South by the company's ships. In fact, the ships' success persuaded the company to convert a large part of its fleet to blockade runners. After establishing intermediate shipping points at Bermuda and Nassau, it had a well-organized system for its new enterprise.

Liverpool was thus a ready ally to the Confederacy, but bringing Europe and even the rest of England over to the Southern cause required the sustained efforts of an army of diplomatic agents and propagandists. Two of the most persistent workers on the South's behalf were James Murray Mason and John Slidell, who worked feverishly to persuade England and France to declare the blockade illegal and to recognize the Confederate States of America as an independent country. Yet all their efforts were for nought, since neither France nor England ever officially acknowledged the existence of the Confederacy. Ironically, Mason and Slidell came closest to this goal by accident when they were snatched from aboard the British mail packet *Trent* by Charles Wilkes. The illegal actions by the United States Navy led many in Britain to cry for war, but it was an empty threat.

Slidell later negotiated a huge loan with the Emile Erlanger Company in France, while Mason worked in England with propagandist and finance specialist James Spence to develop a system of credit based on cotton certificates. A native Britisher, Spence was a loyal advocate of the South's right to secede but was suspicious of the Erlanger Company. He urged the Confederacy to develop another method of financing its European operations.

An influential man, Spence encouraged his high-placed friends to spread the Confederacy's message to members of Parliament and the general population. As a result of Spence's hard work and influence, Judah P. Benjamin, the Confederate secretary of state, named him to oversee all the South's financial arrangements in Europe. Spence began at once to coordinate his efforts with those of Fraser, Trenholm and Company. With Mason's help, he devised a plan to use cotton as a basis for credit through the issuance of cotton certificates, which could

# *The Blockade Takes the Life of Rebel Spy*

Good as they were, even the latest British-built runners faced danger from the growing strength of the blockade toward the close of the war. The following story tells of two such vessels, a renowned Confederate spy, and their strangely intertwined fates off the coast of Cape Fear.

One of the new breed of ships was the *Night Hawk*. She carried British registry and a British crew, which technically classified her as a neutral vessel, but her design showed her kinship to the new steamers built in England to run the blockade, and thus betrayed her true purpose. She was long and low and had two lightly rigged masts and two rakishly swept stacks. She was large enough to transport nearly a thousand bales of cotton at a speed of fourteen knots.

After taking on freight at Bermuda on September 26, 1864, the *Night Hawk* steamed toward Wilmington. As the sun sank below the horizon four days later, she was thirty miles from New Inlet. Just before midnight, and within sight of the mound battery at Fort Fisher, the fast-moving vessel was spotted by a patrolling blockade vessel, the USS *Niphon*. The Yankee gunboat turned at once to attempt to overtake the runner.

The *Night Hawk* gave a burst of speed upon being discovered. When Commander Edmund Kemble of the *Niphon* saw that the target was getting away, he veered his ship to bring her starboard guns to bear and fired a broadside at the fleeing craft. Swerving frantically to avoid the enemy fire, the *Night Hawk* ran too close to shore and went aground just a half-mile from the guns of Fort Fisher. Until the flash of cannon fire and rockets from the Union gunship lit the sky, the vessels had been running without lights and had gone unnoticed by the men at the fort. As a result, the *Night Hawk* was already stranded before the fort's guns could give her protection.

The men of the *Niphon* were quicker. A boarding team headed for the grounded ship within minutes. The crew of the *Night Hawk* lowered their dories, climbed aboard, and rowed desperately in an attempt to escape to shore, but the approaching Union sailors opened fire on them with rifles. Only about half the men escaped. The rest, including the captain and the chief engineer, were captured and taken aboard the blockader. The boarding crew then set fire to the *Night Hawk* and her cargo. At that point, the guns of Fort Fisher opened up on them with grapeshot and explosive shells, driving them back to their own vessel.

Although the captured crewmen and officers were British neutrals, they were detained as prisoners of war. The patience of the United States Navy was growing thin at the barely disguised efforts of private British firms to engage in illegal trafficking of arms for the Rebels.

The British complained to Secretary of State William Seward that the blockaders had fired on unarmed sailors who had not resisted capture and had only been trying to flee. They also objected to the treatment of the officers and crew of the neutral vessel as prisoners of war. The officers of the *Niphon* were later called upon to justify their actions, but this did not result in an apology to the British. It was clear that the United States would make its own rules when it came to enforcing the blockade.

As for the unfortunate *Night Hawk*, she was left stuck in the sand at the edge of the foaming surf north of Fort Fisher.

Meanwhile, another blockade runner was bearing down on the North Carolina coast. This one carried not only cargo for the Confederacy, but also a woman whom some considered partly responsible for one of the South's great land victories early in the war. Still considered a threat by those in the North, she was fresh off a European trip to win support for the Confederate cause.

Rose O'Neal Greenhow's brief career as a Southern spy had already exposed her to danger. Her husband, Dr. Robert Greenhow, had been a native Virginian whose position in the

Secret agent Rose O'Neal Greenhow and her daughter
Mrs. Greenhow was drowned after the blockade runner *Condor*,
which had brought her from England, was chased ashore near Fort Fisher.

COURTESY OF THE U. S. NAVAL HISTORICAL CENTER.

State Department had brought him to Washington. There, Rose quickly endeared herself to members of government and the city's elite. After her husband's death, she continued to reside in Washington, although her heart was in the South.

When the war broke out, she resolved to do all in her power to help the Rebels. Upon learning details of the North's plan to attack at Manassas in July 1861, she passed the word to Confederate general P. G. T. Beauregard. Some say this information allowed the Rebels to make the advance preparations that led to a major triumph.

Greenhow was later held under arrest in Washington and nearly thrown in prison for passing information to Southern military leaders. At her trial, she was given the option of swearing allegiance to the United States, but she haughtily declined. Uncertain what to do with such a woman, the Union eventually agreed to pardon her if she would at least swear to leave the North and never return. To this, she agreed.

But that did not mean she would abandon the cause. Greenhow understood the importance of good relations between England and the South. She decided to try her hand at being a Confederate agent in Europe.

First, she had to cross the Atlantic. Her reputation as a spy and the risks of traveling through the blockade made her nervous. Her trip from Wilmington to Bermuda aboard the blockade runner *Phantom* proved a frightening experience, for blockaders pursued her ship all the way to the harbor at St. George's.

The USS *Niphon*
One of the most aggressive and successful ships of the North Atlantic Blockading Squadron assigned to Wilmington, she made several captures, assisted in others including the destruction of the *Cornubia*, and participated in numerous chases.

Courtesy of the U. S. Naval Historical Center.

Her trip to Europe proved more successful than even she had hoped. Honored by high officials in both England and France, Greenhow also won popularity among the residents of those two nations, especially the British. While in England, she published her memoirs, entitled *My Imprisonment and the First Year of Abolition Rule at Washington*. The book was well received all over England, helping further her goal of influencing public opinion in favor of the Confederacy. Copies were snatched up eagerly by people anxious to read a firsthand account of the war across the Atlantic—and especially to hear the story of such an attractive and popular spy.

Now, as she prepared to travel back to Wilmington, Greenhow carried several thousand dollars in gold coins, her share of the profits from the book's sales. Of all the Southern patriots who came across the sea to win over the English, it's unlikely that any

The blockade runner *Condor*
One of the largest ships to try the blockade, the triple-stacked steamship ran aground while trying to dodge enemy fire near New Inlet on her maiden voyage.

BY PERMISSION OF THE ARTIST, MARTIN PEEBLES

was as well liked as she, and it was with some regret that she was leaving. Yet she missed her friends back across the Atlantic and wanted to see them again in spite of the dangers of the forthcoming voyage. Also, it was rumored that she carried secret dispatches for President Jefferson Davis.

She stepped aboard the new blockade runner *Condor*—a magnificent gray behemoth with three stacks and remarkable speed—as the vessel prepared to leave Scotland in September 1864. The captain was a furloughed British naval officer using the alias Samuel Ridge.

It was fear of capture that caused Greenhow the most dread, for she was *persona non grata* in the United States and was unlikely to be freed again. She knew the story of Belle Boyd, another Southern spy, who had been captured aboard a blockade runner just a year earlier and thrown into prison for six months, and who might have faced a death sentence for treason but for the efforts of a Union officer who worked to have her released. The cagey Boyd had charmed the young man while a captive aboard his blockading ship, and they had later gotten married. Greenhow knew she might not be so lucky.

The *Condor* reached Halifax, Nova Scotia, without incident. The American consul there, like those in Bermuda and Nassau, habitually alerted the blockading fleet off Wilmington of suspicious vessels headed its way. When he sent word of the *Condor*'s departure, the men of the blockaders knew she would be coming soon, at high tide on a moonless night. Usually, dark skies offered an advantage in eluding the Union gunboats, but they would be no friend to the runner on this trip.

It was the first week of October when the *Condor* reached the vicinity of New Inlet. Guiding her was Thomas Brinkman, one of the small cadre of Smithville pilots who helped blockade runners reach the Cape Fear River through the maze of sand bars and shoals. Brinkman directed the shadowy vessel along the shoreline, taking advantage of her seven-foot draft to cruise at the very edge of the surf. The skies were stormy that night, and although waves rocked the ship, the crewmen were thankful for the additional cover.

The blockading force had a multitude of small steamers lurking close to shore, ringed by faster chase vessels encircling the inlet. These ships attempted to patrol every possible route, their crews eager to take a Rebel vessel as a prize. All their lights were extinguished or shielded, and their crews stood watch in silence, hoping for concealment from the equally dark and hushed runners.

In the darkest part of the night, just before dawn, the *Condor* increased speed as she approached the mound battery at Fort Fisher, now faintly visible a couple of miles ahead. Unfortunately, the omnipresent *Niphon* was waiting, and the sharp-eyed men on watch picked out the blockade runner's outline, although it barely showed above the background dunes. The blockader turned rapidly toward the *Condor*, firing rockets and burning calcium lights, which brightened the sky and blinded the eyes of the sailors on both ships for a few moments. Projectiles from the *Niphon*'s bow gun struck so close to the speeding three-stacker that great fountains of water sprayed over the ship.

Captain Ridge called for maximum power from his engines. He was confident that the *Condor*'s spectacular speed, slight draft, and proximity to Fort Fisher would allow her to escape. Already moving at a rapid clip, the ship leapt forward as her engines went to their highest revolutions. Suddenly, directly in her path, the masts and superstructure of another ship emerged—apparently a blockader attempting to cut the *Condor* off. Without time to do more than dodge the craft, Brinkman gave the wheel a desperate clockwise whirl, hoping to pass the ship safely to port, but there was no room. The *Condor* plowed into the sandy bottom at high speed, hurling her crew to the deck. Surprisingly, no men were seriously hurt, but the vessel was hopelessly stuck. Bow resting with a slight uphill tilt and decks canted crazily, she waited at the mercy of the enemy.

As the *Niphon* steamed closer, her calcium flares lit the area like an early dawn—but they also exposed her to the alert gunners at Fort Fisher. A few well-placed rounds drove the Yankees back to sea.

The "enemy" ship that had blocked the *Condor*'s path was at that point revealed to be the still-smoldering wreck of the *Night Hawk*. She might as well have been the enemy, for she had destroyed the *Condor* as surely as any broadside. The two would now share a common grave.

Rose O'Neal Greenhow was desperate, believing that the enemy would board the *Condor* momentarily and that she would be arrested. She pleaded with Captain Ridge to take her to shore, but he tried to reassure her that once daylight arrived, they could make it to the beach safely. He explained that the stormy weather made the sea too dangerous for an attempt in the dark. Still, she begged him until he finally relented.

The captain asked three of his most experienced crewmen to launch a lifeboat and deliver her to shore. As soon as they were aboard the small craft, a monstrous wave overturned it, and all aboard were tossed into the swirling waters. The men all surfaced and made their way to land. But Greenhow was never seen alive again, as the heavy gold coins she carried in her garments pulled her to the bottom. Her body washed ashore the next day. Ironically, it was discovered by a former crewman of the *Night Hawk*.

Greenhow had given her life in the service of the Confederacy. Her body was delivered to Wilmington, where she was given a hero's funeral and buried in Oakdale Cemetery in the heart of town.

be used to subsidize purchases of arms and supplies by Huse and Bulloch.

Meanwhile, in France, the Erlanger Company proposed a loan based on cotton bonds that would provide the Confederacy with $25 million. When Slidell sent the proposal to Secretary Benjamin, the terms were judged to be so glaringly unfair that it was rejected in spite of the South's desperate need. In pushing for a smaller loan, Benjamin insisted on reducing the outlandish percentage the Erlanger Company was seeking. Finally settling on a loan of $15 million, the South got only a little more than half the proceeds after the Erlanger Company got its cut.

By this time, Huse and other purchasing agents had spent all their money, extended their credit, and run up massive debts with several European companies. At the end of 1862, merchants were showing themselves hesitant to extend further credit until the Confederates paid for goods already received. Mason pleaded with Slidell to see to the release of the Erlanger funds, which were inexplicably still unavailable.

The Erlanger loan, finalized in September 1862, was not released until the summer of 1863. Spence was outspoken in his criticism of the terms of the loan and the delay in the release of the monies. The Erlanger Company was in turn piqued by Spence's criticisms and made its displeasure known to Slidell and Mason. Slidell wrote Secretary Benjamin denouncing Spence's tactics and pushing for his removal. Anxious to avoid any interference with the consummation of the loan, Benjamin assigned the responsibility for overseeing the Erlanger deal to C. J. McRae, leaving Spence in charge of transactions in England only. Power over the Erlanger loan gave McRae considerable sway over most Confederate purchases in Europe. Spence was pushed out of power in spite of all the favors he had done for the South.

By the summer of 1863—with the Erlanger loan approved, cotton certificates and treasury bonds available, and companies prepared to sell almost anything the Rebels needed—the South was ready to supply its war efforts.

Many of the companies that ran the blockade were British owned, and it was natural for them to look for their fleets of runners among their own ships. They found what they were seeking in the boats that plied the rivers of England and Scotland. There was an existing force of medium-sized steamers that were fleet, had a shallow draft, and were designed for the short voyages between ports along the Clyde River. Most of them were sidewheelers ideal for slipping across the treacherous sand bars of the Carolina coast. Very quickly, almost all such steamers began to disappear from the Clyde River.

These "off the shelf" vessels were too unstable for ocean voyages from England to the South. But they were excellent for the three- and four-day jaunts between Wilmington and the island ports; more than fifty of them were making the trip by 1863. Their biggest drawbacks were their limited coal and cargo capacities. Since the vessels were designed for ferrying passengers or transporting small loads, they were capable of storing only 100 to 200 tons of coal. A round trip between Wilmington and Nassau required about 125 tons of coal and a round trip between Wilmington and Bermuda even more, so the ships operated on a narrow fuel margin.

Several shipbuilding firms in England were prepared to construct new blockade runners. In fact, some were able to produce a ship in less than three months. Once the ready supply of river steamers was exploited, orders for new vessels burst upon the British shipyards. For the first time, the specific design characteristics needed to run the blockade could be incorporated into construction from the outset. This resulted in a new class of ships that were capable of moving significant freight at a reduced risk of capture.

The unique characteristics of the family of ships built in England during the last couple of years of the Civil War included shallow draft, low freeboard, decks bare of vertical structures that could make the ships more visible, long, slender hulls with considerable cargo capacity, and steam engines ensconced far below the water line. Most were streamlined and had long, sweeping curves, lending them an air of beauty and sleekness. Some firms built several sister ships from the same blueprints, simplifying construction and speeding up production. Four or more such vessels constituted a class of ships. Some vessels were so strikingly similar that they could be distinguished only by their names.

The British, ever conscious of their status as a great naval power, knew they must constantly investigate new technology if they wanted to maintain their dominance of the world's oceans. If they had not already perceived the demise of the great sailing men-of-war, there could have been no greater demonstration than the War Between the States. A single homemade ironclad, the CSS *Virginia,* sent the Federal ships of Chesapeake Bay reeling in panic when she steamed at will among them in March 1862, wreaking destruction on the vulnerable wooden warships.

The use of metal for the framework and skin of seagoing craft proved a quantum leap in the construction of merchant ships as well as warships. A ship made of iron had a much smaller supportive framework and considerably thinner walls than a wooden ship of the same length and width, making it significantly lighter and capable of greater speed from the same horsepower. And since interior space was no longer consumed by the massive wooden beams needed in old-style ships, there was more cargo space as well. British shipbuilders had done extensive testing of metal ship designs before the war. Now, they applied the results to the problem of producing better blockade runners.

Some experimentation took place before the ideal model evolved. Although ultimately a successful blockade runner, the first all-steel ship, the *Banshee,* had serious flaws. Her plates were only an eighth of an inch thick in portions of the hull and deck. When put to the test at sea, these plates buckled, showing that steel could fail if pushed to extremes. Many of the new ships had iron frames and iron hulls, some had iron frames and steel hulls, others were all steel, and a few had wooden frames with iron plates. All were built with several watertight compartments, giving them great flotation capability even after they suffered hull damage through collision or gunfire.

Theories of streamlining developed from studies showing how bow-generated waves interacted with the hulls of moving ships. The best evidence indicated that long, narrow shapes produced less drag than short, wide ones. The *Banshee* was built with a beam less than a tenth of her length. The average ship had a beam-to-length ratio of about one to six, showing what an extremely slender hull configuration the *Banshee* possessed. However, such a narrow beam gave the ship an alarming tendency to roll, and cargo space suffered from the narrow hull confines. A more practical ratio of about one to nine was eventually selected for most of the new ships, still delivering a very sleek form.

# *Twin Propellers Rescue the Don*

The *Don* was one of the blockade runners equipped with two propellers designed for counterrotation. Her captain used that capability on several occasions to turn his ship quickly and avoid being spotted. Once, the *Don*'s propellers even broke her free after she was grounded on a sand bar close to an enemy gunboat.

On that occasion, the blockade runner was harried by deepwater cruisers of the North Atlantic Blockading Squadron before she reached the shallow waters near the North Carolina coast. When she finally arrived off Cape Fear, her crew prepared to make their run through the inner gauntlet of gunboats.

The moon, in three-quarter phase, was due to arrive in the eastern sky around midnight, giving the crew a four-hour interval between last twilight and early moonlight for their attempt to pass through New Inlet. Unfortunately, the evasive detours forced upon them by the blockading cruisers had delayed their arrival. Before they could race through the Union ships, the sky was already growing bright from the first pale rays of the rising moon.

The crew pulled the *Don* in toward shore as closely as they dared, stopped her engines, and quietly lowered her anchor into the shallow water near the beach. They then watched in horror as a Union gunboat steamed up and anchored only a stone's throw away, so close that they could clearly understand casual conversations aboard the enemy vessel. Masked by the sand dunes and low trees in the background, the *Don* lay perpendicular to the enemy, facing the shore. This afforded her adversary the barest end-on view. Only the gentle slap of the waves on her hull spoke of her presence. Her crew scarcely dared to breathe.

After hours of tense waiting, unable to speak or smoke, the crew of *Don* realized they could not wait to be exposed by the first rays of sunlight. The captain, Augustus Charles Hobart-Hampden, ordered the twin screws engaged, one to turn forward and the other in reverse, a maneuver designed to whip the vessel around like a spinning bottle. But to the crew's considerable alarm, the bow hit the beach and stuck firmly in the sand. Several powerful thrusts from the engines—whose sound was masked by the roar of the surf—nudged the ship against the sea bottom until she suddenly broke free, turned, and streaked away up the coast.

Incredibly, the enemy still had not spotted the low, gray form of the *Don*. Before they steamed out of sight, the *Don*'s crew saw the blockader weigh anchor and move slowly away in the opposite direction, oblivious to the fact that she had been within spitting distance of a heavily loaded blockade runner. The Union officers and crew would have been dismayed to learn that they had allowed considerable prize money and booty to slip through their grasp. Meanwhile, the *Don* safely entered New Inlet and headed up the Cape Fear River toward her destination.

To keep the ships' profile low, freeboard was minimized and smokestacks were either inclined at a steep angle or telescoped down near deck level. Although small structures to enclose the pilot and the wheel were sometimes provided at the stern or amidships, very little deck structure was incorporated into the design. Most of the new ships had two masts, fore and aft, but they were slender staffs that could generally be lowered to the deck to further reduce the ships' profile.

Such ships were commonly referred to as "auxiliary steamers," but sails were of little consequence to their locomotion. What sails were provided were used more to keep the ships stable than to propel them on their course. In case of engine failure or an exhausted coal supply, the sails might provide slight headway, allowing the runners to reach port if they weren't too far at sea.

The prows of the innovative vessels were designed to pierce the waves, rather than porpoise up and down over them. This enabled the ships to run level and keep their decks low to the sea. To repel the water that washed onto the decks, convex covers were built over the bow to help shed the water. Called "turtlebacks" because of their shape, these covers added to the streamlined appearance of the new class of blockade runners.

Steam engineering was still a new science in the 1860s. Many American riverboats used what was called a "walking beam" engine, but this was not the best engine for blockade runners for several reasons. In this type of engine, what looked like a giant seesaw was located atop the deck in the middle of the ship; it rocked (or walked) up and down as it transferred the motion of the piston to the paddle wheel. The elevated position of the apparatus made it vulnerable to gunfire and raised the ship's center of gravity so high as to produce instability during ocean travel. Better suited to river passage, the walking beam engine had a short life in the blockade-running trade and was soon replaced by other types, some of which could be completely enclosed in the hull and located below the water line.

The placement of the cylinder was one of the variables tackled by engineers trying to design the most effective engine for steam-powered blockade runners. One of the simplest plans was to place the cylinder vertically, so the piston moved up and down. The walking beam engine employed this style, as did the side lever engine. The side lever engine worked much like the walking beam except that the piston was fixed to a horizontal bar that was linked to two rocker arms placed below deck. The two arms transferred power to the sidewheels. This solved the instability problem and reduced the exposure of the engine to gunfire, but since the side lever engine employed twice the number of beams as the walking beam, it added to the weight of the drive train and was soon discarded in favor of more efficient models.

One design widely used on blockade runners was an improved version of the oscillating engine. In this design, the cylinder itself rocked, and the piston was connected directly to the crankshaft of the sidewheels. The engine was pivoted at the base, allowing the cylinders to oscillate and enabling shipbuilders to keep the entire mechanism below the water line.

Propeller-driven ships were better suited to an engine in which the piston's connecting rod emerged from the bottom of a vertical cylinder

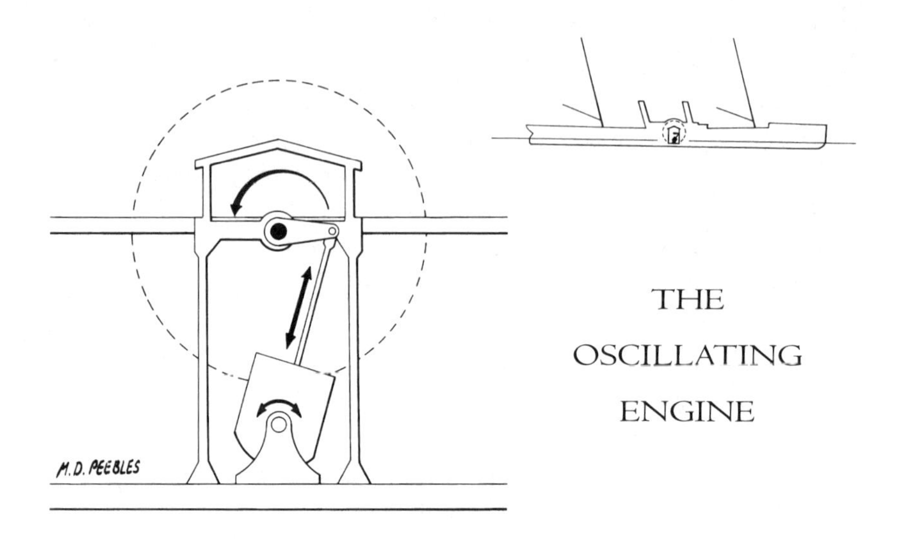


THE
OSCILLATING
ENGINE

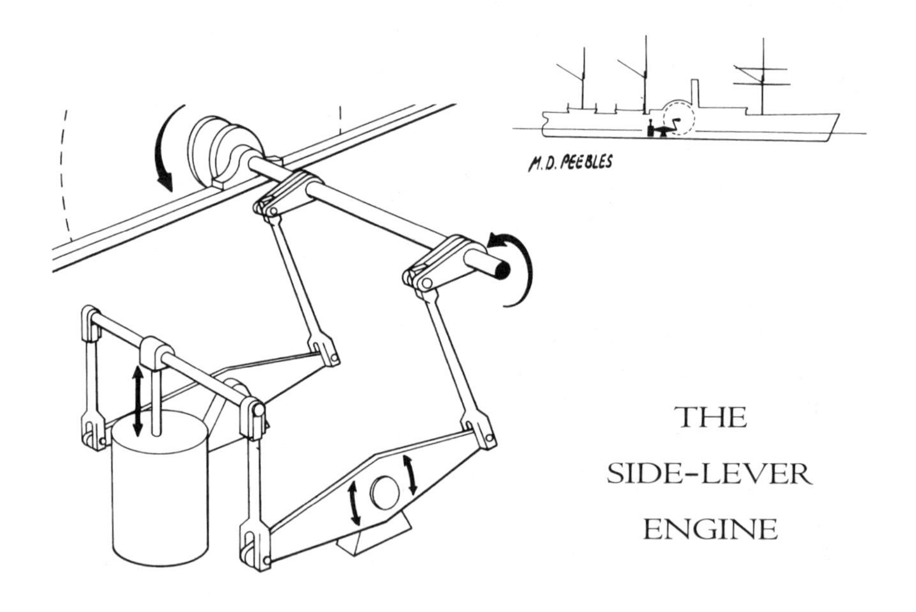


THE
SIDE-LEVER
ENGINE

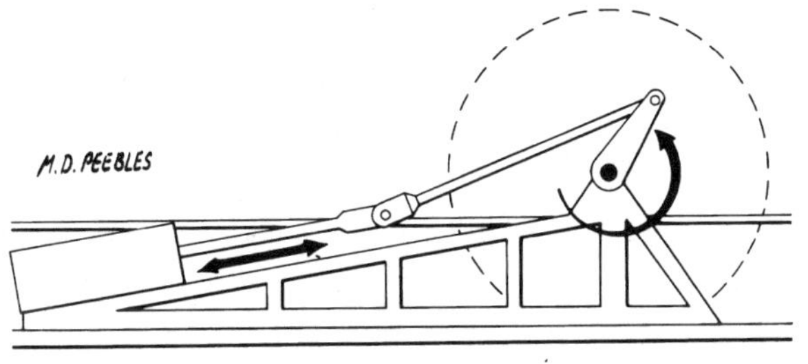


THE INCLINED
DIRECT-ACTING
ENGINE

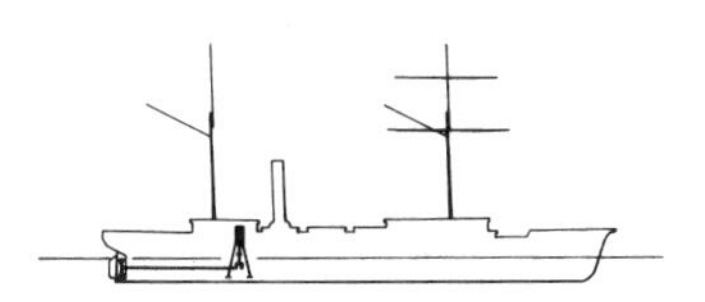

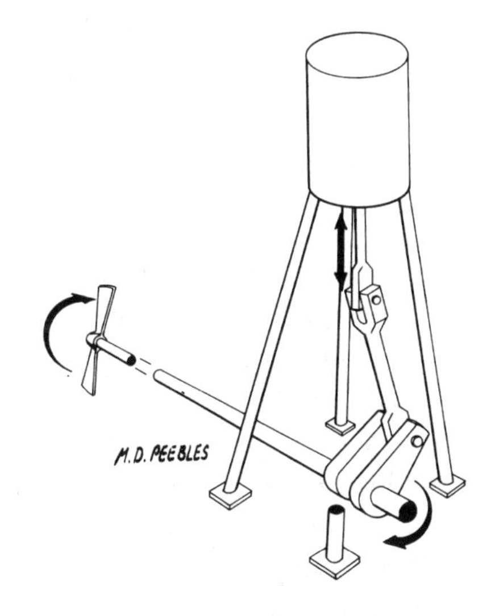


THE INVERTED
DIRECT-ACTING
ENGINE

The most popular steam engine designs of British-built ships used to run the blockade are pictured above. The oscillating engine, the side-lever engine and the inclined, direct-acting engine were more suited to sidewheelers. The inverted, direct-acting engine was adapted to propeller-driven craft.

Drawings by Martin Peebles.
Taken from "Hidden Beneath the Waves," by permission of the Division of Underwater Archaeology of the North Carolina Department of Archives and History.

and was linked directly to the drive shaft. This clean, efficient design allowed easy maintenance and suffered very little power loss in the linkage, producing great speed.

The most efficient engine for sidewheelers proved to be the inclined, direct-acting model. The cylinder was fixed in an almost horizontal position but with a slight incline in the direction of the piston's power stroke. This engine had several advantages. It was located below the water line, had very simple linkage, and was even more efficient than the vertical, direct-acting style. Most important, it produced the speed needed by blockade runners.

The boilers that powered the various engines were for the most part low-pressure types rated at twenty-five to thirty pounds of pressure per square inch. Embellishments of the basic design introduced preheated water supplies and techniques for blowing off steam underwater.

Although sails and sternwheels propelled some of the early blockade runners, the vessels that endured were driven by twin sidewheels or propellers. Though many ships of the blockading squadron were propeller driven (as were a number of runners), the most common means of propulsion for blockade runners was sidewheels.

Sidewheel design progressed during the war. Some improvising blockade-running captains placed canvas over their wheel housings to reduce noise. But the ultimate solution to eliminating the loud thrashing of the wheels was provided by a feathering mechanism that not only muffled the sound but made the wheels more efficient in moving ships.

The essence of the feathering technique lay in allowing the blades to pivot so that they always entered and left the sea perpendicular to the water's surface. A blade entering the water horizontally used its power to force the water downward, which had the effect of lifting the bow of the ship; when emerging at the end of the rotation, the blade pushed up on the water, causing the stern to lower. This not only wasted power but also resulted in a loss of speed. Feathering kept the blades vertical upon entering and exiting the water and set them for maximum contact with the sea only when in position to propel the ship forward. Preventing the fast-moving blades from striking the water flat upon their entry resulted in a major reduction of sound and allowed the ships to run nearly silently at high speed.

In 1863, about sixty of the hundred or so Clyde River steamers slipping into and out of the Carolina ports were sidewheelers. Of the other forty, many were propeller driven. Captains differed in their opinions of the better method for powering blockade runners. Some felt that sidewheels gave their vessels the best chance of clearing the sand bars and maintained that sidewheels were better than propellers for shaking stranded ships free when they went aground. Others such as the famed John Wilkinson felt that twin screws were superior, since they could be counterrotated to turn a ship within its own length, allowing sudden, drastic changes of course. Counterrotating the twin blades, he argued, could also help wrench stranded runners off sand bars. There were ample opportunities to test such theories, for the grounding of blockade runners in the shallow Cape Fear waters was a common event.

Propeller-driven steamers were produced with single or double screws. Early single-propeller vessels were often listed as auxiliary sailing ships; the sails could be used to save fuel or if the engine became inoperable. Some of these were true sailing vessels whose crews fired up the engines only when they encountered a blockader. Most such ships were designed so the propeller shaft could be hoisted clear of the water while the vessel was under sail, eliminating the fearful drag created as the propeller was hauled through the water.

Single propellers had to be large to produce adequate speed and required deep submergence to perform properly. This presented a problem in running the blockade through shallow inlets. When the propeller struck bottom, the blades, the shaft, or even the engine might suffer damage. A single propeller could embed itself so firmly that a ship could be left irretrievably on a sand bar.

It was the advent of the double-screw steamer that made propellers more acceptable for the blockade-running trade. With two propellers, the diameter of the screws could be reduced, allowing the shallow draft necessary for entering Southern ports. Twin-propeller vessels were more fuel efficient than sidewheelers. But although they were fast, they could not match the speed of the sidewheelers and lacked their quick acceleration. Still, they were the choice of many captains and companies. Their great maneuverability made them formidable antagonists for the ships of the blockading squadron.

The largest blockade-running vessel built during the war was the *Colonel Lamb,* named for Fort Fisher's enterprising commander. The ship was completed at Jones, Quiggin and Company, and her powerful oscillating engine was developed by James Jack and Company at Birkenhead. Although the *Colonel Lamb* made only two successful runs into Wilmington before Fort Fisher was taken, she was a steel-hulled colossus reaching nearly a hundred yards from bow to stern. In spite of her great size, she could skim the waves at great speed.

Long, low, and lean, the new breed of ships had much greater cargo capacity than the Clyde River steamers. Some could transport more than a thousand bales of cotton. Their speed was phenomenal, several of the best models reportedly attaining more than twenty knots.

Before the new steamers were sent out to meet the ships of the North Atlantic Blockading Squadron, they were painted from top to bottom in pastel colors designed to blend with the seascape and make them virtually invisible in the misty regions of Cape Fear. Light blue, pale green, and off-white were sometimes used, but shades of gray dominated the camouflage schemes of the vessels. One Union captain claimed that they could not be spotted at a distance greater than two hundred yards.

On one occasion, as a blockade runner anchored off Old Inlet at dusk to await favorable conditions for crossing the Western Bar, the crewmen were surprised to see a Yankee vessel pull up just a few dozen yards away, drop her own anchor, and go about drills as if the Rebel ship were not there. No one dared make a sound. As dark began to settle, the Union ship weighed anchor and started off on her patrol, leaving the nervous men of the blockade runner greatly relieved.

The immense shipbuilding effort in Scotland and England produced a significant number of excellent blockade runners. The new ships included technological advancements that made them superior to most of the ships of the blockading squadron. Much of the success of the illicit trade in the later years of the conflict can be attributed to the fast, elusive vessels built at such places as Merseyside and Glasgow.

Although most ships made several successful runs before they were lost, almost half the vessels trying the blockade were captured or destroyed by 1864, when the use of new, streamlined runners was at its peak. This cut sharply into the number of ships available to the South. The losses kept British shipbuilders actively employed in the continuing production of additional ships, which sold at a high price.

Further serious inroads to blockade running were made when the Union began converting captured vessels and sending them out to join the blockading fleet off Wilmington. The advantage enjoyed by those trying to penetrate the blockade was diminished when they had to compete with the speed and stealth of their own ships, now turned against them. The United States Navy also adopted many of the tactics employed by blockade runners.

In the latter stages of the war, the vigilance of the North Atlantic Blockading Squadron posed a serious threat to efforts to break the blockade of Wilmington. Yet the great technical advances incorporated into the dozens of new steamers coming out of England and Scotland parried the very best Northern efforts, and ships continued to make their way into and out of Old and New Inlets. More than a hundred ships—almost every one a swift, camouflaged steamer—were still plying the seas between Wilmington and the transshipment ports.

Slow wooden vessels propelled by canvas sails at the whimsy of currents and breezes were the mainstay of navies and merchant marines at the beginning of the Civil War. In an amazingly brief interval, they were replaced by a new class of ships. Steel vessels that provided their own locomotion and could carry significant loads of freight came to dominate the Atlantic. They made the old-style navies of the world—including the United States Navy—obsolete almost overnight.

Chapter 5

# WILMINGTON: CENTER OF THE STORM

"This remarkable traffic through the beleaguered city of Wilmington . . . almost wholly sustained the Confederate States commissariat during the last two years of the war."

JAMES SPRUNT

# WILMINGTON: CENTER OF THE STORM

THE ILL-FATED STEAMER *Kate* quietly approached Cape Fear. Having departed Nassau three days earlier, the small ship, ably commanded by Captain Thomas Lockwood, arrived off Wilmington at the edge of night, planning to use the shroud of darkness to cover her entrance into the river despite the intensified efforts of the blockaders to stop her.

Still smarting from public criticism after the widely publicized escape of the *Thomas L. Wragg* (formerly the *Nashville*), the men of the Union vessels were doubly alert in hopes of preventing the *Kate*'s entry. Yet aboard the widely spaced vessels of the sparse Union fleet, it was impossible for even the sharpest eyes to penetrate the blackness and distinguish the *Kate*'s drab, stealthy form. The elusive steamer crossed the bar undetected and moved up the narrow, winding channel that zigzagged through twenty-five miles of sandy shoals and man-made obstacles on the way to the still-sleeping port town. Especially frustrating to Commander Goldsborough of the North Atlantic Blockading Squadron was the fact that he and his men were completely unaware that the ship had slipped by them until a small group of runaway slaves they rescued told them of the *Kate*'s safe arrival.

If they were like most blockade-running crews, the men of the *Kate* halted their vessel just two miles below Wilmington, where the Brunswick River enters the main channel. There, crews liked to toast their safe arrival at the site of an old, weathered cypress covered by Spanish moss. Known as the "Dram Tree," the aged sentry was a welcome sight to men who had just faced down the challenges of the fickle weather and the United States Navy.

And if it was like most predawn mornings in Wilmington, the smell of pine lingered in the air as wisps of smoke from nearby turpentine distilleries drifted over the marshy areas west of the river and settled along the riverfront, blurring the outlines of the half-dozen or so blockade runners already moored at the docks. Men scurried about the wharf unloading cargo from newly arrived ships and loading others with hundreds of bales of cotton from the huge stacks lining the riverside.

It was mid-1862, and Wilmington was evolving into the busiest seaport in the South. The North Carolina town would soon become the center of the Confederacy's international commerce, proclaimed illegal by the United States government. That traffic would feed and equip the armies of the Confederacy in spite of all efforts to prevent it. As other, larger Southern ports were strangled by the blockade, Wilmington emerged as the final hope for maintaining the lifeline with Europe. In fact, the city came to be called "the Gateway to the Confederacy."

Wilmington had been settled by European colonists after attempts to establish colonies nearer the mouth of the river had proven unsuccessful. The town was first called New Town or Newton but was later renamed Wilmington in honor of Lord Spencer Compton, earl of Wilmington. It was the most inland point of the Cape Fear River navigable by large, deep-draft ships.

The Cape Fear drains rainwater from across the interior of North Carolina. Inland from Wilmington, the river is divided into small tributaries that fan out like long, sinuous fingers across the state. Flowing generally eastward, the tributaries merge near Wilmington and turn abruptly southward, where, for the last twenty-five miles, the tannin-stained waters flow nearly parallel to the Atlantic shoreline, cutting a channel to the sea and emerging at Cape Fear. A narrow fringe of land separates Wilmington from the ocean, providing a sheltered passage for ships and protecting the port from ocean storms.

The 1860 census numbered the population of the town at 9,552, including around 4,400 free blacks and slaves. Wilmington was thus the largest town in North Carolina, as well as the state's busiest port. Frequent contact with travelers from Europe gave the town a cosmopolitan flair. It bore all the signs of aristocracy and culture that form the typical image of the Old South.

Several churches, some of exquisite architectural design, were located a few blocks from the docks. Flowering shrubs and shade trees lined the neat, rectangular web of streets and screened the stately homes from the menacing sun. Thalian Hall, a large auditorium in the heart of Wilmington that boasted seating for 10 percent of the town's residents, was the site of frequent plays and musical performances. Stores offered fine wines and expensive clothing that were rare or unavailable in other towns in the state. Crime was not unheard of, but it was uncommon.

Wilmington already had a well-established shipping trade when the war began. North Carolina's extensive forests of pine, oak, and cypress were well suited to the production of lumber, shingles, and turpentine. Corn, tobacco, and cotton were grown extensively on the state's farms; the plantations around Wilmington also grew rice. Such a wealth of natural and agricultural products generated a booming export business. In fact, Wilmington ranked first in the nation in the shipment of naval stores.

In spite of its status as a secondary port before the war, the town had all the requisites for becoming a refuge for blockade-running ships. Wilmington had a thriving shipping trade with other states, as well as with Europe and the Caribbean. Local businesses also ran a regular steamer service to Smithville and even up the Cape Fear River to Fayetteville, a hundred miles away. Dozens of steamers and sailing craft operated out of the port town, exchanging timber and farm products for imported goods and creating a prosperous commercial trade. Large oceangoing ships, small barges, and ketches all frequented the Wilmington piers. The steady river traffic provided work and income for locals. It also demanded the services of a large number of river pilots, whose expertise would be invaluable when the Cape Fear River became a conduit for ships during the blockade.

Wilmington was blessed with arteries for transporting goods between its piers and the interior. By 1861, three railroads radiated outward from town, carrying freight and passengers across the state.

The Wilmington and Weldon Railway led almost directly north to Weldon, North Carolina, a small town near the Virginia border. From there, the Petersburg Railroad of Virginia led straight to Richmond. This pipeline provided Lee's Army of Northern Virginia with half its arms and provisions until Northern troops disrupted the Petersburg tracks just six months before Wilmington was captured. After that, detours along the North Carolina Railroad at Goldsboro led through Greensboro and Danville to Richmond.

The Wilmington and Manchester Railroad, a less critical but still important railway, reached southward to Charleston. It served as a thoroughfare for transporting reinforcements from other Southern states and sending wounded soldiers back home. It also brought in cotton from states farther south.

The Wilmington and Rutherford Railroad stretched to the western regions of North Carolina. While it was an important line for the state, it ranked low on the Confederacy's list and was sometimes raided for rails to replace those on other tracks.

This network of railways was supplemented by several plank roads linking Wilmington with surrounding counties. And the Cape Fear River's numerous inlets gave the town access to the vast inland waterways of the state, which served as avenues of trade to the state's scattered coastal settlements.

In a ten-day period during late April and early May 1861, before the United States placed a blockading force around Cape Fear, thirty ships arrived at Wilmington and twenty-three cleared its docks. Of those leaving Wilmington, six were headed for in-state ports, but the rest sailed for Northern states, England, and the Caribbean.

Once the blockade was instituted, Wilmington's geographical location

*Opposite*: North Carolina Coastal Railroads.
The Wilmington and Weldon railroad, with its connections to Richmond along the Petersburg railroad of Virginia, was key to the delivery of supplies brought in by the blockade runners. After the Federals cut the Petersburg line, a detour was established via the North Carolina and Danville Railroads.

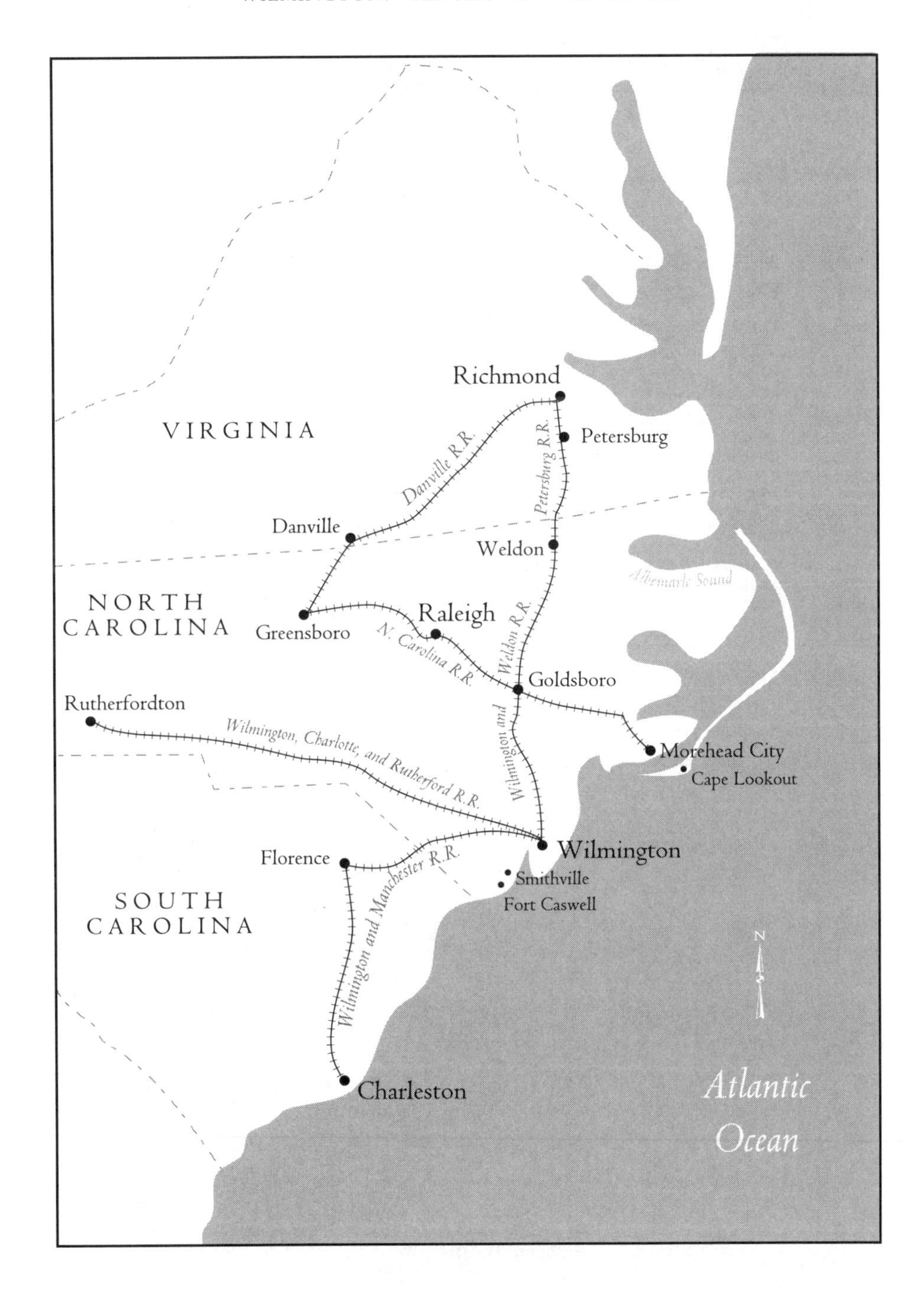
Richmond
Petersburg
VIRGINIA
Danville R.R.
Petersburg R.R.
Danville
Weldon
Albemarle Sound
NORTH
CAROLINA
Greensboro
Raleigh
N. Carolina R.R.
Weldon R.R.
Goldsboro
Rutherfordton
Wilmington, Charlotte, and Rutherford R.R.
Wilmington and
Morehead City
Cape Lookout
Wilmington
Florence
Wilmington and Manchester R.R.
Smithville
Fort Caswell
SOUTH
CAROLINA
N
Charleston
Atlantic
Ocean

## *A Pilot Saves the* Mary Celestia

The men who knew the waters of Cape Fear best were the river pilots who lived around Wilmington and Smithville and worked the Atlantic shore and the Cape Fear River. Their knowledge and skills were essential to running the blockade. Maneuvering a fast-moving ship through the shallows and into the narrow inlets of the river in pitch-black darkness would have been impossible without the guiding hands of pilots.

The Federals, also wary of the sand bars, frequently tried to persuade captured pilots to help them navigate the coastal waters, which would have enabled their gunboats to follow blockade runners as they approached the shore. Rewards were offered for the pilots' cooperation, yet almost none agreed. Admiral Lee demanded that pilots who declined his offer be imprisoned for the duration of the war, although other sailors and even captains were usually released after a short stay behind bars.

Men like John Julius Dosher of the *North Heath* and Joseph Bensel of the *City of Petersburg* had already established their standing before the war and did not hesitate to pitch in when the conflict began. Most pilots worked unheralded, but those aboard runners that acquired great notoriety became well known also. Among those who acquired unwanted recognition because of their association with such vessels were Archibald Guthrie aboard the *Robert E. Lee;* C. C. Morse, who piloted the *Cornubia*, the *Advance*, and the *Kate;* and Tom Burruss of the *Banshee*.

Pilots risked their lives to help the South. However, even their great knowledge could not always save their ships under the extreme hazards they encountered. Experienced professionals like Thomas Brinkman—who lost the *Condor* when she ran aground while trying to dodge the wreck of the *Night Hawk* in the darkness—were occasionally defeated by the heavy odds against them.

Perhaps one of the best examples of the courage and unselfish devotion of the Cape Fear pilots is seen in the story of John William Anderson.

Bermuda found itself under siege in July 1864 as the *Mary Celestia* lay at anchor in the harbor at St. George's. Yellow fever raged through the local population and invaded visiting ships. The plague felled many aboard the blockade runners, killing some. Like others awaiting a load of armaments to deliver to Wilmington, the officers and crew of the *Mary Celestia* were exposed to the clouds of mosquitoes that drifted over the docks at the whim of the wind. Unaware of the danger, the men regarded the insects as just one of the nuisances to be endured in the tropics.

Anderson had been in town only a few days before he was taken by the chills and fever that frequently mark the onset of the deadly disease. The few medical facilities on the island were already overflowing with sick natives. Since few knew how to combat the disease anyway, Anderson chose to stay with his ship and help her get back to Wilmington.

After the *Mary Celestia* left St. George's, Anderson's condition worsened until he was unable to rise from his bunk. Indeed, he was almost too weak to talk. By the time the vessel reached the outer ring of blockaders off Cape Fear, his skin had taken on the ghastly yellow hue that gives the disease its name.

As the swift little steamer picked up speed and began a run toward New Inlet, she was spotted and fired upon by a blockading ship. Although the *Mary Celestia* had a head start, the enemy seemed to be gaining. Shells from her bow cannon splashed dangerously close.

Anderson was the only man on board who knew the channels well enough to get the *Mary Celestia* in safely, but he was too weak to rise. Realizing the desperate state of the mission, he pleaded with the captain to let crewmen carry him onto the deck. Not knowing if they could catch the fever by touching him, two men lifted Anderson gently and carried him to the wheelhouse. They held his shaking, burning body upright so he could see the shoreline. Despite his fever, he scanned the coast until he recognized the area. Pinpointing the channel's path, he gave a slight nod of his head and barely audible directions to show the crew how to cross the bar.

Refusing to lie down until the *Mary Celestia* reached her anchorage, he continued to guide the helmsman through the river's hidden obstacles. When the anchor was finally dropped just north of Smithville, the adrenalin that had kept him going subsided, and Anderson collapsed and died within sight of his home.

Although few pilots had to sacrifice their lives, all of them risked their safety and their liberty on every trip through the blockade.

proved ideal for receiving blockade runners. The two widely spaced inlets into the Cape Fear River confounded Union ships trying to plug the "Rathole," through which blockade runners scampered almost at will. And the town's proximity to Nassau and Bermuda allowed cargo to be transported quickly with limited fuel.

In 1862, at the time of the *Kate*'s arrival, the rules of polite society still prevailed in Wilmington. After two years of conflict, things were still relatively normal for a town at war. However, a demon was waiting in the wings, for the *Kate* brought more than munitions and provisions on her inward voyage.

When the blockade runner had left Nassau, yellow fever had been rampant there. But the crew of the ship seemed well enough and were anxious to leave. A couple of men felt feverish and out of sorts but were able to handle their work. It was hoped that the fresh sea air would cleanse them of their disorder. Yet by the time the vessel arrived at Cape Fear, they were seriously ill.

When the ship tied up in Wilmington, most of the crewmen wandered along the waterfront, while those who were sick remained on board. Dockhands removed the heavy load of fruit, liquor, clothing, and munitions and began reloading the vessel with cotton and resin for the trip back to sea.

The *Mary Celestia*
An effective blockade runner, she was once rescued from the Yankees by her gravely ill pilot, who brought her safely into the Cape Fear River in spite of being near death from yellow fever. She later struck a rock and sank in the harbor at St. George's, Bermuda.

COURTESY OF THE MUSEUM OF THE CONFEDERACY.

Nearly three weeks later, the *Kate* pulled away from the wharf and slowly made her way down the river to Smithville, where she dropped anchor. After waiting briefly to watch for blockaders, the crew brought the ship out of the inlet as effortlessly as she had entered. In three days, the *Kate* was back in Nassau. No one on board nor anyone in Wilmington knew the damage done by her brief visit.

In mid-August, a German lumber worker whose job brought him near the docks fell ill with a fever and soon died. He was the first in a string of victims who succumbed to a mysterious disease over the next weeks, all struck down by similar symptoms that included a peculiar yellowing of the skin.

Local physicians, careful not to jump to conclusions and not wanting to start a panic, said the disorder was jaundice. It was not until the middle of September—after several residents had died from the malady—that doctors finally declared Wilmington to be in the grip of the dreaded yellow fever. By then, dozens were falling ill daily, the infection spreading in widening circles from the docks, where it had begun. Some residents, suspicious about the mystery illness and fearful of the killer "Yellow Jack," were already abandoning town.

Citizens began a desperate attempt to eliminate the filth and decaying vegetation they believed was fouling the air and causing the fever to spread. Resin was burned in tar pots along the brick sidewalks throughout town to purify the "bad" night air, but the dark, acrid clouds of smoke only added to the gloomy atmosphere pervading the empty streets.

By the first of October, the number of new cases had climbed to fifty a day. Only a few businesses continued to operate, since most merchants were either too ill or too frightened to open their doors. Those who did try to keep their stores open moved their places of residence to the nearby sounds, traveling to their shops after dawn and returning to the safe areas before nightfall. The editor of the *Wilmington Daily Journal* was forced to reduce publication to a single page once a week. He stacked copies by the doorway of the printing office, to be picked up by any who were fit enough to walk there, since no delivery boys were available.

The rampaging pestilence forced hundreds of locals to abandon their homes. Many headed for the countryside or nearby towns like Smithville. Doctors and nurses were not immune. It was not long before they, too, fell prey to the scourge, leaving many of the sick to care for themselves. Wilmington's mayor pleaded for help from Charleston. A few physicians and Catholic nuns came to help the stricken town, in spite of great personal risk.

Trains stopped running due to a lack of healthy personnel to keep them going. In turn, the loss of rail traffic interrupted mail delivery and left the cargoes of blockade runners piled on the docks. Even the telegraph offices shut down. More critical for Wilmington residents was the disruption of food delivery into town. Those who had small gardens held off hunger by living on their meager crop of vegetables. Mayor John Dawson established a central food depot to distribute the sparse supplies to all who could get to the site. But often, every member of a family was prostrated by the fever, leaving no one to go for help.

The city had not experienced yellow fever in almost fifty years, and remedies and treatments were unknown. The town's only hope was for

## *The Banshee's Nighttime Escape*

Sometimes, a heavy load of cotton taken on in Wilmington could nearly prove the death of a blockade runner. On those occasions, it took a combination of the captain's daring, the runner's superior speed, and a measure of luck to provide a narrow margin of escape.

Before twilight one evening, the *Banshee* eased up to the anchorage near Fort Fisher, preparing for a run through the blockade. It was to be a night without moonlight, perfect for an escape into the Atlantic. The thin metal skin of the vessel's deck was pressed by the weight of hundreds of bales of cotton, which were stacked in three layers and reached upward for fifteen feet. More cotton was stashed in the holds below, as was tobacco. The great weight of the cargo brought the deck so close to the water that a crewman might have reached down to touch it. Only the *Banshee*'s light draft would permit her to pass through the shallow waters of the inlet.

Usually, it was easier to evade the blockade on the outgoing voyage from Wilmington than on the incoming trip from the islands. Captain Jonathan W. Steele's plan was to skirt close to the blockading squadron's flagship, anchored at a fixed position just offshore. As the other ships patrolled in the darkness, a small circle of safety would be left around the stationary vessel. The *Banshee* should be able to steam right through the enemy lines by passing between the flagship and the patrolling gunboats.

Steele and his officers rowed over to Fort Fisher to confer with Colonel Lamb, who kept close watch on the United States fleet. He informed them that the flagship was the USS *Minnesota*. The men from the *Banshee* carefully checked the flagship's location through their glass, knowing she would still be there when they emerged from the river.

When twilight faded into darkness, the crew of the *Banshee* weighed anchor, headed out of the inlet, and slipped by as close to the *Minnesota* as they dared. If the watch on the sixty-gun frigate saw them as they eased by, there was no indication. Either the stealth of the *Banshee* prevented her being sighted or the admiral's crew felt vigilance was solely the duty of the patrolling vessels. The runner was soon past the first line of picket ships and well into the middle cordon of blockaders.

There, the *Banshee*'s luck ran out, as one of the cruisers started after her, firing as she came. Ordinarily, the *Banshee* was a fast ship. Now, however, she was little more than a bulky, slow-moving pile of cotton that had a tendency to roll and responded sluggishly to the helm. Yet Steele felt his vessel was still swift enough to outrun the ships of the blockading fleet, and he pressed his engineers for the maximum knots she could attain.

As the two vessels plowed on through the darkness, the blockader fell farther and farther behind, until the crew of the *Banshee* could no longer make out their pursuer's form. At that moment, Steele ordered a radical change of direction that took them ninety degrees off their original course. Minutes later, he called for all engines to stop. Rocking gently in the silence, the *Banshee* sat in waiting, all action suspended, until the enemy reappeared. The gunboat soon loomed out of the shadowy distance, still headed on her original course and still firing randomly into the empty sea ahead.

When the flash and rumble of the blockader's cannon receded into the distance, the runner picked up speed and continued toward Nassau. Thanks to Captain Steele's tactics, the *Banshee*—encumbered as she was by her weighty cargo—had emerged victorious. And Steele's company reaped enormous profits, as the cotton on this single voyage alone was worth more than $125,000.

an early frost to stay the spread of the deadly disease. Unfortunately, Wilmington was experiencing an unusually warm autumn, and the onset of freezing temperatures was later than anyone could remember. Finally, on November 10, a hard frost spread a welcome silvery coating across Wilmington and put an end to the worst plague the town had ever known. Although a few unfortunate individuals who had been infected earlier continued to fall ill, the deadly mosquito that was the unsuspected culprit had been eradicated.

Two things are necessary for the transmission of yellow fever: an infected person and the *Aedes aegypti* mosquito, which spreads the virus by biting the infected person and then moving on to another person. The mosquito normally survives only in semitropical zones. No one knows whether the *Aedes aegypti* mosquito was already in Wilmington or whether it was delivered aboard a ship from the islands, but the disease was certainly transmitted to the local population through the infected sailors aboard the *Kate*.

Records list 1,505 known cases and 550 deaths, but since many were too poor or ill to seek medical care, their illness went unreported. It is believed that the actual cases might have topped 2,000, with fatalities numbering close to 700. At least 30 people who traveled outside Wilmington after becoming infected were reported to have died. Many of the deceased, some unidentified, were buried in mass graves in Oakdale Cemetery. Within three deadly months, the town lost nearly 10 percent of its population to the lethal hemorrhagic fever, which causes victims to bleed internally and often suffer a final "black vomit" of blood from the stomach.

By Christmas, most of the town's population had returned, although some would stay away until after the war. As a testament to the goodwill among the local people, the editor of the *Wilmington Daily Journal* stated that even during the epidemic, when there had been virtually no policemen patrolling, little theft had occurred. He said that during the months when the fever left streets and homes unguarded, he himself had lost just two ducks to theft, one so old and tough that he felt sorry for the thief. Only near the end of the war, when greed and speculation pushed the town to the edge of starvation and mean, tough out-of-towners moved in, did such things as the vegetables from backyard gardens become subject to looting.

Rail traffic and shipping soon resumed, but a quarantine station established on the river between Smithville and Wilmington during the epidemic was maintained throughout the rest of the war. All ships arriving from infected ports were required to stop there on their way upriver and wait for several days before continuing to Wilmington. Health authorities boarded the blockade runners to check for disease before allowing the vessels to proceed to port. No one wanted another bout with the killer disease.

After Charleston Harbor was choked off in 1863, a cotton compress was established on the west side of the Cape Fear River near the wharves. Its potent, steam-powered presses could reduce the volume of cotton by two-thirds and turn out five hundred bales a day. The compacted cubes of fiber, held together by burlap and rope or steel bands, weighed as much as five hundred pounds. By compressing the cotton, more could be loaded on blockade runners. Skilled stevedores used screw jacks to cram the bales into every available space below deck, then stacked layers on the deck until the vessels themselves looked like large, floating bales of cotton. The bales provided a protective barrier against Yankee gunfire and could be dropped overboard as a last resort to lighten the ship during a chase. They occasionally served as a fuel additive when desperate crews dipped them in resin and threw them into the fires to deliver emergency speed.

Large blockade runners could carry as many as a thousand bales of compressed cotton. Thus, when the blockade drove the price of cotton to almost a dollar a pound in Europe, a single cargo could be worth nearly half a million dollars. After the officers and crews were paid and the transshipment merchants received their commissions, profits were still enormous. Even if the cost of fuel and the occasional loss of an entire ship and its cargo are taken into consideration, companies turned a profit if their ships could make just a couple of trips through the blockade. The sale of cotton could keep the South in the war if blockade runners could get it out of Wilmington and into Europe.

The passage of blockade runners into and out of the Cape Fear River grew to massive proportions. Soon, as many as forty ships were entering Wilmington each month. Most captains chose moonless nights for their forays, although a few preferred bright moonlight because it exposed the lurking Union gunboats and helped the swift runners avoid them. Still, during the week of the dark of the moon, traffic into Wilmington surged.

The occupation of the northeastern corner of North Carolina by Union forces early in the war left the strategic Wilmington and Weldon Railway exposed to constant harassment and sabotage. The railway was hard to maintain due to a lack of iron rails, wooden crossties, and manpower. And it was almost impossible to obtain new locomotives from elsewhere in the South's already stressed rail network. Because of the condition of both engines and track, trains crept along at less than ten miles per hour and had to make frequent stops for repairs. As a result, materials piled up at Wilmington, and horse-drawn wagons were used to help deliver goods into Virginia.

Due to such problems of distribution, successful runs of ships through the blockade did not guarantee that Confederate soldiers would have the arms, clothing, and food they needed. Many Rebel troops, unused to cold winters, walked barefoot through snow-covered Virginia fields in tattered uniforms and sat coatless around their small campfires while they stirred a little fatback into their cornmeal gruel. After combat, the Rebels often had to resort to scouring the battlefield, ghoulishly retrieving abandoned rifles to supply their weapon needs.

As the war rolled unabated into its third full year and blockade running into Wilmington continued to grow, the town was forced to expand its port facilities. Additional warehouses were built to hold perishable goods and to protect armaments from the corrosive effects of the salt-laden mists that sometimes drifted in from the ocean. The Confederate government sent agents to supervise the flow of arms, to coordinate the efforts of the blockade runners, and to improve the river's defenses. By then, it had become clear to most among the Confederate leadership that the loss of Wilmington would draw the final curtain on the South's aspiration to exist as an independent nation.

One noteworthy officer present since the early days was William Henry Chase Whiting, appointed by Governor Ellis to prepare Wilmington for war back in April 1861. Upon his arrival, Whiting had started the long process of turning the Cape Fear region into one

## *A Cargo Saved, a Vessel Lost*

Armaments and food were so desperately needed by Rebel soldiers that the cargoes of blockade runners were sometimes more valuable than the ships themselves. If a ship became stranded while trying to reach Wilmington, urgent attempts to salvage the supplies were set in motion by her crew and by soldiers on shore, lest the Yankees destroy the goods or take them as booty. Tugboats transported rescued goods into the city once they were landed from a stranded vessel. Several loads of clothing, munitions, and food were saved in this manner.

For its part, the Union government was rich in war goods. Although it sought to salvage the cargo of stranded runners to keep it out of Rebel hands, its more immediate need was for the vessels themselves. Admiral Lee was anxious to get his hands on speedy runners that could be armed and converted to ships of the blockading squadron.

One dark night, the *Wild Dayrell* grounded when she tried to run too close to the Cape Fear shore. So firmly embedded in the sand was she that her engines stood no chance of refloating her. But tons of supplies were still safe in her holds, and Confederate recovery efforts started at once.

Meanwhile, the pride of the blockade, the USS *Sassacus*, was cruising a few miles out to sea on her wide-ranging patrol. Lieutenant Commander Francis A. Roe noted something suspicious in the distance and turned to investigate.

When the *Sassacus* drew near, Roe found the *Wild Dayrell* beached and her crew busily tossing cargo overboard, where it was being carried to shore in small boats. Not one to relinquish an opportunity, Roe fired his weapons in the direction of the runner, scattering the salvage crew. His men then rowed over and went aboard the derelict, which they found to be fairly intact, with part of her cargo still stored below.

From just before lunchtime until after midnight, the *Sassacus* tried unsuccessfully to tow the blockade runner off the reef. It was early February and the weather was bitterly cold. When a storm blew in, conditions became unbearable, and the *Sassacus* temporarily abandoned the effort and returned to sea.

She returned the next morning despite a blustery wind. The USS *Florida* subsequently showed up and joined the effort to salvage cargo and tow the *Wild Dayrell*. Crewmen were allowed to take anything they wanted from among the blankets, shoes, and provisions aboard the runner. The men of the two ships worked for two fruitless days, during which time the Rebels sniped at them from behind the dunes and the anchor cable of the *Sassacus* parted. After feeling the hull of his ship bump against the sea floor a couple of times, Roe decided it was too risky to continue the operation.

After all the crewmen had returned to the Federal ships with their booty, the two gunboats began to fire into the stranded hulk. A team was later dispatched to set fire to the vessel and any remaining cargo. Leaving the *Wild Dayrell* burning vigorously, the *Sassacus* and the *Florida* steamed back to their stations in the Atlantic.

The ship was a total loss. But that is not to say that her grounding at Cape Fear bore no fruit, since the Confederates brought more than half her cargo into Wilmington the hard way and the Federals enjoyed all her riches they were able to carry.

of the most heavily armed sites of the war.

As a member of the Confederate army, Whiting could not be ordered by the governor to remain in Wilmington, and he was soon transferred to another assignment. He was replaced by Brigadier General Joseph Anderson, who was superseded by General Samuel French within less than a year. Hardly six months later, in November 1862, newly promoted Brigadier General Whiting was ordered back to Wilmington.

When he relieved French, he was dismayed to find what little progress had been made in his absence. He was quite pleased, though, with the efforts of Colonel William Lamb, who had made Fort Anderson a formidable defensive site. He sent Lamb to Federal Point to expand Fort Fisher.

Lamb and Whiting formed a dedicated team, respectful of each other and devoted to saving Wilmington from capture. At the end, when other general officers abandoned Lamb and Fort Fisher, it would be Whiting who joined the battle, at the cost of his own life.

Though Whiting succeeded in turning the Cape Fear region into a mighty bastion of earthworks armed with modern weaponry, he never was able to obtain sufficient troops to defend against a determined Northern ground attack. As a result, he and most of the citizens of Wilmington endured three years of invasion jitters, knowing that the area's small contingent of Rebel soldiers could be overwhelmed.

Several factors delayed the feared Union attack on Wilmington. Rumors of underwater traps in the river, uncertainty about the capabilities of the many forts defending the Cape Fear region, and "ram fever"—the fear of Confederate ironclad ships—was enough to stay military initiatives by the Union. But perhaps the most crucial factor that kept Wilmington safe from assault until 1865 was the failure of Northern government officials and military planners to recognize the role the city played in sustaining the Confederate war effort.

Actually, this was a failing that United States and Confederate authorities shared. The Confederate naval flotilla at Wilmington was a mixed array of underpowered, poorly armed vessels whose movements and functions were weakly coordinated. Several locally owned steamers—among them the *A. P. Hart*, the *J. T. Petteway*, and the *Kate McLaurin*—were already regulars on the Wilmington waterfront when war broke out. These were used to transport troops and to deliver supplies to the coastal fortifications. And the Northern tug *Uncle Ben* was appropriated when she entered the harbor immediately after Fort Sumter was attacked. Later, her engine was removed to power the ironclad CSS *North Carolina*. Tugs were used to help stranded ships break free and to carry cargo off blockade runners that found themselves hopelessly grounded.

Three U. S. Naval officers
On the left is Commander Sidney S. Lee, who joined the Confederate Navy; in the center is Captain Samuel F. DuPont, who would head the South Atlantic Blockading Fleet; and on the right is Lieutenant David D. Porter, commander of the North Atlantic Blockading Fleet. Porter also led the attack that brought down Fort Fisher.

COURTESY OF THE U. S. NAVAL HISTORICAL CENTER.

The Committee of Safety, a self-proclaimed defense group organized for the protection of Wilmington and headed by Mayor Dawson, prodded the inattentive Confederate navy into authorizing the construction of two ironclads at local shipyards. The larger vessel, the *North Carolina,* was built at the port's major yard, Benjamin W. Beery and Sons, located on Eagle Island at the west bank of the river. The other vessel, the *Raleigh,* was constructed by Cassidey Boat Builders, located across the river at the edge of town.

The purpose of the ironclads was to provide river defense. Neither

## *The Charge of the* Robert E. Lee

John Wilkinson was one of the most daring of the Confederate naval officers who captained blockade runners. Wilkinson served aboard warships as well, and he also did a stint of land duty in Wilmington, where he reorganized the lights and the signal system to help runners pass through the two inlets of the Cape Fear River.

He is probably best known for his command of the *Robert E. Lee*, one of the most effective of the Confederacy's runners. Wilkinson's ingenuity and daring saved the ship from capture on several occasions. Once, when his escape from Wilmington was blocked by a Union gunboat, he did the only thing he could—he charged right at the vessel and forced her to give way.

After clearing Old Inlet one dark evening, Wilkinson directed the *Robert E. Lee* at full speed close along the shoreline. He hoped the low silhouette of his sidewheeler would blend into the background of trees and dunes until he could safely turn out to sea and set a course for Bermuda.

Unfortunately, his ship was soon spotted by the vigilant crew of a patrolling blockader. The Federal ship was so close that the crew of the *Robert E. Lee* clearly heard the enemies' cries to man the cannon and open fire.

Wilkinson's helmsman was a fierce old salt by the name of McLean, a man just as daring as his captain and just as unlikely to shrink from a challenge. When Wilkinson gave the command to turn directly toward the blockader and "run her down," McLean never hesitated. He aimed the speeding vessel directly at the enemy ship, which lay just a few dozen yards before the *Robert E. Lee*.

The crew of the blockader scrambled to take evasive maneuvers to avoid being hit. Their ship had barely steamed out of the way when the runner whisked by, missing the blockader's stern by a hair's-breadth. Wilkinson said later that if the blockader had not moved so expeditiously, his sidewheeler would surely have sliced her in two.

By the time the rattled gunners recovered their composure and brought their weapons to bear, Wilkinson and his ship were receding rapidly into the night. The errant missiles discharged toward them splashed harmlessly into the ocean nowhere near the target.

Clearly, Wilkinson had not been bluffing. But on other occasions, he proved himself equally adept at scheming his way through the blockade. No runner was ever captured while under the command of John Wilkinson, although he served on several vessels and had a record of more than two dozen successful trips.

was suited to attacking the Union fleet. The *North Carolina,* encased in more than fifty tons of iron, rode so low in the water that she could hardly maneuver in the river, much less cross the bar into the Atlantic. Fortunately, such facts were unknown to the crews of the blockading vessels, who watched the construction of the *North Carolina* and the *Raleigh* nervously.

The *Raleigh* did make one foray out of New Inlet, charging in among the ships of the Union blockade and scattering them in alarm. Both sides fired several salvos, but none of the Northern shells found its mark, and only one shell from the ironclad caused any damage, perforating the smokestack of an enemy vessel. Although it was clear that the *Raleigh* was no *Virginia,* it was hoped she could at least remain in the river and offer supporting fire to the guns of Fort Fisher. Unfortunately, upon reentering the Cape Fear River, the ship became stuck halfway over a sand bar. With the sand bar as a fulcrum, the downward force of the heavy armor on the two ends of the ship broke the *Raleigh* in half. Salvaging her guns and iron was all that could be done. The *Raleigh* had sailed her last voyage.

Late in the war, the CSS *Chickamauga* and the CSS *Tallahassee* briefly used Wilmington as a base for their forays against Northern shipping. Although the two vessels had some success, many in Wilmington, including General Whiting, feared their attacks would bring retribution on the town. Whiting pleaded with President Jefferson Davis to discontinue the sorties, but Davis felt that the ships could serve to reduce the pressure of the blockade by luring Union ships to pursue them. Generals Robert E. Lee and Braxton Bragg supported Whiting, believing that if the two vessels remained on the river, their firepower could help protect Wilmington against attack.

Bowing to the will of Bragg and Whiting, the Confederate command returned the *Tallahassee,* renamed the *Olustee,* to Wilmington after a successful commerce-destroying raid. Once again, the steamer was renamed, this time becoming the *Chameleon.* Her guns were removed, and she was converted into a blockade runner under the command of John Wilkinson.

The *Chickamauga* was converted into a defensive vessel and remained in the Cape Fear River for the duration of the war. Later, during the attack on Fort Fisher, the sailors of the *Chickamauga* were the only men who knew how to fire the new Brooke rifles deployed at Battery Buchanan. Coming to the soldiers' aid, they fired the guns with such effectiveness that even Union officers remarked on their skill. Their bravery under fire and their accurate shooting earned them the respect of the fort's defenders. When the sailors were finally relieved, soldiers who had once wanted to fight them on the streets of Wilmington applauded them for their efforts.

But incidents like this were the exception rather than the rule during the latter part of the war. Morale was low among Confederate naval officers, who were unimpressed with the quality of the Cape Fear fleet. And the crews had little to do, since the vessels remained at anchor a large portion of the time. To overcome boredom, the navy men spent much of their time strolling Wilmington's streets, looking for entertainment or creating their own. Their apparently lazy lifestyle and their rowdiness irritated locals and stirred hostility among army troops, who were constantly training or building fortifications and resented the sailors' free time.

There were frequent fights along the waterfront. Soldiers and sailors fought with the crews of blockade runners and with each other. Some of the men rounded up in foreign ports to serve as temporary crewmen on the runners were rogues. They had none of the polish and class of the British officers and men who commonly manned the ships. These criminals robbed and even killed with little compunction. It soon became unsafe for law-abiding citizens to walk the streets, especially near the docks.

Much of the suspicion and jealousy that developed between navy and army men in Wilmington likely resulted from the friction between the navy's local commander, Flag Officer William F. Lynch, and General Whiting. Lynch and Whiting continually fought for control of the port. Lynch also antagonized North Carolina's new governor, Zebulon Vance, by taking the best coal for his ships, leaving only the low-grade variety to fuel the state's own blockade runners, which lost speed and smoked heavily as a result.

Things got so bad that at one point, Lynch threatened to have one of his vessels deliver a broadside to one of the state's blockade runners. On another occasion, Whiting sent troops to remove marines who had been ordered by Lynch to take control of a blockade runner at the docks.

Irked by the continual bickering, Jefferson Davis called both men to Richmond to try to reach a solution. Eventually, he replaced Lynch and sent Braxton Bragg to take charge of the region's defenses. Although this eliminated the quarreling between Lynch and Whiting, many felt the arrival of the hapless Bragg spelled disaster for Wilmington. Later, when Bragg did little to reinforce and defend Fort Fisher during the Union attack, some believed their fears had been justified.

Against this background, the women of Wilmington formed their own organization to help the war effort. The Ladies' Soldiers' Aid Society raised money and provided food to soldiers. Its special cause was the seriously injured men who stopped briefly at the train station on their way through town. Mrs. Armand J. deRossett served as president of the group. Under her leadership, the women fed soldiers, made socks, sewed cartridge bags, and tended to the wounded.

The riches to be had from blockade running attracted speculators and scalawags into town. After Wilmington became the South's major depot for contraband, the moneychangers and hard-edged, salty crewmen who arrived in large numbers changed the quality of local life. Speculators came from Charleston, New Orleans, and other ports where the blockade had put them out of business. As they gradually took control of the auctions of food and other nonmilitary goods arriving on the incoming ships, prices were driven up and the value of Confederate money dropped. The cost of locally produced food items rose as well, until those with fixed incomes could barely obtain enough nourishment to survive. It was said that anyone hoping to fill a food basket in Wilmington's markets had best bring along a basket of money.

Food was always available for those with plenty of money, including the crews of the blockade runners and the rich speculators. Young, well-dressed British sailors paid outrageous prices to rent some of the best local homes, where they held parties throughout the night. The ability and willingness of blockade-running crews to pay high prices helped fuel local inflation, but it was the speculators who were the worst culprits.

Outside groups conspired to pool their bids at public auctions, which allowed them to obtain most of the goods brought in by blockade runners. Unable to compete, local businessmen got little, and what they did acquire came at a cost that few residents could afford. The inflation rate skyrocketed to more than 1,000 percent on common merchandise such as salt. Luxury items like coffee were well beyond the reach of most who lived in wartime Wilmington.

A diet of sweet potatoes, cornbread, and greens was the fare for the majority of residents, who had to rely on their own gardens and the few vegetables brought in from nearby farms. They obtained seafood by fishing in local streams and the ocean, and they brewed a poor imitation of coffee by parching wheat, rye, or even okra seeds. Molasses and sorghum syrup were about the only sweets available, and flour biscuits with butter were a treasured luxury.

When a blockade runner arrived, many rushed to the docks hoping to share in the celebration of the crew, who sometimes invited locals on board for a little champagne or a few oranges and bananas. Exquisite fare including hams, potted meat, cheeses, sardines, and fine wines were brought to Wilmington's docks almost daily. But in the midst of plenty, most residents suffered malnourishment, and few Southern soldiers in the fields had enough to eat.

Some in town and in the government began to view blockade running as an evil for the ruinous effect it was having on the South's economy. It was clear that the companies involved in running the blockade were catering to the wants of speculators at the expense of the Confederacy, and that the needs of Rebel troops took second place to expensive luxuries that brought high profits to investors. Soon, North Carolina began looking into running its own ships to assure that the state's soldiers would have the food and clothing they needed, and leaders in Richmond began considering restrictions to give the South control of the blockade-running trade.

None of this helped the beleaguered natives of Wilmington. But as the war progressed, the harried locals grew even tougher. They remained loyal to the Southern cause until Union troops marched into the city and forced them to swear an oath of allegiance to the United States. The town served the Confederacy well. And although hunger, poverty, and disease were common, Wilmington suffered little physical damage from the war. It was spared the destruction felt by other Southern towns that happened to find themselves in the path of Sherman's March to the Sea.

At least half the arms and provisions supplying the Rebel armies during the final years of the war passed through Wilmington. Without the goods brought in aboard blockade runners, there would have been little hope for Southern troops, who were outnumbered by more than two to one. Some claim that except for Richmond, Wilmington was the most important city in the Confederacy. They may be mistaken; toward the end of the war, Wilmington might have been the most important.

Chapter 6

# NORTH CAROLINA TAKES A ROLE

"I don't like to be troublesome
but if you have an opportunity
I would be glad if you would
send me a box of something to eat.
Our fare is pretty rough."

A NORTH CAROLINA SOLDIER
*in a letter to his mother*

# NORTH CAROLINA TAKES A ROLE

ONLY THE THINNEST sliver of new moon hung in the darkened summer sky. Conditions were ideal for the blockade runner *Modern Greece* to make it safely into New Inlet. But as the large, gray ship steamed toward Cape Fear, everyone on board was tense. Sailors have always been a superstitious lot.

Even after a full year of war, everyone said the Northern blockade of Wilmington was ineffective. Ships passed through the scanty collection of sluggish Union vessels unscathed almost every day, bringing goods to the needy South and returning high profits to investors. Still, the crew of the *Modern Greece* knew that eager Yankee sailors were on watch out there in the darkness, itching for the chance to take a rich cargo.

Measuring over two hundred feet from bow to stern, the *Modern Greece* was one of the largest vessels to attempt to run the blockade into Wilmington, and her holds were packed with two million pounds of gunpowder, hundreds of Enfield rifles, and four of the latest Whitworth long-range, rifled cannon.

Had the blockaders known, there were items aboard the runner that would have stirred even greater excitement—hundreds of barrels and kegs of "spirituous liquors." The grog ration for the crews of blockading ships would not be eliminated for another two months, but sailors were always anxious to expand their liquor stores and never hesitated to sample the wares from wrecked or captured blockade runners. The elegant clothing and other choice civilian goods that typically made up a large portion of incoming contraband could be evaluated by the prize courts, which would then tender large monetary rewards for all to share. These were reasons enough to motivate the Northern sailors and to keep the men on the blockade runner nervous.

The *Modern Greece* moved southward toward Fort Fisher. By four o'clock, an early-morning haze had settled over the waters near Cape Fear. With New Inlet and safety a mere five miles ahead, the captain hoped the fog might conceal his ship during the last twenty minutes of the voyage and allow her to reach the river without being discovered. Once the ship was under the guns of Fort Fisher, no Yankee cruiser would dare try to take her.

The pilot guided the ship along the Atlantic's choppy edge, ready to make a hard turn to starboard upon reaching the inlet. So far, the men aboard the runner had not spotted a single ship as they cruised along the shoreline. Their ship was difficult to detect, and if they could not see any blockaders, then the enemy was unlikely to see the *Modern Greece*.

The *Modern Greece* was truly modern, having been built in England just three years earlier. She was a propeller-driven, iron steamer, yet like most steamships of the day, she was also rigged for sails. Her pilot probably would have preferred paddle wheels to a propeller, for he could not approach the shallows with the same confidence afforded by shallow-draft sidewheelers. If her deep-running propeller happened to encounter one of the constantly migrating sand bars, the *Modern Greece* would be left exposed to the enemy when daylight arrived.

Forced to run along the deeper portion of the coastal shelf, the ship steamed too close to the USS *Cambridge*, which was also running within a mile of the beach. In spite of the veil of mist, one of that ship's lookouts spotted the stacks of the *Modern Greece* and yelled the alarm.

The *Cambridge*'s fires were already hot, since the ship was on her nightly patrol. Her well-trained gun crews were also ready. Within seconds, she was in pursuit of the heavily laden blockade runner. Although Union men like those on the *Cambridge* liked to complain about the constant training routines they endured, their practice made them efficient, and now they had a chance to put the results to good use.

Captain William A. Parker fired rockets to signal other blockaders that the *Cambridge* was in hot pursuit of a runner and to indicate the direction of the chase. This also alerted the captain of the *Modern Greece,* who barely had time to hoist British colors before receiving a more urgent notification of danger—a shot from the *Cambridge*'s Parrot gun that rattled through his ship's rigging. It was clear that the ruse of claiming to be an innocent English merchant vessel was not working, and the captain ordered full steam ahead. As the Union gunboat continued to fire, shells began to splash all around the zigzagging *Modern Greece.* Soon, they began to find their mark, plunging into the blockade runner and penetrating her hull in several places.

Any hope of evasion was thwarted when another Union cruiser, the *Stars and Stripes,* moved to head off the runner and prevent her entry into the inlet. The gods of good fortune were not with the *Modern Greece* that day, for Captain Roderick S. McCook of the *Stars and Stripes* also opened fire with every weapon available. Although the harried runner had come within range of Fort Fisher's guns, it was too late to get away. McCook could not close on his quarry due to the accurate fire from the fort, but he was able to fire his long-distance, rifled cannon at the *Modern Greece.* He even tried skipping cannonballs from his eight-inchers across the water into the blockade runner.

It was clear the vessel would never reach New Inlet, which lay just a tantalizing mile ahead. As a last resort to save the cargo, the captain ordered the pilot to aim the *Modern Greece* directly toward shore. Steaming at her maximum speed of almost fifteen knots, the ship grounded with tremendous force and drove well up into the shallows.

Battered and shaken, the crew realized their ship was hopelessly lost. Struggling to their feet, they lowered the boats over the side, scrambled aboard, and rowed to shore. Troops from Fort Fisher rushed out to meet them and help them into the earthen enclosure, where they would be safe from gunfire and could change into dry clothing.

The overcast sky that morning revealed a panorama of disaster. The *Modern Greece* lay like a stranded whale just outside the breaking surf, while the two Yankee gunboats circled a couple of miles offshore, still hopeful of salvaging the ship or her goods. The light of day improved

## *The* Cornubia *Beats Five-to-One Odds*

To overcome some of the problems of dealing with privately owned blockade-running firms, the South began to buy some ships of its own early in the war. Although the Confederate government's control of the trade would not fully blossom until later, the few ships acquired in the early days rendered great service to the Rebels by making a number of successful trips into Wilmington.

One of the most productive such vessels was the twin-stack sidewheeler *Cornubia*, a former passenger ferry. Purchased in late 1862 by Caleb Huse for the Ordnance Division of the War Department and turned into a blockade runner under the command of Lieutenant Richard Gayle of the Confederate navy, she would rack up one of the best records of the war, though her term of service would span less than a year.

The *Cornubia* had her share of narrow escapes from the ships of the North Atlantic Blockading Squadron. One of her many successful evasions came on an early Sunday morning in 1863, when she arrived off Topsail Island four days out of Bermuda. The light of day exposed her smoke to the enemy while she was still more than a hundred miles from Fort Fisher. She was first sighted by lookouts aboard the USS *State of Georgia*, who signaled the USS *Mount Vernon* to take up the chase. The *Cornubia* sped on toward the coast at fourteen knots as the *Mount Vernon* swung toward her. The pursuit was then joined by the *Cambridge* and the *Daylight*, both of which had been patrolling nearby. A couple of hours later, lookouts aboard the USS *Iroquois* noted the smoke, and that vessel, too, took out after the *Cornubia*.

Captain Gayle was disappointed to have been discovered so far from his goal. He ordered full speed from his engines, hoping to elude the chasers until nightfall, when he believed he could escape. But nightfall was a long way off.

All the pursuers trailed the *Cornubia* by at least four miles, but the closest seemed to be gaining. Around nine o'clock, the blockade runner entered a fog bank. As soon as his ship was enveloped by the blanket of mist, Gayle ordered a course change, heading the *Cornubia* directly for shore.

Lieutenant James Trathen, commander of the *Mount Vernon* and a man wise to the ways of blockade runners, set a course to head off the Rebel ship. Within an hour, when a westerly breeze sprang up and cleared away the haze, the *Cornubia* reappeared exactly where Trathen had anticipated. The Yankee captain ordered barrels of pitch and rancid pork tossed into his boiler fires to extract a few more knots from his vessel.

Such tricks were common among blockade runners. So common, in fact, that when Captain A. Ludlow Case of the trailing *Iroquois* saw clouds of black smoke belching from the fast-moving *Mount Vernon*, he assumed it to be another blockade runner. He ordered full sail in hopes of catching at least one of what he now believed were two juicy targets. But the *Iroquois* could eke out only twelve knots, and the other ships gradually widened the gap. After five hours, Case's ship had fallen a good ten miles behind, and he was forced to give up the chase.

In the meantime, the *Mount Vernon*, which had gained on the *Cornubia*, opened fire on her, but the distance remained too great, and the shot fell at least a half-mile short. Still, Trathen was heartened by the advantage he had gained and ordered full sail. The quarry managed to stay just out of cannon range.

Aboard the *Cornubia*, Captain Gayle was disappointed that his ruse had not fooled his pursuers. Determined to escape, he ordered the crew to toss some of the heavy cargo into the sea. The men struggled to bring about half of the six hundred barrels of gunpowder up from below and drop them over the side, where they were left bobbing like corks in the ship's foamy wake. Despite their value, most of the one hundred ingots of lead on board the *Cornubia* were also surrendered to the deep, since they proved the easiest way to get rid of weight quickly. Now several tons lighter, the steamer seemed to take on new life as she surged ahead.

On the *Mount Vernon*, Trathen was surprised to see his prey begin to widen the space between them, but he realized what had happened when his ship passed through a large mass of floating debris. Although he managed to stay within view of the *Cornubia* until sundown, darkness eventually swallowed the pale gray quarry. Trathen knew that further pursuit was useless. He ordered his ship's hot, straining engines slowed.

The *Cornubia* steamed on unscathed through the night and arrived off Masonboro Inlet by early morning. James Burroughs, the pilot on this voyage, steered her in close to shore, where the crew got word to Colonel Lamb of their presence and their intent to pass through New Inlet. Lamb immediately ordered the guns of Fort Fisher readied. The gunners watched for the approaching ship, ready to provide cover for her entry into the Cape Fear River.

Whipping along the very edge of the breakers at better than fifteen miles per hour, the ship completed the last twelve miles in just forty-five minutes. To avoid fire from the fort, the Union gunboats had moved out to sea at the first hint of daylight, and the *Cornubia* passed into the river before they could attempt an interception. Although she had jettisoned cargo valued at around twenty thousand dollars, the *Cornubia* still carried supplies worth many times that amount into Wilmington.

Within three weeks, the blockade runner departed for Bermuda carrying more than three hundred bales of cotton and several casks of tobacco and turpentine, to be sold at high prices for the Confederate government.

Before finally being captured in late 1863, she completed eighteen runs on behalf of the Ordnance Department. It was the performance of vessels like the *Cornubia* that helped convince officials in Richmond to acquire Confederate-owned ships to move war goods through Bermuda and Nassau to Wilmington.

the accuracy of Fort Fisher's gunners, whose occasional near misses kept the *Cambridge* and the *Stars and Stripes* at a distance, although they maintained a desultory firing at the stricken ship.

The crews of the two blockaders had fired more than two hundred shots and had pierced the runner's hull in about ten places. They were surprised when the guns at Fort Fisher were also turned on the *Modern Greece*. The rescued crew had warned Colonel Lamb of the tons of gunpowder aboard the *Modern Greece*. He knew he must puncture the ship to let water in, or else the hot shells from the blockaders would set off an explosion that would eliminate any possibility of saving the other cargo.

After a brief stop for breakfast, the Yankees opened fire again, but they could see that their shooting was having little effect. Feeling that the ship and her load had been adequately destroyed, Captains Parker and McCook took their ships back to their daytime anchorage three miles from shore, leaving the derelict to the Rebels.

Soldiers from the fort and volunteers from Wilmington soon gathered on the shore and set up a salvage operation to retrieve cargo from the *Modern Greece*. They were pleased to see that the Union attackers had left prematurely, for much of the cargo was still intact. The ship's high resting place had kept water from damaging the contents in the upper portion of her holds. Gunpowder was almost always loaded in the bottom of a ship's hull to protect it from gunfire. Although most of the gunpowder aboard the *Modern Greece* was lost to water damage, the remaining goods were safe.

What followed was one of the most successful recovery operations of the war. A rich windfall of goods was saved for the Confederates and the merchants. Having lost both his ship and his cargo, however, the *Modern Greece*'s unfortunate British owner was forced into bankruptcy.

The most important items rescued were four Whitworth rifles. Colonel Lamb used them to extend Fort Fisher's protection for blockade runners to five miles. Along with the British-made Whitworths, Lamb recovered a supply of the twelve-pound, hexagonal bolts they fired. The retrieval of the accurate breechloaders saved numerous blockade runners from the fate of the *Modern Greece*. Several hundred pounds of gunpowder were also recovered, much of it protected inside wooden casks. A large number of British Enfield rifles were found, but not all of them could be saved.

Of more interest to local businessmen were the barrels and kegs of fine alcoholic beverages left intact aboard the *Modern Greece*. Expensive clothing was also pulled from the derelict and offered at auction in Wilmington.

At that point in the war, local merchants were still able to bid successfully for the cargoes of blockade runners, and much of the finery and alcohol from the *Modern Greece* was offered for sale on the local streets. Wilmington auctioneer Wilkes Morris advertised forty casks of aged Scotch whiskey, a hundred casks of regular Scotch, twenty cases of pale cognac and twenty of dark, a hundred casks of champagne, twenty casks of brandy, and five cases of sparkling Burgundy. He also offered three casks of Epsom salts and twenty kegs of bicarbonate of soda, possibly for use by those who bought all that alcohol.

O. S. Baldwin's store advertised 150 dozen fine shirts, 200 dozen pairs of men's hosiery, 12 dozen fine English razors, 50 dozen umbrellas, and 50 dozen pairs of dress gloves. The store also listed 10 gross of buttons, a case of doeskins, a case of linen handkerchiefs, and 20 reams of English letter paper. The editor of the *Wilmington Daily Journal* reported seeing large numbers of seasonal undergarments salvaged from the *Modern Greece* stacked on shelves at Baldwin's store. He encouraged local soldiers to stop in and purchase what they needed before out-of-state merchants came in to buy up the lot.

The Whitworths, rifles, and gunpowder aside, it's easy to see that a very large portion of the *Modern Greece*'s cargo consisted of luxury items of no use to the war effort. Since doctors had little to offer to ease the pain of soldiers facing surgery, the Confederate government imported some liquor for use as anaesthesia, but most of the alcohol brought in aboard blockade runners was intended for civilian consumption. The companies that owned blockade-running ships made their own decisions regarding the cargoes, leaving the Confederacy to settle for whatever it could get.

It was political infighting and jealousy that had put the South in this predicament.

Early in the war, Stephen Mallory, secretary of the Confederate navy,

# *The* Don *Makes Another Escape*

On their runs to Wilmington, North Carolina's blockade runners—the *Don*, the *Annie*, the *Hansa*, and the *Advance*—delivered thousands of pairs of shoes, hundreds of bundles of blankets, and enough material to keep the state's textile mills humming as they turned out uniforms by the tens of thousands.

The *Don* was said to be capable of fourteen knots. She proved her swiftness by outrunning the formidable USS *Quaker State* on one occasion. But she had a greater problem eluding the USS *Dacotah*, although that was a slower ship.

In eight months of joint service for North Carolina and Alexander Collie and Company of England, the 162-foot blockade runner made several round trips between Wilmington and the islands, bringing supplies to North Carolina and delivering cotton on the return voyages. But strain on the *Don*'s engines from numerous chases and her long time at sea without maintenance left her boilers fouled and her water pipes clogged. Also, her skilled master, Augustus Charles Hobart-Hampden, turned the ship over to a new man and left for England to live off his accumulated wealth—although he would return within six months, unable to resist the siren call of adventure.

Captain Cory took the twin-screw iron steamer out of port on the first leg of her sixth round trip with a load of shoes, clothes, blankets, and munitions destined for Wilmington. For the first three days of the *Don*'s voyage, she was shielded by mist and thick clouds. But when she was a hundred miles from the North Carolina coast, the skies suddenly cleared and her heavily smoking stacks were spotted by the steam sloop USS *Dacotah*, which took up the chase.

Her full-rigged sails capturing the stiff wind, the blockader began overtaking the struggling *Don*, which also had all her canvas set. The crew of the blockade runner was despondent at being unable to get away. Making less than ten knots, the *Don* maintained her southerly heading until the *Dacotah* narrowed the gap to less than a mile.

Aboard the *Don*, the engineers tried desperately to force a few more knots out of the laboring engines. Their vessel was being pursued by a blockader that was moving at no more than twelve knots, and they could not outrun her. It was disheartening to crawl along at such a pace on a ship designed to show her heels to the Union blockaders.

Aboard the *Dacotah*, Commander A. G. Clary ordered his gunners to stand by their weapons in preparation for forcing the enemy to a halt. The unknown vessel was flying British colors, so there was still some doubt as to her identity, but her desperate attempt to escape left little doubt as to what she was up to.

Unable to raise more than a third of the normal steam pressure in the *Don*'s dirty boilers, her crew had little hope of eluding the *Dacotah* or of reaching shore without being riddled by canister and solid shells. The blockader approached to within half a mile, and it seemed capture was inevitable.

When the *Dacotah* was almost upon his vessel, Captain Cory sent several of his men aloft. On a signal from him, they suddenly furled the sails, and the helmsman gave the wheel a vigorous spin, causing the *Don* to whip around 180 degrees, directly into the wind—and into the face of the enemy ship.

Caught by surprise, the crew of the *Dacotah* could only watch as the *Don* steamed saucily by them in the opposite direction, less than fifty yards separating the vessels. The men on the *Dacotah* had been prepared to fire their bow gun, but the other guns were not set, and not a single shell was sent in the *Don*'s direction as she moved past.

By the time the heavy, three-masted blockader lost enough momentum to complete a turn of her own, the *Don* was well away. Although the *Dacotah*'s bow gun was discharged at last, the distance was too great, and the blockade runner cruised out of sight as night descended.

When the *Don* was finally captured by Yankee blockaders not long after this incident, she was hauled into port at Beaufort. The *Dacotah* happened to be anchored there, and Commander Clary came over to shake the hand of the man who had cleverly outwitted him.

had assigned James Bulloch to Europe as a civilian purchasing agent. Once there, Bulloch had joined forces with Major Caleb Huse and Major Edward C. Anderson to buy military supplies. The men soon came to understand that they needed their own ship to transport goods through the blockade.

Bulloch negotiated for the purchase of the Scottish-built steamer *Fingal*. After registering the vessel under false British ownership and hiring a British captain, he had a large cargo of arms placed on board. He and Anderson went aboard for the initial voyage. Despite a few minor mishaps, the load of fourteen thousand rifles, twelve tons of gunpowder, half a million cartridges with percussion caps, swords, blankets, and miscellaneous military paraphernalia arrived safely in the harbor at Savannah, Georgia. This was clearly a coup for the Confederate government, for it had brought in a large load of purely military goods on its own ship and avoided the prohibitive freight charges demanded by private ship owners.

Anderson believed a fleet of Confederate blockade runners could operate successfully under control of the Southern navy to solve the immense problems of supporting the army and supplying the civilian population, and do so at a reasonable price. With its own ships, crews, and cargoes, the Confederacy could eliminate having to negotiate for priority of its shipments over the luxury items preferred by investors. Even the high shipping charges the South paid barely allowed it to compete for the limited space aboard privately owned blockade runners.

Buoyed by their triumphant arrival through the blockade, Bulloch and Anderson headed for Richmond to report to government leaders. There, Anderson enthusiastically presented a plan for a Confederate role in running the blockade, but he was thwarted by divisiveness among the various government departments. And he was shocked to find that the disarray extended to Jefferson Davis himself.

As a last resort, he pleaded with Secretary of the Navy Mallory. Anderson's plan for a system of government-controlled blockade runners to feed, clothe, and arm the South was designed to put the Confederacy in control of its supply line. In hindsight, it might have prevented spiraling inflation and the devaluation of the Southern currency. But he spoke to a deaf ear. Mallory was unimpressed with the idea and was opposed to an underling—especially an army man like Anderson—involving himself in high-level navy decisions. He dismissed Anderson without further ado, thereby making one of the many serious blunders that hastened the South's downfall. Mallory wanted the navy to put its resources into ships that could attack the Northern merchant marine. He liked ships that could fight, not lumbering freighters that had to sneak past warships in the night. His plan was to let private companies assume the responsibility for supplying the South. When Confederate naval leaders finally came to their senses and took control of running the blockade, it was too late to change the course of the war.

Josiah Gorgas, the inventive and energetic head of the Confederate Ordnance Bureau, was not so lacking in foresight. He understood that despite his best efforts, the South's industries would be unable to meet wartime needs for several years. His progress in organizing a Southern effort to manufacture rifles, cannon, and powder and produce food, salt, and clothing was frustrated by a lack of manpower and by the Northern strategy of sealing off the states west of the Mississippi. A steady stream of victories gave the Union control of the territory that held the Rebels' scant sources of strategic materials such as copper, salt, and saltpeter, which further stifled Confederate efforts to be independent of external supply.

Gorgas had little confidence in the government's plan to rely on private business to meet the South's need for foreign imports, and he was quickly proven right. Even patriotic firms like John Fraser and Company of Charleston and Fraser, Trenholm and Company of Liverpool, which went out of their way to help the Southern cause, were in business for profit first. Established British trading companies and new firms organized by enterprising stockholders were behind the bulk of the blockade-running business. They were clearly out to reap the rewards of hauling expensive contraband, thereby relegating the South's military needs to second place.

After garnering support from Secretary of War James Seddon, Gorgas sent Major Norman S. Walker to Europe. Walker was to look into the possibility of purchasing steamers that could transport supplies for the Ordnance Bureau. He met with Caleb Huse to discuss Gorgas's plan. Huse then arranged for the purchase of sidewheelers to run between Bermuda and Wilmington. By the late fall of 1862, Gorgas had established a supply line. He assigned Walker to Bermuda. There, Walker worked with local merchant John Tory Bourne to transship the goods to Wilmington. The two coordinated the movement of cargo with Major Thomas Bayne and J. M. Seixas, the Ordnance Bureau's agents in Wilmington.

The sidewheeler *Cornubia* became the first of the Ordnance Bureau's ships to enter Wilmington when she passed safely through the blockade in mid-December 1862. During the following year, the swift steamer established an enviable record of success, arriving in North Carolina as regularly as clockwork in the middle of each month. She was finally captured by the USS *Niphon* in November 1863.

The *Merrimac,* another of the Ordnance Bureau's blockade runners, was less fortunate, making only one trip from Bermuda to Wilmington. Among her cargo, however, were three powerful Blakely rifled cannon, one of which was sent to Fort Caswell and another of which went to Fort Fisher. Difficulties with the ship's engines could not be remedied in Wilmington, and Gorgas was persuaded to sell the sidewheeler after the one successful voyage.

Three other ships—the *Eugenia,* the *Phantom,* and the popular *Robert E. Lee*—were added to the Ordnance Bureau's small fleet. Although British captains were sometimes used, the Richmond government allowed some Confederate officers and men to serve as captains and crew.

By the time the *Modern Greece* grounded on the North Carolina shore, the state's contribution of troops to the Southern cause was nearing seventy thousand. The Confederate government was not able to furnish these

# *The Capture of the* Cornubia

November 1863 was a disastrous month for the Confederate government's fleet of blockade runners. The South was doomed to lose several of its ships in less than four weeks.

The first to fall was the *Cornubia,* a 190-foot sidewheeler that had made eight round trips between Wilmington and Bermuda. Much of her success may be attributed to the qualities of her captain. But he eventually grew tired of the intense stress and asked to be relieved.

With her new commander, Richard S. Gayle, the *Cornubia* left the docks at Bermuda around lunchtime on Wednesday, November 4. She dropped off her local pilot after clearing the harbor, then pointed her bow for Wilmington on the first leg of her ninth voyage.

The trip across nearly seven hundred miles of the open Atlantic was uneventful. The crisp fall weather was clear. Although the crew of the *Cornubia* sighted a number of ships, they all appeared to be sailing vessels and constituted no threat to the powerful steamer.

With perfect timing, she arrived off the Cape Fear coast a few miles northeast of New Inlet around midnight. A favorite ploy of experienced captains was to stop outside the ring of blockading ships and reconnoiter until they were assured the way was clear, then to build up speed for a sprint right through the Union barrier. But the new captain headed the *Cornubia* toward the inlet without bothering to pause. She was soon seen by lookouts aboard the USS *James Adger,* which was patrolling nearby.

Realizing his vessel had been spotted, the captain ordered full speed ahead, and the blockade runner sped away and was soon out of sight of the slower *James Adger.* If she had only moved out to the open sea, the swift *Cornubia* might have lost her pursuer, but instead she headed for shore to run southward along the beaches toward the inlet.

The wily commander of the Federal gunboat anticipated this move and headed toward the southwest to cut off the enemy's escape. Within minutes, his ship was in position to intercept the fleeing runner, which soon appeared exactly where he had expected. A few miles away, the crew of the USS *Niphon* saw the rockets fired from the *James Adger* and moved their ship to prevent the *Cornubia*'s escape.

When the men of the *Cornubia* saw they were cornered by the converging Union ships, their concern bordered on panic. Although neither Federal vessel had discharged its weapons, it was likely that shelling would begin at any moment. Instead of taking a chance and running into the inlet—which was now within easy range—the *Cornubia* was deliberately run aground. Her crew jumped over the side and made their way to shore as the two blockaders moved in to take charge.

While the *Niphon* shelled the beach to prevent sniping, the *James Adger* attached a hawser to the *Cornubia* and pulled her out of the sand within an hour. Not content with capturing the ship, her cargo, and her captain, who had nobly remained on board, the commander of the *Niphon* dispatched his boats to bring back the crew and passengers who had reached the beach, where they believed they were safe. Along with the wet, miserable men of the *Cornubia*, the Union sailors hauled in several bags of letters and secret papers, retrieved from where they had been hastily hidden behind the dunes.

In one fell swoop, the Yankees had captured one of the South's most notorious blockade runners, as well as secret documents of the Confederate government. The papers disclosed information regarding the extent to which certain companies and ships were involved in blockade-running operations, details heretofore only guessed at. They also divulged that some British crewmen were used to man the Confederacy's blockade runners. The most telling piece of information found in the ship's papers revealed that the *Cornubia*'s true owner was James Seddon, the Confederate secretary of war.

> The capture of one of the War Department's few ships and her cargo of rifles, ammunition, saltpeter, and lead was a serious loss for the Rebels. But far greater damage was done by the failure of the crew of the *Cornubia* to destroy the secret correspondence.

soldiers with the materials they needed. It was up to the men or to their state government to supply their weapons and uniforms. Women made socks and cartridge bags, and soldiers were expected to buy their own underwear.

North Carolina officials—Adjutant General James G. Martin in particular—were fearful of being unable to supply their men under arms. They suggested to Governor Henry Toole Clark that the state get involved in the blockade-running business in order to acquire essential supplies. The governor had only a few months left in his term and did not take an aggressive approach to solving the problem of equipping the soldiers, postponing a decision until the incoming governor, Zebulon Vance, could take office.

Something of a firebrand and a man intensely loyal to his state, Vance was not so hesitant. At Martin's continued urging, he began investigations into establishing a process for assuring that the state's troops would be the best equipped in the South.

Vance contracted with George Nicholas Sanders to buy war supplies in Europe. Sanders proposed that the goods be transported aboard sailing vessels, which he felt could slip through the blockade by flying a foreign flag. But Duncan Kirkland McRae, the state's inspector in Wilmington, wrote Vance that steamers were the only viable vessels for defeating the blockade. He cited the "universal sentiment" that sailing ships had little chance of penetrating the Union fleet. Captain William Muse, the man in charge of the Cape Fear River steamers that North Carolina had turned over to Confederate control, stated his opinion that it was safer to trust all the state's merchandise to one steamer than to distribute it over ten sailing ships, as it was unlikely that even one of

North Carolina's first blockade runner, the *A. D. Vance*
The state eventually sold half interest in the steamer, but she still brought tons of supplies for North Carolina's soldiers before finally falling to the enemy just six months before the end of the war.

COURTESY OF THE U. S. NAVAL HISTORICAL CENTER.

the older ships would make it to Wilmington.

McRae suggested that the best plan would be to work with companies that agreed to grant the state preferred status and a low shipping rate of only fifteen dollars per ton aboard their steamers. But when Vance assigned John White and Thomas Morrow Crossan to Europe as agents for the state, they had orders to acquire a steamer to haul North Carolina's cargo through the blockade. The new governor, it seemed, trusted neither private businessmen nor officials in Richmond.

In late 1862, Crossan bought the *Lord Clyde* and, using a play on the governor's name, renamed it the *A. D. Vance*, although the vessel was usually simply called the *Advance*. Built by Caird and Company of Scotland the previous year, the *Advance* was more than 230 feet in length and was capable of steaming at seventeen knots. The powerful sidewheeler proved she was an excellent choice by making nine round trips between Wilmington and Bermuda before being captured four months before the fall of Fort Fisher.

Though North Carolina was already developing the textile industry that would one day be among the best in the nation, it lacked cloth and yarn to produce uniforms. On the *Advance*'s first trips, the cargo holds were filled with shoes and with fabric that could be turned into thousands of uniforms for North Carolina regiments. Also delivered from England were innumerable pairs of cotton cards—hand-held, flattened brushes with short wire bristles. They were used to roll cotton and wool fibers into strands for spinning into yarn. The indispensable cards were not available locally because the state had neither the proper metal nor the ability to draw it into wire.

The *Advance* completed her first successful mission into Wilmington during the last week of June 1863. Governor Vance was delighted and traveled to the port to visit the ship. Found to be free of disease, the *Advance* was granted a waiver of the usual waiting period at the quarantine station. Moving on to Wilmington, she arrived victoriously at the wharves amid the cheers of those who had come to welcome the state's own blockade runner. The governor boarded the vessel in triumph. Planning to deliver a speech in honor of the occasion and then tour the vessel with the captain, he was stayed by commands from a Confederate officer who appeared suddenly at the bottom of the gangplank.

It appeared that the officer in question, Lieutenant Colonel Thornburn, knew more of regulations than politics. He maintained that the ship was in violation of the quarantine guidelines and that everyone on board must remain on the *Advance* for the normal two-week waiting period. The resulting altercation between the red-faced Vance and Thornburn quickly deteriorated into a pomposity contest, Vance stating that the upstart officer must not realize he was the governor and Thornburn replying that he didn't care if Vance was Jesus Christ, that he was absolutely not leaving the ship.

To back up his authority, Thornburn assigned a squad of soldiers to the dock with instructions to shoot and kill anyone attempting to disembark. Someone hurriedly managed to locate Thornburn's superior officer, who hastened to the docks, overruled Thornburn, and had the troops stand down.

# *The* Robert E. Lee *Joins the Union Blockade*

The *Robert E. Lee* was one of the most successful and famous of the Confederate-owned blockade runners. It was finally captured, renamed USS *Fort Donelson,* and sent to join the blockade fleet.

COURTESY OF THE MUSEUM OF THE CONFEDERACY.

The Confederates' bad luck continued in November 1863, another important vessel falling within a week of the *Cornubia.*

The *Robert E. Lee* was popular in the South for her successful career as a blockade runner—and also for her very name. General Lee had proven he could whip the Yankees, and the vessel bearing his name showed the blockaders a thing or two as well.

A 268-foot steamship with two large sidewheels and two rakish stacks, the *Robert E. Lee* was built in Scotland in 1860. Originally called the *Giraffe,* she was renamed for the well-liked general when the Confederacy purchased her in late 1862. Captained by the highly competent John Wilkinson, the ship carried the hopes of those who believed the South could win the war.

She made her first trip from Bermuda in December 1862. Over the next nine months, she completed nine round trips to and from Wilmington, successfully eluding the blockading squadron time after time to bring military supplies for the Confederate forces. The *Robert E. Lee* proved well worth the $160,000 paid for her.

In the late summer of 1863, Wilkinson learned that he was to be reassigned. On his last trip commanding the *Robert E. Lee*, he took her to Nova Scotia. Aboard were a band of marines who were to participate in a clandestine operation to rescue Southern soldiers from a Northern prison at Fort Johnston, Ohio. But before the ship reached port, the secret mission was spelled out in detail in Northern newspapers, and the plan had to be abandoned.

Wilkinson said a sad farewell to his old ship. He was replaced by Captain John Knox, who took the vessel to Bermuda for some much-needed maintenance. Two months later, with cleanly scraped hull and reconditioned engines, the blockade runner crossed the Atlantic toward Wilmington once again. Within four days, she arrived off the North Carolina coast just as the sun rose above the horizon.

At six o'clock that morning, the *James Adger* was cruising about twenty miles off Bogue Inlet, southwest of Cape Lookout, when her lookout sighted a steamer off the port bow. The unidentified ship lay northwest of the blockader, and her southwesterly course allowed the Union gunboat to cut the corner and intercept her.

Within an hour, the *Robert E. Lee* was within range of the *James Adger*'s bow gun. Although he had already made at least one critical error, Captain Knox might yet have escaped, for it was difficult to hit a moving target from the deck of a speeding blockader. Or he might at least have run his ship aground, which would have saved the crew from capture and given the Confederates some chance of refloating the *Robert E. Lee* or saving her cargo. However, when the first shells whistled across his bow, Knox decided to heave to and surrender ship, cargo, and crew to the victorious *James Adger*.

The Yankees were delighted when they discovered the captured runner to be the elusive *Robert E. Lee.* The ship had hundreds of cases of blankets and shoes on board, as well as rifles, salt, lead, and saltpeter, none of which would ever reach the Rebels. She also carried seventy-six officers, crew, and passengers, including a foreign consul and some British military officers. Almost all the captives were sent north for confinement.

The officers of the blockade runner had made several mistakes. First, they tried to make their run to the Cape Fear River in daylight. Second, instead of showing the enemy their stern and heading out to sea, they tried to outrun a ship already in position to head them off. Finally, they gave up without an attempt to elude the only enemy ship anywhere on the horizon. It was an episode filled with error and timidity, one that never would have happened under the *Robert E. Lee*'s former commander. When Wilkinson heard of the capture of his beloved ship, he was inconsolable, blaming the captain for poor tactics and declaring the loss unnecessary.

The *Robert E. Lee* was drafted into service for the Union navy. Renamed the *Fort Donelson*, she was soon chasing runners as part of the North Atlantic Blockading Squadron. It was a tragic loss for the South.

The indignant governor stepped off the deck and onto the wharf. After venting his fury to the cheering crowd, Vance returned to Raleigh, where he fired off a scorching letter to President Jefferson Davis. General Whiting had been out of town at the time of the incident. Upon his return, he was horrified to learn of the debacle and wrote Vance a profuse apology.

After the yellow-fever tragedy the town had suffered just a year earlier, it would appear that Thornburn's actions were appropriate. But no young, officious upstart was going to trample Zebulon Vance, a man who openly challenged Richmond's authority and was not hesitant to chastise the president of the Confederacy. Thornburn capped his undoing by being a Virginian. He was removed from his post and was out of the army within two months. He was replaced by Major Thomas Sparrow of the Tenth Regiment of North Carolina troops, who took command of the city and river defenses of Wilmington.

In her first six months of service, the lucky *Advance* made four successful round trips between Wilmington and Bermuda. Governor Vance then elected to sell a half-interest in the vessel. Not wanting to risk the state's enterprise on just one ship, he bought a partial interest in four additional steamers.

Almost as important as the procurement of the state's first blockade runner was the relationship that John White established with the English trading firm Alexander Collie and Company. That company assisted the state's agents in the purchase and shipment of nearly all the merchandise obtained by North Carolina during the rest of the war. It was Alexander Collie and Company that agreed to sell Vance a partial interest in four of its ships. Two of these, the *Don* and the *Hansa,* were already in operation. Another, the *Annie,* was nearly ready for launching. The last was still on the drawing board.

With partial ownership of a small fleet of blockade runners, Vance was now prepared to test the blockade and supply North Carolina troops in a manner unmatched throughout the Confederacy. It was to be a bumpy voyage, for Vance would frequently butt heads with Seddon, Mallory, and even Jefferson Davis himself. The governor was suspicious of leaders in Richmond. He believed that North Carolina officers were overlooked in military assignments, too many appointments within the state being granted to Virginians when equally capable Tar Heels were available. He traveled to Virginia to check on rumors that North Carolina troops were not as well provided for as Virginia troops and came away even more determined to supply his state's soldiers with adequate food and clothing.

The first inkling that the state's blockade-running venture was in for trouble came when competition developed between Gorgas's fleet and Vance's handful of ships. Both used Wilmington as their center of operations, and they competed with private blockade runners for limited dock space. All three groups also vied for cotton to carry on their return trips, for scarce space on the rail cars, and for the scrimpy stockpiles of good coal. It was hard for North Carolina to match the high prices paid by private enterprise, and the Confederate army and navy demanded priority over state needs.

And worse trouble was on the way, for around August 1863, the Confederate government began a belated effort to take firm control of blockade-running operations. This came in the wake of General Lee's defeat at Gettysburg and his serious loss of men and arms. The urgency of the situation forced a reconsideration of the way procurements were made in Europe and the inefficient way supplies were delivered. From that point until early 1864, the government in Richmond gradually assumed more and more power over the trade passing through Wilmington.

One of the first moves unified the dispersement of funds among the agents operating in Europe. C. J. McRae was granted the authority to oversee all the South's business operations there. McRae was daunted by the disarray he discovered in the South's credit arrangements and by the disjointed manner in which buyers operated, often competing against each other. But he soon established order, and the exchange of cotton for munitions showed almost immediate improvement.

Another action came from Secretary of War Seddon, who was disappointed at the inability of the Confederate government to obtain the number of cotton bales it needed and to find space aboard departing blockade runners to carry them to European markets. In the late summer of 1863, Seddon imposed a restriction on all private blockade runners. It required that any ship leaving a Southern port reserve at least half its cargo space for Confederate cotton.

Although North Carolina's ships were successfully supplying the state and its troops with food, clothing, and ordnance, freeing the Confederacy from that burden, Richmond determined that Vance's ships would have to adhere to the same restrictions imposed on privately owned vessels.

It soon appeared that the governor's decision to sell a half-interest in the *Advance* and to invest in partial ownership of other ships had been a flawed choice. Since Alexander Collie and Company owned 75 percent of North Carolina's other vessels, it was hard to argue that

## *North Carolina Loses the* Advance

North Carolina's 25 percent share of the cargo space aboard the *Don*, the *Annie*, and the *Hansa* amounted to about a hundred gross tons each—less than the four hundred tons comprising the state's 50 percent ownership of the *Advance*.

Shortly after the *Don* was captured in March 1864, the Confederate government in Richmond demanded half the state's cargo space, leaving Governor Vance with only a fraction of the carrying capacity North Carolina had once owned. The feisty governor was uncertain who would put him out of the blockade-running business first, the Yankees or the Rebels. It was the Union, though, that struck him the cruelest blow.

In early September 1864, the *Advance*, the pride of the state's blockade-running fleet, was loading at the Wilmington docks in preparation for a run to Bermuda. Stevedores packed over four hundred bales of cotton in the ship's massive holds, then loaded three hundred more on deck. Barrels of turpentine made up the rest of the shipment. On Friday, September 9, the *Advance* pulled away from the wharf, headed down the Cape Fear River, and anchored near Smithville. As the ship got ready to leave through New Inlet, it was discovered that she was drawing more than the allowable eleven feet, so Captain Joannes Wyllie had the cotton removed from the deck.

The *Advance*, which had cost more than two hundred thousand dollars in gold, was still in fair shape, but her fuel stores consisted of soft coal from the mines in Chatham County, North Carolina. With Confederate naval ships getting first chance at the good coal, Wyllie and other blockade-running captains had to take the dregs of the pile.

By sunset, the *Advance* was ready to cross into the Atlantic, but close passes by blockaders kept her penned in until nearly midnight. When an opening finally appeared between the blockading ships, Wyllie slipped his vessel out into the ocean.

The runner barely emerged from the inlet before being detected by Commander Samuel Huse and the USS *Britannia*. Taking up the chase, the Federal gunboat fired rockets to warn the other pickets and loosed a broadside at the *Advance* as she steamed off to the north.

Handicapped by her poor fuel, the *Advance* could barely make eight knots, but even that was too much for the *Britannia*, whose hull was severely fouled by the sea life that had attached itself to her during her long patrol. After an hour, the Yankee ship lost steam pressure, and two of her cannon malfunctioned. By then, the blockade runner had pulled well ahead, and Commander Huse dropped out of the race.

By morning, Wyllie's vessel was near Cape Lookout and was preparing to turn for Bermuda. In the same region, however, the USS *Santiago de Cuba* was on her way to Hampton Roads for refueling. Around eleven o'clock in the morning, her lookouts spotted black smoke on the horizon. Captain O. S. Glisson ordered the *Santiago de Cuba* turned in that direction.

Within two hours, the blockader was close enough to see that the source of the smoke was a large sidewheeler with two stacks and schooner rigging. Suspecting at once that it was a runner, Glisson called for full speed and ordered that all heavy cannon and all crewmen who could be spared be moved to the stern. The additional weight at the rear of the ship forced the prow higher and increased the sidewheeler's speed.

By four o'clock, lookouts aboard the *Santiago de Cuba* could make out the *Advance*'s hull. By sundown, the blockader was only four miles behind and coming within cannon range. Glisson had one of the ship's eleven heavy guns returned to the bow for action. Just before eight o'clock, with night rapidly falling, the *Santiago de Cuba* sent a shell across the deck of the blockade runner.

Captain Wyllie had done all in his power to increase the speed of his ship, but the *Advance* refused to do any better. With the

Union ship closing rapidly and in position to destroy his vessel, he ordered the struggling engines halted and surrendered the *Advance* to the Yankees.

Clearly, the lack of good coal had done the runner in. Glisson admitted that his ship, powered by an inefficient walking beam engine, could hardly have mastered the mighty *Advance* had she been burning proper fuel.

Admiral Lee had the captured ship's hull scraped and her engines reconditioned. Pennsylvania bituminous coal was loaded on board. The vessel then became the USS *Frolic.* It was an ignominious end for North Carolina's proud ship, which served the enemy in the final attack on Fort Fisher.

those ships were not under private ownership. Yet argue Vance did. He had not endeared himself to the Confederate leaders with his constant criticism of their actions and decisions, and his pleas now for an exception to the rules for blockade runners were disregarded. Even when Georgia's governor, like Vance, began a campaign to have his own state's ships excluded, Seddon remained adamant. Vance protested that if Alexander Collie and Company's ships were forced to allocate half their cargo space to Confederate freight at low, fixed freight charges, and that if the state occupied its own 25 percent, then the owners could hardly afford the risks of running the blockade with the small load left to them.

Vance was soon proven incorrect. By selecting expensive items that brought a good return and by transporting a few hundred bales of cotton on outbound voyages, ship owners still enjoyed a profitable operation. So in spite of vigorous protests by the European and Southern operators of blockade runners, business was pretty much as usual.

The Confederate government continued to experience problems getting enough cotton to fill its half of the cargo space on outgoing ships, and these difficulties were amplified by competition with the Confederate navy, which was buying and shipping its own cotton. William F. Lynch, in charge of the small contingent of naval vessels stationed at Wilmington, constantly sought cotton and space to carry it. This added to the War Department's dilemma and aggravated the rivalry between Lynch and General Whiting.

In February 1864, when the *Hansa* refused to give up any of her available space for the navy's cotton, Lynch was indignant. He took over the ship when she anchored at Smithville in preparation for running the blockade, placing her under the guns of the CSS *North Carolina* to prevent her from sailing. Refusing to bow to Lynch's presumed authority, Whiting sent soldiers to eject Lynch's marines from the *Hansa* and brought the ship back to the wharves in Wilmington.

Responding to the challenge, Lynch ordered the *North Carolina* upriver. Although the heavy ship could barely make it to Wilmington, she brought the blockade runner under her guns once more. To settle the dispute, Secretary of War Seddon demanded that the *Hansa* be turned over to Lynch, and Whiting had to back down.

The *Ella and Annie*
One of the earliest Confederate-owned blockade runners, she ran the blockade from 1861 to 1863 but was captured and renamed the USS *Malvern*.

PAINTING BY R. G. SKERRETT. COURTESY OF THE U. S. NAVAL HISTORICAL CENTER.

Late that winter and into the early spring of 1864, the Confederate Congress passed bills giving President Jefferson Davis the power to refuse the import of luxury items and to force the runners to bring in designated supplies and armaments for the South. To limit the damage likely to be inflicted by these new rules, Davis offered to pay attractive shipping rates for the South's cargo, hoping to encourage a continuing flow of ships.

It is ironic that during a war fought in part over the rights of states to act independently of the central government, the pleas of North Carolina to operate its own blockade-running enterprise without government interference were denied by leaders in Richmond. Yet Seddon knew that if he allowed competition to persist between states and the government in Richmond, the South's struggle would be lost. Most Southern leaders grudgingly accepted this, and Vance was forced to concede, although not without continuing complaints.

Even under the tight regulations imposed by Davis and Seddon, North Carolina's blockade-running venture went on unabated into 1864, bringing so many supplies into Wilmington that the state accumulated a surplus. At the end of the war, nearly a hundred thousand uniforms imported through Wilmington were still stashed in Raleigh warehouses, ready for delivery to troops that no longer needed them.

Luck ran out for some of the state's ships, as they were bagged by the blockaders that surrounded the Cape Fear in increasing numbers. The first ship to be lost to the joint operations of North Carolina and Alexander Collie and Company was the *Don,* which was captured by the USS *Pequot* in March 1864. The fast sidewheeler had completed five round trips between Wilmington and either Bermuda or Nassau before being caught.

The *Advance,* the state's favorite ship, finally fell when the USS *Santiago de Cuba* spotted her smoke, took up the chase, and captured her as she steamed from North Carolina in September 1864. As usual, Governor Vance blamed Richmond. He argued that all the good coal had been appropriated for use in Confederate-owned vessels, leaving only inferior fuel for the *Advance.* In the fourteen months before her capture, the state's ship had carried out thousands of bales of cotton and returned with a treasure trove of supplies for her owners.

Within two months, the *Annie* was lost while departing Wilmington. She was caught on an underwater reef near Fort Fisher, where she was surrounded and towed away by Union ships. Although the *Annie* had not made her first run to North Carolina until March 1864, she had enjoyed an amazing run of luck, penetrating the blockade sixteen times before finally being taken and converted into a gunship for the Union navy.

After the loss of the *Annie*, only the *Hansa* was left to transport the state's merchandise. One of the first ships to operate under the partnership of Alexander Collie and Company and North Carolina, she had a career blessed with good fortune. The *Hansa* completed ten round trips between Wilmington and the islands, making her last run in December 1864, just six weeks before the fall of Fort Fisher. The lone survivor of the war among the state's small fleet, she did more than her part to keep North Carolina soldiers clothed, armed, and fed.

In the last bloody year of war, the Confederate government went still farther in establishing order in its purchasing procedures in Europe. It finally acknowledged the folly of depending on private companies to assume the responsibility for supplying the needs of the army.

James Seddon ordered several blockade runners for the War Department. C. J. McRae established an agreement with Fraser, Trenholm and Company of Liverpool for these vessels. The company agreed to order the ships at its own expense and turn them over to the Confederacy after enough cotton was delivered to pay for them. In addition to receiving cotton, the company received commissions for its services. And should the vessels be lost or captured before they were paid for, the South still had to compensate Fraser, Trenholm and Company.

It seemed the perfect arrangement, for the South would get needed supplies and the company would grow richer. It was flawed, though, for it hinged on the premise that the South would win the war, or that the company would at least recover any losses through reimbursement by the United States or through the sale of ships and supplies left when the war was over. In the end, Fraser, Trenholm and Company paid dearly for its friendship with the South.

Some of the newest and best ships—such as the *Bat*, the *Owl*, the *Deer*, and the *Stag*—were secured through such arrangements. By the latter part of 1864, the South was running its own ships through the Northern blockade.

Regardless of some continuing interservice rivalry, the importing of ordnance, clothing, and food had finally assumed systematic operation. As a result, sufficient supplies were arriving in Wilmington to sustain the army on at least a subsistence level.

North Carolina had far surpassed this, bringing in more than enough to equip its own soldiers independent of the Confederate government. Governor Vance met the challenge when called upon to help his state. Some criticized Vance for his very success, claiming it was wrong to amass a surplus. But the soldiers he supported were an important contingent of the Confederate army. If the Commissary Bureau and the Quartermaster Bureau of the War Department had followed the lead of the Ordnance Bureau, the state might never have had to assume the leadership role in supplying its troops. North Carolina offered a hundred thousand of its young men to the defense of the South, more than any other Confederate state. When the government in Richmond could not meet their needs, the state did not stand idly by while they shed their blood and sacrificed their lives.

# Chapter 7

# CLOSING THE GATEWAY

"You may rest satisfied . . . that the gate through which the Rebels obtained their supplies is closed forever."

ADMIRAL DAVID PORTER,
*January 17, 1865*

# CLOSING THE GATEWAY

DAWN BROKE CLEAR and cold over the Atlantic Ocean on January 13, 1865, displaying a vision of horror to the sentinels staring out from the tall, turf-covered parapets of Fort Fisher. Echelons of warships appeared to stretch from just offshore all the way to the horizon. From ironclads and squat, strange-looking monitors to multimasted, wooden men-of-war, dozens of enemy vessels covered the water as far as the eye could see. It was a portentous way to begin Friday the thirteenth for the superstitious among the fort's defenders.

Less than a month earlier, the Rebels had sent General Benjamin Butler's Union invasion force scurrying back to its ships in disarray and humiliation after the poorly organized and inadequately supplied group had landed on the sandy beach north of Fort Fisher. A heavy bombardment from the Federal fleet had rained thousands of shells on the fort but had failed to do any significant damage. The whole episode had been an exercise in frustration for the United States. But now the Federals were back, and they were more experienced and had a new general in command.

Inside the fortress, Colonel Lamb received word of the ships' return with trepidation. Despite his and General Whiting's desperate requests for troops from Braxton Bragg, only a few hundred had arrived. Lamb's total contingent numbered around fifteen hundred, and it was clear that he could not rely on Bragg to come to his defense. Even had he known that General Alfred H. Terry was at that moment landing nearly ten thousand Federals a few miles up the coast, there was little he could have done except telegraph Whiting of the invasion.

Admiral David Porter commanded the Union flotilla that now sat just offshore. He had great confidence in General Terry and was determined that this attack would complete the job. Porter's plans to support the troops and bombard Fort Fisher centered around the maneuvers of his more than fifty ships. He had assigned specific targets to individual vessels, so their gunfire would not be wasted as in the first assault. There would be no more random firing patterns. Gunners would shoot to disable the enemy's cannon and to rend the earthen walls of the Rebel stronghold. Porter wanted no wasted, symbolic firing at flagpoles.

While Terry's men were being carried to shore by boats from the fleet of transports, Porter assigned the *New Ironsides* and four monitors—the *Canonicus*, the *Mahopac*, the *Saugus*, and the double-turreted *Monadnock*—to a position just half a mile from the northeast corner of Fort Fisher, where the sea face joined the land wall. The little group of vessels commenced firing at the thick ramparts of the fort by eight o'clock that morning.

As the first fifteen-inch projectiles impacted against the inclined walls of the fort, they flung sand and chunks of turf high into the air. The terrific reverberations from the explosions rippled along the mile and a half of bulwarks, inspiring troops to duck into bomb shelters. Crews were already at their guns in anticipation of the attack. Within seconds, Fort Fisher's impressive weapons opened up on the monitors. The trained gunners were soon on target, striking the vessels repeatedly but without noticeable effect. The shells that struck the monitors bounced off the heavy armor plating. Although they created a terrific din inside the ships, it was hardly worse than the damage done to the sailors' ears by the roar of their own large cannon.

It soon became clear that the handful of metal-covered ships could remain there in relative safety while continuing to bang away at the fortress. The firing from the fort's guns soon slowed to an occasional shell lobbed toward the fleet as a reminder that the Rebels knew the ships were still there. Lamb had fewer than twenty-five hundred shells for his big guns, a precious hoard of ammunition too valuable to waste on targets that were impregnable. The fort's gunners turned their attention to the wooden ships and thin-skinned vessels, but even those targets received infrequent attention. The fort had about fifty operable guns, some of them large, rifled weapons, but even if the men had not been kept from their positions by the terrific hail of shells from the sea, Lamb's limited ammunition would have made the fort's firing sporadic.

Porter had no such limits. Once he ordered all his ships to open fire, shells exploded against the fort at the rate of almost one each second, producing a continuous, earsplitting thunder that rocked the ground and addled the defenders. The sounds of battle reached Wilmington within seconds of the opening barrage. The concussion of the heavy shelling rattled windows throughout town. Residents watched fearfully as huge clouds of dust and smoke hung in the air. No one had ever witnessed such an attack. Even the barrage of the previous month had never reached this intensity. It led some to wonder how anyone in the fort could possibly survive.

The guns on board just two of the ships—the *New Ironsides* and the *Minnesota*—nearly equaled the total number in the fort. Porter's squadron outgunned the Confederates by more than ten to one; altogether, the fleet had six hundred guns. With supply ships carrying an almost unlimited supply of ammunition for the fleet's weapons, it made for a very uneven exchange of gunfire between the combatants, the Yankees firing at least twenty-five shells for every one unleashed by the Rebels.

While the ironclads kept the enemies' heads down with their steady barrage, the wooden men-of-war cruised by in a line, firing broadsides at the fort. Porter claimed he did not want the enemy to feel he was unfairly using only armored vessels in the attack.

Since the fleet enjoyed a surplus of guns, and since there had been previous problems with premature explosions among the Union's hundred-pound rifles, Porter recommended that those weapons be used sparingly, if at all. But in the heat of battle, even they were turned on the enemy. Before the barrage ended, several hundred-pounders indeed exploded, killing and wounding a number of Union sailors and inflicting nearly as much damage as enemy gunfire.

The armada fired continually, the monitors maintaining their barrage throughout the night. By late afternoon on Saturday, a few of the fort's guns had been disabled or knocked off their mounts, and several men had been killed or wounded. But the thick walls of the bombproofs were proving all but impenetrable to even the massive fifteen-inch shells hurled by the fleet. Hundreds of cannonballs and a carpet of iron shards from exploded shells littered the interior of the fortress, but the ramparts had sustained little serious damage.

The amazing strength of the fortifications would bear up under the greatest barrage ever unleashed in a naval assault on a land-based defensive structure. Even though the firing would continue for another day, a large number of the fort's guns would survive the battle. Had a land attack not accompanied the invasion, the fleet alone could not have taken Fort Fisher. And even with the accompanying assault by Union army troops, significant numbers of Southern troops on the beach might have kept them from reaching the fort. However, the Rebels sent to counter the assault were too few and too late to create more than an annoyance to the enemy advance.

Eighty-five hundred men under General Terry landed north of Fort Fisher and slowly made their way along the beach. They were well armed, well supplied, and ably led, a far cry from the condition of the troops landed the previous month during Butler's disastrous attempt to capture the Rebel stronghold. Except for a few skirmishes with soldiers of General Robert Hoke's Confederate battalions, there were virtually no obstacles to halt their advance. By midday on January 15, they were within a few hundred yards of the fort. Terry assigned several thousand men to a defensive posture protecting the flanks of his attack force, but he still had more than three thousand soldiers ready for the final assault by three o'clock on Sunday afternoon.

Supply ships stood offshore, their cargo holds filled with food and ammunition in support of the attack. Everything had been planned to assure the success of this assault. Among the vessels were several former blockade runners. The *Advance*, the *Fort Donelson* (formerly the *Robert E. Lee*), the *Emma*, the *Lilian*, and the *Little Ada* were all there, serving a new master. And the gunboats that had been on blockading duty stood ready to offer covering fire for the men as they stormed the fortress.

Sailors aboard the *Keystone State*, the *Santiago de Cuba*, and others had long been forced to sit offshore to avoid the fort's guns but now had a chance to avenge the long months of frustration by helping deliver the final blow against the hated bastion of the Cape Fear.

The eleven- and fifteen-inch guns of the *New Ironsides* and the monitors concentrated on the land wall to soften it up for General Terry's troops. The long mound of sand was soon pockmarked with huge cavities dug out by the massive shells. After two and a half days of continuous shelling, most of the guns along the top of the half-mile embankment had been knocked off their mounts or disabled. The larger guns of the Atlantic wall were still mainly intact, but the army had no plans to attack from that quarter.

Admiral Porter was anxious for his sailors to become even more important players in the game. He decided to send fifteen hundred of his men, accompanied by four hundred marines, in a frontal assault on

Bombardment of Fort Fisher, January 1865
Positions of the monitors can be seen inside the ring of larger warships.

COURTESY OF THE U. S. NAVAL HISTORICAL CENTER.

the sea face of the fort. He asked that sailors from every ship be spared for this task force, so that everyone would have an opportunity to participate in the enemy's final destruction. Only sailors who had some army training were given rifles. Most were supplied with weapons that were more symbolic than effective. Unbelievably, Porter sent more than a thousand sailors untrained in land warfare and armed with only pistols and "well sharpened" cutlasses onto an exposed beach to face the defensive fire of several hundred Rebel sharpshooters. The marines, at least, were armed with Spencer repeating rifles.

After landing about a mile north of the fort, the men attempted to gather into formation for the assault. Of course, they came from different ships and had never trained together. Planning to join the army troops in a two-pronged attack as soon as Terry's men were in position, the sailors advanced within a quarter-mile of the fort, where some who had brought digging tools were ordered to build sand breastworks. They were spotted by the Rebels, who began to unload grapeshot in their direction with devastating effect. Special squads moved forward under the intense fire and dug rifle pits for the marines, who were to provide cover while the sailors attempted to "board" the fort. The nervous marines had an inkling of the indefensible position thrust upon them by the optimistic admiral.

The major part of the force needed to get within about a hundred yards of the sea face, yet there wasn't a single tree on the beach to hide the advance. The waves had cut into the dunes and left an escarpment of sand that stood about four feet high and ran the length of the shoreline. Under this shield of sand, the motley force struggled to reach the jumping-off point near the northeast corner of the fort, where the sea face met the land wall. As they waited for the signal to move against the fort, the air sang with whizzing iron pellets that could tear a fist-sized hole in a body or rip off an arm or leg.

The army signaled its readiness around three o'clock that afternoon. By prearranged plan, every ship in the fleet let loose a blast on its whistle, accompanied by a rousing cheer from every sailor on board. The gunners shifted their aim away from the land wall and toward the southern end of the fortress, to reduce the risk of hitting their own men.

# *The* Sassacus *Proves* *Too Much for the* Nutfield

As the North Atlantic Blockading Squadron increased in strength with the addition of newer, faster steamers, it became increasingly difficult for blockade runners to avoid capture. Many of the Union ships added to the force toward the close of the war were capable of chasing the enemy into the deep waters of the Atlantic. Their swiftness forced the runners to increase their speed as they wended their way through the treacherous shoals near the inlets.

Admiral Lee was pleased when the *Sassacus* became part of his fleet. Assigned to steam along the route that most runners used when traveling between Wilmington and Bermuda, she stood ready to give chase to any Rebel ship that dared enter her domain. It was the misfortune of the blockade runner *Nutfield* to do just that.

Lookouts aboard the Yankee cruiser spotted the *Nutfield* as the first light of day revealed her low silhouette in the distance. The *Nutfield* was about twelve miles away, a lead too great for most blockaders to overcome, but Commander F. A. Roe of the *Sassacus* confidently ordered his ship turned in pursuit. He believed she could catch any runner on the open sea.

By eight o'clock, the chase was on. When the captain of the *Nutfield* was informed of the trailing blockader, he ordered his vessel steered toward land. He hoped to make an easy getaway into the Cape Fear River, but failing that, he would at least be able to beach his ship and save her from falling into the hands of the Yankees.

The *Nutfield* was fast, but the *Sassacus* was faster. Within four hours, the hunter had closed within firing distance. Shell geysers sprouted like mushrooms about the speeding *Nutfield*, inspiring her captain to attempt evasive maneuvers. Commander Roe was near enough now to see that his prey was a medium-sized sidewheeler with a single stack. As he watched, the runner's crew began throwing cargo over the side in a desperate attempt to increase their vessel's speed.

Despite the best efforts of the men of the *Nutfield*, they could not shake their pursuer. A little after noon, the pilot drove the iron-hulled ship directly onto the shore, where it struck with a tremendous jolt. The crew lost no time getting overboard, lingering just long enough to start a fire among the cargo. Leaving the *Nutfield*'s engines running, they lowered the boats and rowed toward shore.

By then, the *Sassacus* was close enough to lower her own boats. Squads of Yankee sailors headed for the smoking steamer. Once aboard, they quickly extinguished the small blaze, which had done negligible damage. In his haste to vacate the *Nutfield*, one of her crewmen had fallen overboard. Now, the Federals pulled him in. He informed them that among the cargo tossed over the side had been several Whitworth rifled cannon.

Alerted to the chase, the USS *Florida* came on the scene, and she and the *Sassacus* made an unsuccessful attempt to salvage the grounded runner. But the Federals were able to capture a quantity of arms, clothing, and medicine, as well as the ship's instruments and charts. A thousand muskets were taken, but a more important loss for the Rebel army might have been the gallon of quinine found aboard the *Nutfield*.

After the Union sailors were allowed to scavenge whatever they wanted from the remaining items, the ship was set ablaze and perforated with gunfire until her hull looked like a sieve. The *Nutfield* would never reach Wilmington.

However, the sailors and marines, held down by enfilading fire from the fort, had not yet reached their point of embarkation. They were still at least two hundred yards from the palisades. Still, they rose to charge across the open beach in four straggling lines.

They immediately came under the observation of the Rebels, who, aware of their presence, had gathered in large numbers along the upper ramparts of the fort. Although Colonel Lamb knew of General Terry's force, which even now was preparing to attack the fort from the northwest, the Rebel soldiers believed the men maneuvering for an assault on the eastern face were the major invasion threat. All along the Atlantic wall, riflemen unleashed a volley that struck with such fury that the running lines of sailors were torn to tatters.

As they led the makeshift force across the open beach, several of the commanders were struck down in the hail of flying lead. The soft sand pulled at the stumbling men's boots. The blistering fire ripped flesh and bone and left dozens of dead and wounded scattered across the sand. The marines in the rifle pits were pinned down. Some deserted the puny sand holes for better protection, but even then, they provided little or no covering fire for the sailors. This left the Rebels free to take unhindered aim at the attacking force. Although the Southern troops may have been ragged and hungry, most were expert shots.

With their officers falling dead or wounded around them and little help available from the marines, the inexperienced sailors—some of whom were coal heavers from the engineering department—abandoned the attack and made a desperate effort to get back to the protection of the dunes. A handful of the extremely brave managed to reach the palisades that ran at a right angle from the northeast corner of the fort to the water's edge. Even those few who reached the fort could do little or nothing with their pistols and cutlasses. The Rebels gave a yell, believing they had turned away a Yankee invasion, just as they had sent Butler scrambling for safety. It was a delusion doomed to a short life.

Used to fighting his battles from a distance, Porter had little concept of close-quarters combat. He apparently had a romanticized notion of his men storming the walls with cutlasses waving. In fact, he had informed them that if they were fired upon, they were to offer no quarter, and that if cannons were turned on them, they were to toss Confederates over the wall in the face of the fire. As it turned out, it was the Rebels who gave no quarter and the panicked sailors who faced lethal fire. If he had known of the deadly meat grinder that awaited his unprepared, untrained men, perhaps Porter would not have been so anxious to send them on what amounted to a suicide mission.

All the same, the sailors' failed attack enabled General Terry's soldiers to break through the fort's defenses. Porter's men temporarily distracted the defenders, and the main attacking force managed to storm into the rear of the fortifications, on the river side of the land wall. The persistent cannon fire of the fleet had breached that wall, leaving an opening large enough to allow hundreds of blue-coated troops to pour through. In the end, the "torpedoes" ingeniously buried around the fort had failed to keep the attackers at bay, for the naval bombardment had shredded the connecting wires leading to batteries inside the fort. When Lamb attempted to set off the charges, not a single one fired.

The Rebels inside Fort Fisher suddenly found themselves in desperate hand-to-hand combat. The mound battery and the large guns of Battery Buchanan were blocked from attacking the Union men by the land wall itself. And once the Yankees were inside the wall, the gunners could not fire for fear of hitting their own men. While guarding the front door, the Rebels had allowed the enemy to enter through the back.

Within a short period of time, the attackers were moving from traverse to traverse, each fiercely contested by the Southern defenders. It was desperate combat, so close that it was impossible to raise and fire a rifle at an antagonist. Admiral Porter later commented on how honorably and well the Rebels fought, declaring their efforts to be deserving of a "more worthy cause."

During the attack, General Whiting traveled to Federal Point and offered his services, although he declined Lamb's offer to take command. Whiting was seen charging around the parapets and shouting encouragement to the men. He was hit twice by gunshots and fell bloody and wounded to the ground. A short time later, Colonel Lamb was trying to lead a counterattack against an enemy-occupied bunker when he was hit in the hip by a lead ball. Whiting and Lamb were carried to a temporary shelter, where they lay side by side, unable to help their men in the final minutes of battle.

They might have wondered where Braxton Bragg was in this hour of need. Despite Whiting's pleas for troop support at Fort Fisher, Bragg's attention was clearly on other matters, perhaps on Sherman's approach through South Carolina. He did little except send a load of ammunition to land at a point already in possession of the enemy. He also dispatched a few reinforcements, who arrived too late to help and who refused to leave their bombproof to come out and fight.

Bragg now foolishly sent a new general to take command of the fort in the midst of battle. As Whiting and Lamb lay helpless and the fort was in its last throes, General Alfred H. Colquitt appeared abruptly and declared his intent to assume control. It is amazing that he managed to reach the fort at all, and even more startling that he arrived in complete ignorance of the state of affairs. A glance at the piles of mangled bodies strewn about the grounds and the hundreds of blue-coated troops swarming over everything told him in an instant that the fort was lost. Colquitt left even more suddenly than he had arrived, taking time only to dispatch a message informing Bragg that Fort Fisher had fallen.

It was a fact Bragg could barely comprehend. Many had warned that his arrival was a harbinger of Wilmington's fall. His surprise upon receiving notification of Fort Fisher's capture might suggest that he had distanced himself from reality and perhaps suffered a relapse of the mental breakdown he had experienced earlier in the war.

Why Bragg failed to offer the support needed to fend off the relatively small group of attackers and preserve Fort Fisher continues to be a mystery. However, had the attack been repulsed, it is unlikely that Sherman could have been pushed aside. After destroying Atlanta and advancing quickly across South Carolina, there is little doubt that he would have headed for Wilmington had that city not already been in Federal hands. After the razing suffered by Atlanta at Sherman's direction, the residents of Wilmington must have felt lucky to be spared his attention.

After seven hours of bloody, close-quarters combat that left gray- and blue-clad dead and wounded lying all over the interior of the fort, the Rebels surrendered. Among those taken were Lamb and Whiting, who were later transported north and imprisoned. Lamb survived the war, but Whiting died unexpectedly while recuperating from his wounds in a New York prisoner-of-war camp.

Following the victory at Fort Fisher, signals were sent to the fleet to halt the firing, and the cacophony of cannon blasts was replaced by a barrage of rockets and rousing cheers from the men on Porter's ships. The mightiest fortress in the South had fallen at last, leaving Wilmington and the forts along the Cape Fear River exposed to imminent destruction.

Fort Fisher was unquestionably the key to the defenses protecting "the Gateway to the Confederacy." Once it fell, the other fortifications followed like dominoes. In fact, the retreating Southern forces put into action a plan to destroy almost all the coastal fortifications they had worked so long and hard to establish. Powder storerooms were blown up. Guns were damaged to keep them from falling into enemy hands. The *Chickamauga* was scuttled and burned and steamers were sunk in the Cape Fear River in a desperate but futile attempt to block the channel and hamper the movement of Union vessels.

Admiral Porter sent his gunboats into New Inlet to take control of the lower Cape Fear River. The Union navy then set about removing or destroying the multitude of "torpedoes" that had been placed in the river. This was not without danger, for some of the "torpedoes" were said to contain several hundred pounds of powder and could tear a gigantic hole in the hull of a ship.

Another full-scale Union attack might have been necessary to conquer Fort Caswell at Old Inlet, but before Northern forces could undertake that mission, the South performed it for them. Within a day of Fort Fisher's collapse, Bragg's command in Wilmington ordered Fort Caswell's destruction. Fort Caswell was second only to Fort Fisher on the Cape Fear coast. Had troops been available to meet the land forces of the Union onslaught, the Confederates might have made a fight of it with the thirty guns well protected within the fort's massive walls.

But Bragg had no such plans. He was rapidly organizing a fighting retreat from Wilmington. At his direction, Fort Caswell's own troops spiked the guns and set fire to everything that would burn, then set off the fifty tons of explosives in the fort's powder magazine. The immense explosion shook ships at sea and was heard a hundred miles away. But the destruction of Fort Caswell was a mere echo of the downfall of Fort Fisher.

Admiral Porter believed that if he could get the *New Ironsides* into the river, he could take Wilmington in a day. With both major forts lost, the two inlets to the Cape Fear River were in control of the United States Navy, a fact that some blockade runners would become aware of too late.

Late in 1864, Captain John Maffitt, experienced blockade runner and former commander of the *Florida,* was transferred from the iron-clad *Albemarle* in Plymouth, North Carolina, to the new Confederate merchant ship *Owl.* Just before Christmas, he went aboard the *Owl* in Wilmington and found her already loaded with 750 bales of cotton destined for Bermuda. At the edge of dark, he ordered the 230-foot sidewheeler away from the wharves and headed slowly down the river toward Smithville.

Maffitt waited at the anchorage until he saw a gap among the block-aders. He stole out through the enemy ships and was soon safely through the inner ring. After turning his vessel to an easterly course, he reached Bermuda on Christmas Eve, just as General Butler was leading the first attack on Fort Fisher. Close on his heels were two other blockade run-ners that had left Wilmington about the same time as the *Owl.*

After discharging the cotton and reloading with military supplies, the *Owl* joined half a dozen other blockade runners sitting idly by the docks as they awaited news of the Union attack on Fort Fisher. When they heard through Northern newspaper accounts that Butler had failed, they prepared to leave for Wilmington, never guessing that the United States Navy would return so quickly.

Upon receiving word from the consuls in Bermuda and Nassau that several blockade runners had departed for Wilmington, Admiral Porter developed a plan to trap them. He ordered Commander J. M. B. Clitz of the USS *Malvern* to take charge of the system of light signals at New Inlet. All signals were to be maintained in the fashion that block-ade runners were accustomed to seeing, so their captains would not suspect Fort Fisher had fallen and could be lured into the navy's net. Thus, the elaborate signaling system installed by John Wilkinson was to be turned against the runners. All the Federal ships anchored in the Cape Fear River were to extinguish their lights, and everything was prepared to look normal to incoming traffic. When the unsuspecting

## *The Last Voyage of the* Chameleon

John Wilkinson attempted a run into the Cape Fear River in January 1865 but was perceptive enough to recognize that Fort Fisher had fallen, at which point he turned his vessel back toward the islands. However, he was not quite done trying to break the blockade. He brought the *Chameleon* out of Nassau one last time and headed for Wilmington, determined to bring food to Rebel soldiers facing a severe shortage of provisions.

Less than twenty-four hours out of Nassau, the vessel was sighted at daybreak by a Union cruiser. Wilkinson, sleeping fully clothed, as he usually did, was startled awake by a loud cry for a course change by his officer of the deck. The wheelhouse was adjacent to Wilkinson's cabin. He jumped up and ran to the bridge. As he looked where the deck officer pointed, he saw a large sidewheeler less than two miles distant headed the *Chameleon*'s way. The runner had been nearly within range of the enemy's cannon when the alert officer on watch had veered from the previous course to take her out of the line of fire.

Wilkinson thought he recognized the oncoming gunboat as the USS *Vanderbilt*, reputedly one of the fastest ships of the North Atlantic Blockading Squadron. It was uncertain whether the *Chameleon* could hold her own against such a formidable antagonist. Wilkinson's vessel was in top shape, as always, and he had standing orders for the fires to be tended to provide a good head of steam before daybreak. Now, with daylight upon her, the ship was as ready as possible for the race ahead.

The *Chameleon* sped over the waves, yet she could not shake the trailing blockader. Indeed, as the day wore on, the enemy gunboat seemed to edge closer.

When the wind became stronger, Wilkinson ordered full canvas, and the chaser followed suit. Soon, both ships had all their sails stretched taut. By keeping close to the wind, the schooner-rigged blockade runner had an advantage over the square-rigged pursuer, and the *Chameleon* began to pull away. By noon, the enemy furled her sails and continued the chase on steam alone. By midafternoon, the *Chameleon* had doubled the distance between the ships, and the situation appeared less critical.

At that moment, the chief engineer came forward to tell the captain that the engines were overheating and that a major breakdown and permanent damage would result if they were not stopped immediately. Wilkinson peered into the engine room to assess the problem and saw great clouds of steam issuing from the bearings, which were being steadily doused with water by the engine crew. He reluctantly gave the order to stop.

The ship slowed to a crawl, only the wind on her sails providing any forward motion. The persistent Yankees—still following the *Chameleon* "like a bloodhound," as Wilkinson put it—could be seen closing the distance. Several tense minutes passed before the chief engineer was satisfied that the engines were cool enough to continue.

Once the wheels began turning with renewed vigor, the enemy was again left far astern. Less than an hour later, the blockader conceded defeat and changed course back toward the coast to continue patrolling. The victorious Wilkinson altered his course, too, following in the Union ship's wake toward shore and irritating the crew of the blockader. But there was little the Yankees could do.

When night fell, the *Chameleon* attempted to get the supplies to shore, but the delay caused by the long chase had put her almost a full day behind schedule, and it was low tide when she approached the coast. In consideration of the many blockading cruisers now moving freely up and down the waters along North and South Carolina, Wilkinson accepted the impossibility of reaching any harbor. He regretfully turned his runner back toward Nassau for the last time.

runners anchored inside the inlet, they would be boarded and seized by Union men.

Before the Yankees could put their ruse into operation, Maffitt brought the *Owl* into Old Inlet and cruised close by Fort Caswell before anchoring near Smithville. Had the lights been set, Maffitt might have remained complacent and off guard. But when he saw no signals where signals ought to be, and when some of his men noticed large fires on nearby Smith Island, he became suspicious. Then some Smithville men rowed a boat out to Maffitt's ship and warned him that the Yankees had taken control of Cape Fear. Maffitt dropped off his pilot for a brief visit to his home, located just a short distance away. When the Smithville native returned, he confirmed that Fort Fisher had fallen and that the Rebels were evacuating. Hoisting the anchor hastily, the crew turned the *Owl* back toward the sea and easily slipped by the inattentive crews of the few blockaders in sight. It was a narrow escape. If the *Owl* had arrived just one night later, she might not have been so lucky, for the trap was well laid by then.

Close behind Maffitt were the *Rattlesnake*, the *Blenheim*, the *Charlotte*, and the *Stag*.

Like the *Owl*, the *Rattlesnake* arrived before the Union was ready. Captain Michael Usina spotted fires on Smith Island as well as what appeared to be scattered campfires from Federal Point northward for nearly two miles. Since there were five times the usual number of Federal vessels surrounding New Inlet, he reasoned that Fort Fisher had been captured. Most of the Union ships anchored nearby were not blockaders, and the distracted crews, still celebrating their victory, did not notice as the *Rattlesnake* slipped back out to sea and away from Porter's snare. Realizing it was impossible to deliver his cargo to Wilmington, and with Charleston still held in a tight noose, Usina headed back to Bermuda. His alertness had prevented the loss of his ship and cargo and saved his crew and himself from capture.

In mid-December, the Confederate navy had converted the *Olustee* (formerly the *Tallahassee*) from a merchant raider into a blockade runner and renamed her the *Chameleon*. The ship was placed under the command of John Wilkinson, who took her directly to Bermuda with a load of cotton. Rations for Lee's hungry soldiers were then placed aboard for the return trip. After hearing of the Butler debacle at Fort Fisher, Wilkinson set out for Wilmington. But upon his arrival, he became suspicious of the fires, the military activity visible on shore, and the unusually large collection of ships nearby. He, too, guessed that Fort Fisher had fallen and turned his ship back toward Bermuda.

Wilkinson, Maffitt, and Usina most likely passed the word and saved other ships from falling into Union hands. But a few that had already sailed were not so lucky. Some fell into the Union trap even as they believed themselves safe in the haven of the river.

After forcing captured Confederate signal officers to divulge the secret codes used to guide blockade runners into the inlets, the Yankees put their decoy plan into effect. Within four days of the fall of Fort Fisher, the snare was set.

The *Stag*, one of the latest blockade runners to come out of England, was the first to fall. The slender ship had a length of 230 feet and was built for great speed. Her draft was so slight that even when she was loaded with five hundred tons of military cargo, she could still slide easily into the inlets at Cape Fear.

The *Stag* had been turned over to the War Department just a month earlier. Under the command of Richard Gayle of the Confederate navy, she was en route from St. George's to deliver arms, blankets, shoes, and other items for the Ordnance and Quartermaster Departments. The ship was spotted by a blockader as she headed toward Old Inlet. Several shots were fired as the *Stag* sped by, but only three struck the vessel, and they did no major harm. As Gayle approached the inlet, he had his signalman flash the usual dim lights toward land, and lights from shore came on in response.

Everything seemed in order as the *Stag* entered the inlet and anchored near another ship already there. Unfortunately, the ship was the USS *Malvern*, the flagship of Admiral Porter of the North Atlantic Blockading Squadron. As the crew of the blockade runner prepared to relax after their safe passage, their vessel was boarded by a squad of United States sailors, who informed them that they were now in the charge of the Union navy.

Stephen Mallory, secretary of the Confederate navy, had instructed Gayle to destroy the vessel if she was in danger of being lost to the

Yankees, but there was no time to even light a fire. The flabbergasted crewmen barely managed to toss their secret papers overboard. The consternation of the *Stag*'s crew was viewed with great delight by Admiral Porter, who was ecstatic at having deceived the deceivers.

Another blockade runner, the *Charlotte,* followed closely on Gayle's heels. Only slightly less streamlined than the *Stag,* she had entered the business just two months earlier. Capable of transporting even more cargo than the *Stag,* the *Charlotte* had a slightly greater draft. Still, her sidewheels enabled her to pass over the bar and into Old Inlet on the night of January 19. She pulled up beside her sister runner and one other ship.

A handful of English passengers were aboard on a joyride. They joined the crew in a champagne toast to their safe arrival. It was another celebration doomed to be brief, as a boarding crew from the *Malvern* interrupted the revelry to place them and their ship in the custody of the United States.

Admiral Porter thus made two major captures within hours. And several more runners were rumored to be on their way in.

Six days later, the blockade runner *Blenheim,* whose crew had not received word of the capture of Fort Fisher, put into New Inlet before dawn and dropped anchor. The crew could see only the vague outline of Fort Fisher and did not notice the many Union ships scattered around. The fifteen-year-old sidewheeler was not a Confederate vessel, and it is unknown whether false signals fooled the English crew. Nevertheless, when the sun rose, they were shocked at the number of United States ships within easy rowing distance of their anchorage.

The engineers jumped into action, attempting to get the ship under way. But before the anchors could be raised, a dory from the USS *Tristram Shandy* bumped against the hull, and a squad of armed sailors leapt onto the deck. Within minutes, a boarding party from the *Gettysburg* was also on hand to claim a share in the capture. A third group rowed over from the *Lilian* and took charge of the ship, since the *Lilian*'s crew included the senior officer now on board the *Blenheim.* Soon, there were more captors than captives on the runner. Two other ships would also claim part of the award from the prize courts. It was a woeful ending for the *Blenheim,* the last ship to be caught trying to run the blockade into Wilmington during the Civil War.

Shortly after the capture of Fort Fisher, Lieutenant William B. Cushing of the USS *Monticello* conducted a reconnaissance of the coastal defenses. He found that Battery Shaw had been destroyed, as had Fort Holmes on Bald Head Island. Fort Campbell had been abandoned. Fortifications that Admiral Porter reluctantly called the best-built earthworks he had ever seen thus fell without so much as a shot being fired. When Porter's men raised the Stars and Stripes over the ruins of Fort Caswell, the small Rebel force in nearby Smithville quickly evacuated the town, leaving Fort Johnston in good condition except for spiked cannon. The scrappy admiral boasted that what had taken the Rebels four years to build had been captured in four days. Yet from another perspective, the formidable works had in fact kept the United States Navy at bay for four entire years.

After the major forts at the inlets were eliminated and the river's mouth was sealed against blockade runners, the battle for the river itself commenced. The *Malvern,* a sidewheel steamer with three guns, moved upstream, accompanied by a dozen other steamers armed with nearly a hundred large cannon. They proceeded to shell both sides of the river. They also shelled Fort Anderson, the only major fortification still preventing their passage to Wilmington.

Soldiers fired at the ships from the bluffs above the river, and Fort Anderson maintained intermittent but strong fire through the first weeks of February. As the concentrated shelling by the Union vessels continued unabated, the Rebels on the bluffs were gradually forced from their entrenchments all along the lower Cape Fear River. Eventually, only Fort Anderson endured. Finally, on Sunday, February 19, 1865, that proud bastion capitulated to the overwhelming power of the Union fleet.

As the Union army mopped up the few remaining Rebel holdouts on its way toward Wilmington, the naval vessels moved up the winding channel that had been the pathway for so many blockade runners during the past four years. At noon on Wednesday, February 22, the ships were a mere two miles from Wilmington. They announced midday by firing thirty-five of their guns in jubilation.

A couple of hours later, as the flotilla steamed victoriously into what had been the Confederacy's major supply port, it announced its arrival by loosing a twenty-one-gun barrage in salute to its conquest. The banging of the Yankee cannon sounded the death knell of the Civil War citadel of Wilmington and closed the doors of "the Gateway to the Confederacy."

# EPILOGUE

THE RESIDENTS OF Wilmington did not ask for their city to become "the Gateway to the Confederacy."

In 1860, Wilmington was a peaceful, cultured town. Its worldly air was bolstered by an infusion of visitors and foreign contacts, thanks to the town's thriving international trade. The residents loved music and the arts, lived in comely homes beside clean streets bordered by brick sidewalks lit by gas lamps, and enjoyed access to elegant clothing and exotic foods. Their weather was warmed by the nearby Gulf Stream, which kept winters relatively mild. For those who liked the clean, salty smell of the ocean, the Atlantic was just a short ride away by boat or wagon.

Their happy existence was shattered by the Civil War. Heated debates raged throughout town as to whether North Carolina should join the secessionists. The population was about evenly divided, but once North Carolina's hat was in the ring, the citizens united and rendered to the state and the South their services, their devotion, and sometimes their lives.

For most of the war, the Union fleet sat perched in easy view on the Atlantic surrounding Cape Fear, strung out like a pack of hungry wolves waiting to pounce on any unwary trespasser. Few in Europe and even fewer in the South believed the United States could effectively blockade the Confederacy's thousands of miles of inlet-rich shoreline.

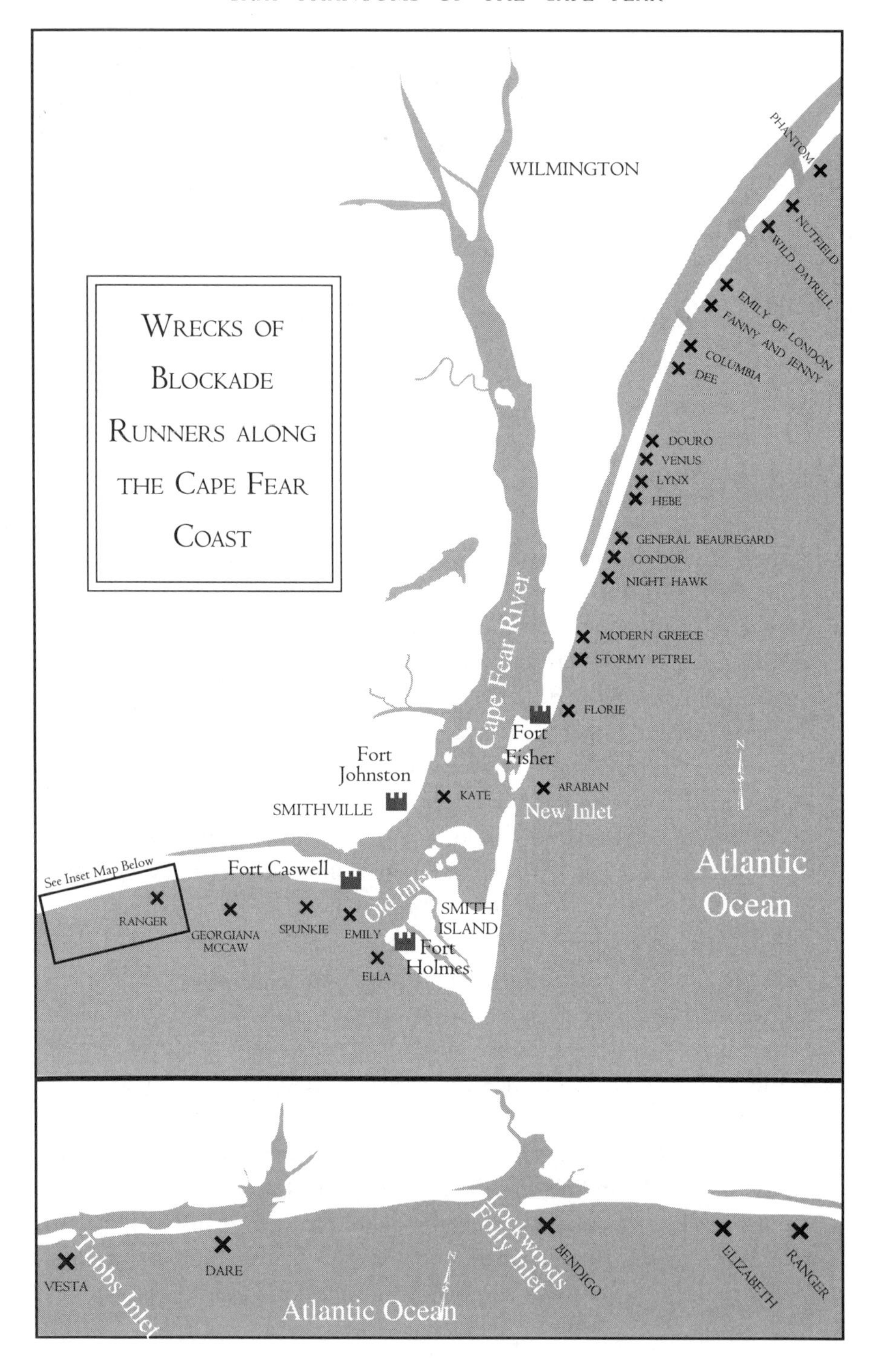
WRECKS OF BLOCKADE RUNNERS ALONG THE CAPE FEAR COAST
WILMINGTON
PHANTOM
NUTFIELD
WILD DAYRELL
EMILY OF LONDON
FANNY AND JENNY
COLUMBIA
DEE
DOURO
VENUS
LYNX
HEBE
GENERAL BEAUREGARD
CONDOR
NIGHT HAWK
MODERN GREECE
STORMY PETREL
FLORIE
Cape Fear River
Fort Fisher
Fort Johnston
SMITHVILLE
KATE
ARABIAN
New Inlet
Atlantic Ocean
See Inset Map Below
Fort Caswell
RANGER
GEORGIANA MCCAW
SPUNKIE
EMILY
Old Inlet
SMITH ISLAND
Fort Holmes
ELLA
VESTA
Tubbs Inlet
DARE
Lockwoods Folly Inlet
BENDIGO
ELIZABETH
RANGER
Atlantic Ocean

In a way, they were right, for even though the initially weak Union navy grew fantastically strong by war's end, it was not the blockade that stopped the flow of blockade runners. Rather, it was the capture of the ports themselves, beginning with New Orleans and ending with Wilmington. If the South had owned enough vessels, it might have tried to block Northern ports or lift the blockade around its own harbors. But the Confederacy was never able to acquire ships in great enough numbers to challenge the might of the Federal navy.

In the early days, running the Cape Fear blockade brought excitement to the participants and inspired the people of Wilmington. A holiday atmosphere prevailed around the wharves. Crowds gathered to cheer the arrival and departure of runners with hurrahs and choruses of "Dixie." What patriotic Southerner could fail to be heartened by the arrival of such beloved vessels as the *Advance* and the *Robert E. Lee*? The town helped make heroes of men like John Maffitt, Thomas Lockwood, and John Wilkinson.

Such gaiety was supplanted by a more sinister air as the blockade-running trade began to attract an undesirable element into town. Thieves and murderers soon strolled the streets around the docks. Disease took its toll. Avaricious out-of-town merchants assumed control of cargo auctions, driving prices beyond the reach of local vendors and inflating the price of even domestically produced food and goods. In the midst of plenty, Wilmingtonians suffered deprivation.

When Federal troops finally marched triumphantly into Wilmington in late February 1865, they found a hungry town where the residents dressed in patched clothing and paint was peeling from their formerly well-kept homes. Luckily, the conquerors spared the city the destruction suffered by other Southern towns.

*Opposite*: Wrecks of blockade runners at Cape Fear. The approximate locations of known wrecks of steamers gives evidence of the routes the ships followed and the hazards they faced in trying to evade the Union blockade of Wilmington. Many wooden ships also fell to the combined dangers of shoals and Yankee gunboats.

COURTESY OF THE NEW HANOVER COUNTY PUBLIC LIBRARY.

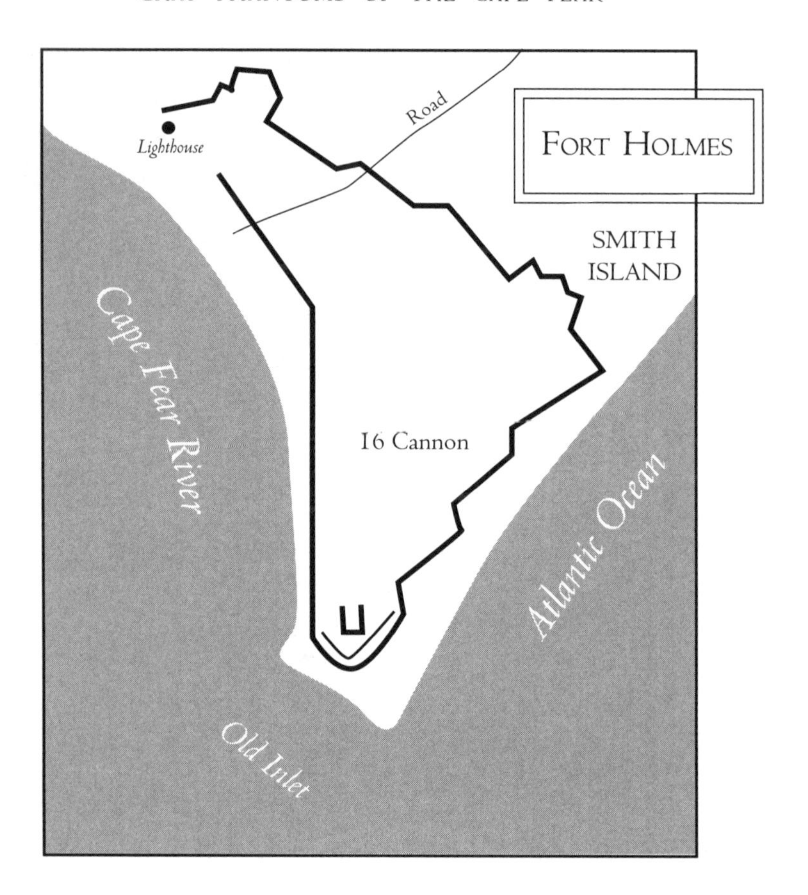
FORT HOLMES
Road
Lighthouse
SMITH ISLAND
Cape Fear River
16 Cannon
Atlantic Ocean
Old Inlet

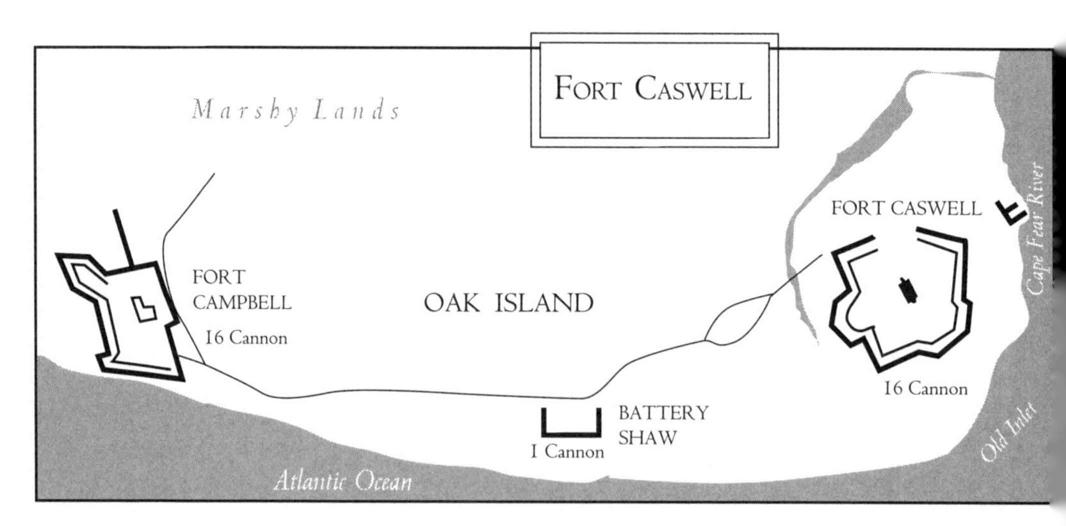
FORT CASWELL
Marshy Lands
FORT CASWELL
Cape Fear River
FORT CAMPBELL
16 Cannon
OAK ISLAND
16 Cannon
BATTERY SHAW
1 Cannon
Old Inlet
Atlantic Ocean

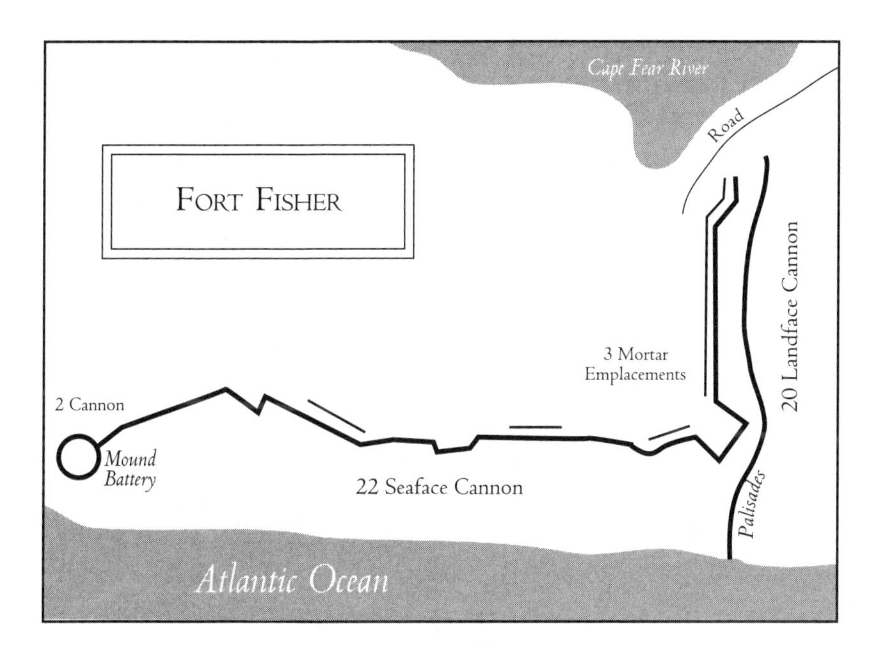
Cape Fear River
Road
FORT FISHER
20 Landface Cannon
3 Mortar Emplacements
2 Cannon
Mound Battery
22 Seaface Cannon
Palisades
Atlantic Ocean

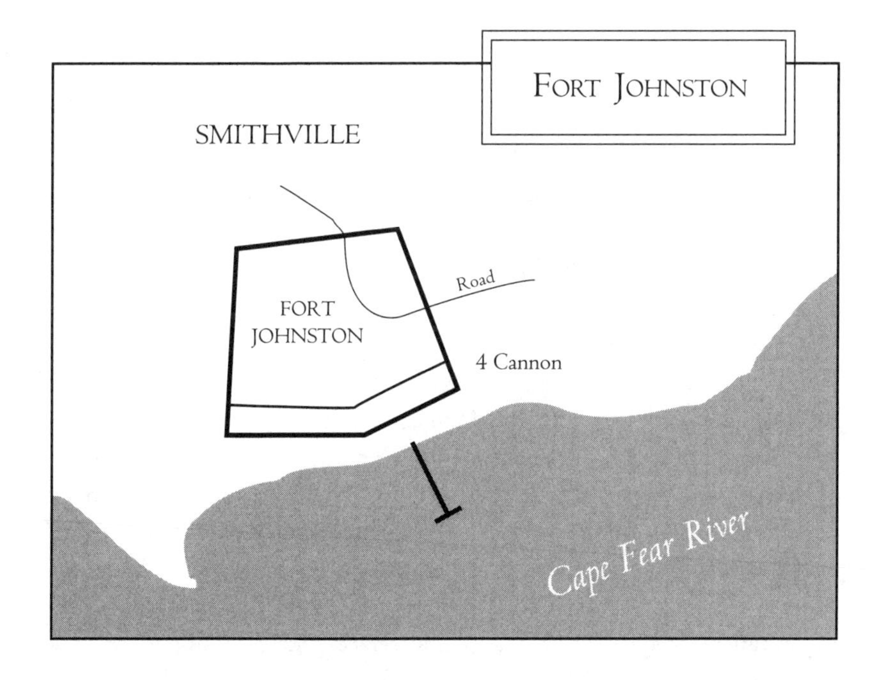
FORT JOHNSTON
SMITHVILLE
Road
FORT JOHNSTON
4 Cannon
Cape Fear River

Wilmington had suffered only minor damage during the war. An occasional fire had broken out around the docks, destroying bales of cotton, lumber, and other commodities. Some blamed Northern sympathizers, but accidents were the more likely culprit. Stacked everywhere around the piers were thousands of bales of dry cotton wrapped in combustible burlap. Sparks flew from the stacks of steamers, and darkness was lit by candles, lanterns, and other open flames. It's a wonder there were not more conflagrations.

At war's end, Wilmington's historic churches and other major buildings remained intact. The worst damage came at the hand of General Bragg, who ordered the burning of forts, ships, supplies, cotton, and even the cotton compress as he exercised his own brand of scorched-earth policy during the Confederate retreat.

Under the conqueror's heel, the residents were forced to swear an oath of allegiance to the United States. They still faced severe shortages of food and other goods, but that was nothing new to people who had endured years of war-induced poverty.

When Wilmington was closed, so was the blockade-running business. General Robert E. Lee had expressed the fear that if Wilmington fell, he would have to evacuate Richmond. It was a prophetic prediction. Within three months of the port town's capture, Lee surrendered to Grant at Appomattox. The long, deadly war that had lasted four years and cost more than half a million American lives was finally over.

Not all of those who suffered from the Confederate defeat were Southerners. Some of the businesses that had invested heavily in ships and credit on the South's behalf became rich. But others—like John Fraser and Company and its Liverpool branch, Fraser, Trenholm and Company—suffered bankruptcy when they were unable to collect the huge debts owed them by the former Southern government; George Alfred Trenholm, who joined the Confederate government as secretary of the treasury late in the struggle, was jailed. British companies hoped to reduce losses through the sale of blockade runners and undelivered cargoes, but United States Consul Thomas H. Dudley, who had been galled by their subversive activities during the war, did all in his power to prevent any recovery of assets. He seized and sold ships and supplies and sent the proceeds directly to the United States.

After the war, blockade runners were converted to peacetime uses by their owners or were taken over by the United States and sold. Whether they had served for monetary gain or out of loyalty to the Southern cause, the crews had to seek new work. Although Augustus Charles Hobart-Hampden went on to become a hero in the Turkish navy, most officers and crewmen of the runners never again knew such stimulating and financially rewarding times as in the heyday of the Southern blockade-running contest.

Altogether, almost a hundred blockade-running steamers were captured during the war, and nearly three dozen were stranded or forced ashore on the treacherous reefs at Cape Fear. Men lost their lives or were tossed into Northern jails when their ships were taken.

In spite of the monumental odds against them, the sleek blockade runners, propellers or sidewheels churning, glided through the fog-shrouded waters of Cape Fear and slipped through the enemy's clutches like phantoms in the night. Built for a unique mission at a brief moment in time, they performed their role with exceptional success. But when the war ended, they faded into the mists of history, disappearing as they had done so well so many times. There had never been ships like the blockade runners, and their kind will never be seen again.

Today, the rusting, coral-encrusted relics of more than thirty blockade runners inhabit the surf from the South Carolina border to Topsail Island, North Carolina. They have been left at the mercy of the currents, to be tumbled about by hurricanes and storm waves until little is left to show. Cargo holds that once carried munitions, food, and uniforms for Confederate soldiers are filled with sand, and the compartments where sailors huddled to escape cannon fire serve as hiding places for fish.

Few except fishermen and boaters know where they rest. Soon, when all the woodwork has decayed and the last metal plate has rusted away, they will vanish entirely. But when they were new, bearing fresh coats of gray paint, traveling with speed and stealth, they were the arteries of the Confederate States of America. And when those arteries were severed, the lifeblood of the Southern armies ebbed away.

# APPENDIX:

## *Sample Cargo of a Confederate-Owned Blockade Runner*

THE FOLLOWING IS a list of the cargo delivered by the *Robert E. Lee* in one trip to Wilmington in July 1863. This information comes from the John Payne Papers ("Wilmington Manifest") and is reprinted by permission of the Eleanor S. Brockenbrough Library, Museum of the Confederacy, Richmond, Virginia.

200 cases Enfield rifles
1 case Tower muskets
375 cases Enfield cartridges
10 cases percussion caps
50 bales cartridge paper
25 cases cartridge paper
3 cases ammunition paper
28 cases leather
1 case pouch meddlings
19 cases cavalry saddlery and equipment
18 cases knapsacks
6 cases stationery
1 case shellac
1 case verdigris (toxic green paint used as a wood preservative)
11 cases steel
1 case bristles

15 cases brushes
3 cases sewing thread
4 cases shoe thread
13 bales white serge
21 bales horse blankets
6 bales numnahs (squares of coarse felt from India)
113 bales greatcoats
32 bales trousers
48 bales cloth
2 bales gray cloth
2 bales blue cloth
1 bale knapsack lining
1 bale scarlet cloth
5 cases cavalry swords
9 cases cavalry accoutrements
4 casks ink
1 keg red arsenic
1 barrel saltpeter
5 casks files
3 casks zinc
100 boxes sheet tin
59 bundles steel ramrods
4 cases mess tins
3 cases cavalry belts
250 pigs lead

# BIBLIOGRAPHY


Axelrod, Alan. *The War Between the Spies: A History of Espionage during the American Civil War.* New York: Atlantic Monthly Press, 1992.

Aycock, Robert, and Elsie J. Aycock. *The Civil War Letters of W. D. Carr of Duplin County, North Carolina.* Raleigh, N.C.: privately printed, 1995.

Barrett, John G. *The Civil War in North Carolina.* Chapel Hill, N.C.: University of North Carolina Press, 1963.

Black, Robert C. *The Railroads of the Confederacy.* Chapel Hill, N.C.: University of North Carolina Press, 1952.

Bonham, Milledge L., Jr. *The British Consuls in the Confederacy.* New York: Columbia University, 1911.

Brown, Jim, and Ken Burns. *Songs of the Civil War.* New York: Ginger Group Productions, Inc., and American Documentaries, Inc., 1991. Documentary film.

Browning, Robert M. "The Blockade of Wilmington, 1861–1865." Master's thesis, East Carolina University, 1980.

Curtis, Walter G. *Reminiscences of Wilmington and Smithville (Southport), 1848–1900.* Southport, N.C.: Herald Job Office, 1901.

Daly, Robert W., ed. *Aboard the USS* Florida: *1863–65.* Annapolis, Md.: United States Naval Institute.

Davis, George B., ed. *The Official Atlas of the Civil War.* New York: Arno Press, 1978.

Edwards, William B. *Civil War Guns.* Harrisburg, Pa.: Stackpole, 1962.

Foster, Kevin J. "The Search for Speed under Steam: The Design of Blockade Running Steamships, 1861–1865." Master's thesis, East Carolina University, 1991.

Gorgas, Josiah. "Notes on the Ordnance Department of the Confederate Government." *Southern Historical Society Papers* (1884): 68–75.

Gragg, Rod. *Confederate Goliath: The Battle of Fort Fisher.* New York: HarperCollins Publishers, 1991.

Greenhow, Rose O'Neal. Papers. Special Collections Library, Duke University.

Hattaway, Herman, and Archer Jones. *How the North Won: A Military History of the Civil War.* Chicago: University of Chicago Press, 1983.

Herring, Ethel, and Carole Williams. *Fort Caswell in War and Peace.* Wendell, N.C.: Broadfoot's Bookmark, 1975.

"Hidden beneath the Waves: Engine Information." Unpublished paper available through the North Carolina Underwater Archaeology Unit and the Cape Fear Museum.

Hill, Daniel H. *A History of North Carolina in the War Between the States: Bethel to Sharpsburg.* Raleigh, N.C.: Edwards and Broughton, 1926.

Hobart-Hampden, Augustus C. *Never Caught.* London: John Camden Holton, 1867.

Jones, John B. *A Rebel War Clerk's Diary.* New York: Sagamore Press, 1958.

Jones, Virgil C. *The Civil War at Sea.* Vol. I, *The Blockaders.* New York: Holt, Rinehart & Winston, 1960.

Lamb, William. *Colonel Lamb's Story of Fort Fisher*. Carolina Beach, N.C.: Blockade Runner Museum, 1966.

Loy, Wesley. "10 Rumford Place: Doing Confederate Business in Liverpool." *South Carolina Historical Magazine* 98 (October 1997): 349–74.

Maclay, Edgar Stanton. *Reminiscences of the Old Navy*. New York: G. P. Putnam's Sons, Knickerbocker Press, 1898.

Morgan, James M. *Recollections of a Rebel Reefer*. New York: Houghton Mifflin, 1917.

*Official Records of the Union and Confederate Navies in the War of the Rebellion*. Series I. Washington: GPO, 1899–1901.

Owlsey, Frank. *King Cotton Diplomacy: Foreign Relations of the Confederate States of America*. Chicago: University of Chicago Press, 1931.

Payne, John M. Papers. ("Wilmington Manifest.") Eleanor S. Brockenbrough Library, Museum of the Confederacy, Richmond, Va.

Porter, David D. *The Naval History of the Civil War*. New York: Sherman Publishing, 1886.

Price, Marcus W. "Masters and Pilots Who Tested the Blockade of Confederate Ports, 1861–1865." *American Neptune* (April 1961): 81–106.

———. "Ships That Tested the Blockade of the Carolina Ports, 1861–1865." *American Neptune* (April 1948): 196–241.

Robinson, Kenneth W. "North Carolina's Blockade Running Partnership: An Effort toward Self-Sufficiency during the Civil War." Master's thesis, North Carolina State University, 1974.

Rye, Scott. *Men and Ships of the Civil War*. Stamford, Conn.: Longmeadow Press, 1995.

Shingleton, Royce. *High Seas Confederate: The Life and Times of John Newland Maffitt.* Columbia, S.C.: University of South Carolina Press, 1994.

Soley, James R. *The Blockade and the Cruisers.* New York: Scribner's, 1883.

Sprunt, James. *Chronicles of the Cape Fear River.* Raleigh, N.C.: Edwards and Broughton, 1916.

———. *Derelicts.* Wilmington, N.C.: Lord Baltimore Press, 1920.

———. "Running the Blockade." *Southern Historical Society Papers* 24 (January-December 1896): 225–29.

———. *Tales of the Cape Fear Blockade: Being a Turn of the Century Account of Blockade Running.* Raleigh, N.C.: Capital Printing, 1902.

Stick, David. *Bald Head: A History of Smith Island and Cape Fear.* Wendell, N.C.: Broadfoot Publishing Company, 1985.

———. *Graveyard of the Atlantic: Shipwrecks of the North Carolina Coast.* Chapel Hill, N.C.: University of North Carolina Press, 1958.

Still, William N. *Iron Afloat.* Nashville, Tenn.: Vanderbilt University Press, 1969.

Taylor, Thomas E. *Running the Blockade.* London: J. Murray, 1896.

Trotter, William R. *The Civil War in North Carolina.* Vol. 3, *Ironclads and Columbiads.* Winston-Salem, N.C.: John F. Blair, Publisher, 1989.

Usina, Michael P. "Blockade Running in Confederate Times." In *Addresses Delivered before the Confederate Veterans Association.* Savannah, Ga.: United Confederate Veterans, 1895.

Vance, Zebulon Baird. *The Papers of Zebulon Baird Vance.* Vols. 1 and 2. Raleigh, N.C.: North Carolina Division of Archives and History, 1963, 1995.

Vandiver, Frank, ed. *Confederate Blockade Running through Bermuda, 1861–1865: Letter and Cargo Manifests.* Austin, Tex.: University of Texas Press, 1947.

Wilkinson, John. *The Narrative of a Blockade Runner.* New York: Sheldon and Company, 1877.

"Wilmington and the Blockade Runners." *Confederate Veteran* 29 (January-December 1921): 258–59.

*Wilmington Daily Journal,* 1861–65.

Wise, Stephen R. *Lifeline of the Confederacy: Blockade Running during the Civil War.* Columbia, S.C.: University of South Carolina Press, 1988. I consider this to be the definitive work on blockade running. Wise's carefully compiled bibliography is the most complete I have seen.

Wood, Richard Everett. "Port Town at War: Wilmington, North Carolina, 1860–1865." Ph.D. diss., Florida State University, 1976.

# INDEX

*A. D. Vance*. *See Advance*
*Advance*, 132, 163, 171-72, 176-80, 182, 190, 209
*Aedes Aegypti* mosquito, 139
Alexander Collie and Company, 176-77, 180, 182-83
Anaconda Plan, 10
Anderson, Edward C., 102, 165-66
Anderson, John William, 133-34
Anderson, Joseph, 143
Anglo-Confederate Trading Company, 95
*Annie*, 163, 176, 178, 183
*A. P. Hart*, 144
*Arabian*, 35
*Arctic*, 62
Armstrong gun, 50, 58
Army of Northern Virginia, 49, 130
Atlantic Blockading Squadron, 14, 16, 25 *See also* North Atlantic Blockading Squadron

Bahamas, 71, 73, 81, 82, 84-85, 93
Bahamas Channel 69, 73
Bald Head Island, 205. *See also* Smith Island
*Banshee*, 95-99, 101, 114, 132, 137-38
Barbados, 71
*Bat*, 101, 183
Battery Bolles, 56
Battery Buchanan, 62, 148, 196
Battery Gatlin, 62
Battery Holmes, 51
Battery Shaw, 51, 205
Bayne, Thomas, 167
Beaufort, N. C., 7, 11-12, 14, 24-25, 37, 46-47, 60, 165
Beauregard, P. G. T., 106
Benjamin, Judah P., 103, 112
Benjamin W. Beery and Sons, 145
Bensel, Joseph, 132
Bermuda, 4, 16, 37, 73, 80-81, 88, 134; blockaders guard route to, 34, 193, 203; Charles Wilkes resents actions of, 71-72; coal shortages at, 31, 76, 113; Rose Greenhow visits, 107; serves as port for blockade runners, 146, 158, 168, 172-74, 176, 178-79, 182, 202; transhipment of supplies through, 82, 84-87, 93, 103, 160, 167; U. S. consuls report on activities of, 109, 199; yellow fever strikes, 133
*Bermuda*, 102-4
Birkenhead, 101, 122
Blakely gun, 38, 58, 167
*Blenheim*, 202, 204
Bogue Inlet, 174
Bourne, John Tory, 84-85, 87, 167
Boyd, Belle, 109
Bragg, Braxton, 148-49, 187, 196-98, 212
Braine, Daniel L. 8, 27-30, 34, 91-92
Bridgetown, Barbados, 71
Brinkman, Thomas W., 109-10
British Parliament, 99
Brooke gun, 51-52, 58, 148
Brunswick River, 127
Bulloch, James, 101-2, 112, 165
Burroughs, James, 160
Burruss, Tom, 96-98, 132
Butler, Benjamin, 47, 187, 190, 195, 199, 203

Caird and Company, 171
Cantwell, John N., 44
Cape Fear District, 56
Cape Lookout, 174, 179
Caribbean, 129-30
Case, A. Ludlow, 5, 31, 77-79, 159
Cassidey Boat Builders, 145
Caswell, Richard, 46
*Chameleon*, 148, 200-201
Charleston, S. C., 3, 14-15, 80, 101-2, 130, 136, 150, 166, 202
Charleston Harbor, 15, 84, 102, 140
*Charlotte*, 202, 204
Chase, Samuel P., 75
Chatham County, N. C., 77, 178
Chesapeake Bay, Va., 14-15, 114
*City of Petersburg*, 132
Clark, Henry Toole, 70
Clary, A. G., 164-65
Clitz, John M. B., 199
Clyde River, 113, 121-22
*Colonel Lamb*, 101,122
Colquitt, Alfred H., 197
Columbiad gun, 51-52, 58
Committee of Safety, 145
Compton, Lord Spencer (earl of Wilmington), 128
*Condor*, 109-11
Confederate Commissary Bureau, 184
Confederate Congress, 182
"Confederate Embassy," 100
Confederate Navy, 202-3
Confederate Ordnance Bureau, 158, 160, 166-67, 203
Confederate Point, 56-57
Confederate Quartermaster Bureau, 184, 203
Confederate States of America, 10, 44, 56, 69, 88, 103, 213
Confederate War Department, 170, 181, 183, 203
*Cornubia*, 132, 158-60, 167-70, 173
Cory, Captain, 163
Cotton compress, 140
Cox, G. V., 35
Coxetter, Louis M., 53
Crosby, Pierce, 54
Crossan, Thomas Morrow, 171
*CSS Alabama*, 70
*CSS Albemarle*, 199
*CSS Chickamauga*, 147-48, 198
*CSS Florida*, 70-71, 101, 199
*CSS North Carolina*, 64, 144-45, 147, 181
*CSS Olustee*, 148, 202. *See also CSS Tallahassee*
*CSS Raleigh*, 145, 147
*CSS Tallahassee*, 147-48
*CSS Virginia*, 64, 114, 147
Cushing, William B., 38, 205

Dahlgren gun, 38
Danville, Va., 130
Dardingkiller, Frederick, 43-44
Davis, Jefferson, 14, 51, 109, 148-49, 166, 175-76, 182
Dawson, John, 136, 145
Declaration of Paris, 10, 13-14
*Deer*, 183
DeHaven, Joseph E., 23
Department of the Navy, 24-25
deRossett, Mrs. Armand J., 149
*Despatch*, 95
*Desperate*, 71
*Don*, 18-22, 115-16, 163-64, 165, 176, 178, 182
Dosher, John Julius, 132
"Dram Tree," 128
Dudley, Thomas H., 100-101, 212
*Duoro*, 35

DuPont, Samuel F., 25

Eagle Island, 145
Earle, William, 30
Edward Lawrence and Company, 95
*Elizabeth*, 35
*Ella and Annie*, 35
Ellis, John, 43-45, 62, 141
Emile Erlanger Company, 103, 112
*Emma*, 190
*Eugenia*, 167

*Fanny and Jenny*, 53-55
Farragut, David, 14, 88
Fayetteville, N. C., 16, 93, 129
Federal Point, 7, 22, 55-56, 144, 196, 202. *See also* Confederate Point
*Fingal*, 165
Florida, 25
Fort Anderson, 56, 64-65, 205
Fort Campbell, 51-52, 205
Fort Caswell, 30-31, 43-47, 50-52, 59, 62, 167, 198, 202, 205
Fort Clark, 15, 46-47
Fort Fisher, 35, 53, 56, 98, 104, 110, 122, 156, 158, 183; armaments of, 29, 48-49, 62, 99, 105, 111, 147, 161, 167, 188; assault on, 149, 180, 187-88, 190, 196, 199, 203; assists blockade runners, 18, 22, 97, 137, 157; Colonel Lamb heads expansion of, 57-58, 122, 144; Federals' capture of, 88, 172, 197-98, 200, 202, 204-5; number of troops at, 59; Whitworths protect blockade runners near, 54, 60-61
Fort Hatteras, 15, 46-47
Fort Holmes, 51-52, 205
Fort Johnston, N. C., 43-47, 50, 52, 205
Fort Johnston, Ohio, 174
Fort Macon, 15, 46-47
Fort St. Phillip, 56
Fort Sumter, 9, 44, 144
France, 10, 69, 103, 108, 112
Fraser, Trenholm and Company, 84, 101, 103, 166, 183, 212
French, Samuel, 57, 143-44
Frying Pan Shoals, 7-8, 15, 22, 55, 91, 93
*Frying Pan Shoals Lightship #8*, 62, 64-65

Gage, Henry, 92
"Gateway to the Confederacy," 128, 198, 206-7
Gayle, Richard, 158-59, 168, 203-4
German Volunteers, 45
Gettysburg, Penn., 177
"Gibraltar of the South," 57
*Giraffe*, 11-13, 173. *See also Robert E. Lee*
Glasgow, Scotland, 122
Glisson, O. S., 179-80
Goldsboro, N. C., 130
Goldsborough, Louis M., 25-26, 127
Gorgas, Josiah, 83, 166-67, 176
Grant, U. S., 212
Graveyard of the Atlantic, 16
Great Britain, 70, 73, 81, 94, 100-103
Green, Charles, 7-8
Greenhow, Dr. Robert, 105
Greenhow, Rose O'Neal, 105-9, 111
Greensboro, N. C., 130
Grissom, Ron, 28
Gulf Blockading Squadron, 70
Gulf of Mexico, 14
Gulf Stream, 11, 34, 207
Guthrie, Archibald, 132

Halifax, Nova Scotia, 80, 84, 109
Hampton Roads, Va. 15, 22-24, 179
*Hansa*, 163, 176, 178, 181

Hatteras Island, 47
Havana, Cuba, 84
*Hebe*, 35, 60-61
Henry Adderly and Company, 84-85, 92
Heyliger, Louis, 84
Hobart-Hampden, Augustus Charles, 18-19, 87, 115, 163, 213
Hoke, Robert, 190
Holmes, Theophilus, 51
Hooker, Edward, 13
Hotze, Henry, 94, 99
Huse, Caleb, 83-84, 101-2, 112, 158, 165-67
Huse, Samuel, 179

*Index*, 99

James Jack and Company, 122
John Fraser and Company, 15, 84, 101-2, 166, 212
John Laird and Sons, 101
John William Dudgeon of London, 18
Johnston, Gabriel, 45
Jones, Quiggin and Company, 101, 122
*J. T. Petteway*, 144
*Juno*, 35

*Kate*, 25-26, 127, 132, 134-35, 139
*Kate McLaurin*, 144
Kemble, Edmund, 104
Key West, Fla., 14
Knox, John, 174

Ladies' Soldiers' Aid Society, 149
Lamb, William, 56-58, 61, 137, 144, 160, 161, 187, 188, 195-97
Lamsen, Roswell H., 48-49
Lee, Robert E., 15, 85, 148, 173, 177, 202, 212
Lee, Samuel Phillips, 18, 26-27, 31, 34-35, 132, 142, 180, 193
Leffy, Henry, S., 28
*Lilian*, 190, 204
Lincoln, Abraham, 3, 9-10, 13, 44, 54, 81
*Little Ada*, 190
*Little Hattie*, 27-30
Liverpool, England, 84, 95, 101-3, 166, 183, 212
Lockwood, Thomas, 127, 209
Lockwoods Folly, 35
Lookout Shoals, 12
*Lord Clyde*, 171. *See also Advance*
Lords Proprietors, 45
Lynch, William F., 149, 181

MacDiarmid, John, 77
Maffitt, John N., 71, 199, 202-3, 209
Mallory, Stephen, 162, 166, 176, 203
Manassas, 106
*Margaret and Jessie*, 35
Martin, James G., 170
*Mary Celestia*, 131, 133-34
Mason, James Murray, 69-70, 103, 112
Masonboro Inlet, 27, 160
McCook, Roderick S., 157, 161
McRae, C. J., 112, 177, 183
McRae, Duncan Kirkland, 170-71
*Merrimac*, 167
Mersey River, 100
Merseyside, 122
*Minho*, 87
Mississippi River, 10, 166
Mobile, Ala., 3, 14
*Modern Greece*, 61, 155-57, 161-62, 167
Morehead City, N. C., 14-15, 47
Morris, Wilkes, 162
Morse, C. C., 132
Mosquito Fleet, 47

Mound battery, 18, 22, 48, 58-59, 98, 110
Murray, Charles, 48-49
Muse, William, 170

Nassau, 4, 16, 37, 48, 73, 75; as port for blockade runners, 11, 28, 92, 96, 127, 135, 138, 182, 200-201; as transshipment base, 84, 103, 160; Charles Wilkes complains about, 71-72; Civil War improves life at, 85-87; Consuls report on activities of, 81, 109, 199; yellow fever strikes, 80, 134
Naval Pension Fund, 37
New Inlet, 18, 55, 59; blockade of, 7, 22, 26-27, 31, 32, 34, 123; blockade runners aim for, 20-21, 53, 96, 99, 104, 109, 115, 155-57, 160; blockade runners escape into, 12, 28-30, 49, 116, 133; shallow waters cause problems, 147, 178; Yankees take control of, 198-99, 202, 204
New Orleans, La., 3, 14-15, 35, 150, 209
New Providence, 71, 73
New Town (Newton), 128
New York, 69-70, 75, 92, 198
New York Harbor, 75
*Night Hawk*, 104-5, 111, 132
Norfolk, Va., 14-15, 47, 56
North Atlantic Blockading Squadron, 4, 25-27; improvements increase success of, 35, 115, 123, 158, 175, 193, 200, 203; problems of, 4-5, 8-9, 38, 122, 127
North Breaker Shoal, 98
North Carolina assembly, 45
North Carolina Department, 51
North Carolina Railroad, 130
*North Heath*, 132
Northern prize courts, 60
Nova Scotia, 174
*Nutfield*, 193-94

Oakdale Cemetery, 111, 139
Oak Island, 46, 51
Ocracoke Island, 47
Old Inlet, 43, 51-52, 55-56, 64, 122-23, 146, 198; blockaders have difficulty at, 8, 22, 30, 34; Confederates destroy forts at, 198; Maffitt escapes from, 202; Porter captures blockade runners at, 203-4
Ord, H. St. George, 71
*Oreto*, 101. *See also CSS Florida*
O. S. Baldwin's store, 162
Outer Banks, 15, 47
*Owl*, 101, 183, 199, 202

Pamlico Sound, 47
Parker, William A., 157, 161
Parrot gun, 38, 157
Petersburg Railroad, 130
*Phantom*, 35, 107, 167
Philadelphia, Penn., 75
Plymouth, N. C., 199
Porter, David, 27, 188-89, 191-92, 195-96, 198-99, 202-5
Port Royal, S. C., 14-15
Prioleau, Charles Kuhn, 102

Raleigh, N. C., 175, 182
*Rattlesnake*, 202
*Revere*, 92
Revolutionary War, 45-46
Richmond, Va., 4, 47, 50, 130, 149, 165, 212; efforts to control blockade running at, 151, 160, 167; Governor Vance has trouble with, 171, 175-78, 182, 184
Ridge, Samuel, 109-11
*Robert E. Lee*, 13, 31, 76-80, 87, 132, 146, 167, 173-75, 209

Roberts, Captain, 19-21. *See also* Hobart-Hampden, Augustus Charles
Roe, Francis A., 142-43, 193
Royal Navy, 19
Royal Victoria Hotel, 87
Russell, Lord John, 81

Sanders, George Nicholas, 170
Sands, Benjamin F., 24, 26, 31, 35
Savannah, Ga., 14-15, 102, 165
Scotland, 100, 109, 113, 122-23, 171-73
Seddon, James, 167, 169, 176-77, 180-83
Seixas, J. M., 85, 167
Seward, William, 16, 70, 81, 105
Sewell's Point, Va., 50, 56
Sherman, William T. 197
Sherman's March to the Sea, 151
Slidell, John, 69-70, 103, 112
Smith Island, 49-52, 55, 62, 202
Smithville, 43-44, 109, 129, 132, 205; as anchorage for blockade runners, 134-135, 178, 181, 199, 202; quarantine station established near, 140
South Carolina, 14, 25, 73, 197, 201, 213
Sparrow, Thomas, 176
Spence, James, 103
*Stag*, 183, 202-4
Stansbury, Smith, 84
St. George's, 19, 71-73, 75, 77, 80, 81, 84-88, 107, 133, 203
Steele, Jonathan W., 96-98, 137-38
Stone, Edward E., 17
Stringham, Silas S., 16-17, 24-25, 47
Swift, Joseph Garner, 46

Tar Heels, 176
Taylor, Thomas, 96
Tenth Regiment of North Carolina, 176
Terry, Alfred H., 188, 190-92, 195-96
Thalian Hall, 129
Thirtieth North Carolina Regiment, 44
Thirty-sixth North Carolina Artillery, 57
*Thomas L. Wragg* (formerly the *Nashville*), 25-26, 127
Thornburn, Lieutenant Colonel, 172, 175-76
Throwbridge, Edward, 70-71
Topsail Island, N. C., 158, 213
Trathen, James, 159-60
Trenholm, George Alfred, 102, 212
*Trent*, 69-70, 103
*Tubal Cain*, 98-99
Turkish navy, 213
Twenty-four Hour Rule, 71

*Uncle Ben*, 64, 144
United States Blockade Strategy Board, 65
United States Navy, 15, 46, 58, 64, 71, 123, 199, 205; adopts blockade runner tactics, 12, 123; Britain has trouble with, 103, 105; challenges faced by, 3, 4, 19, 28, 34, 95, 128
U. S. Congress, 133, 46, 70
Usina, Michael, 202-3
*USS Britannia*, 179
*USS Cambridge*, 23, 26, 32, 156-58, 161
*USS Canonicus*, 188
*USS Chocura*, 23
*USS Cumberland*, 25
*USS Daylight*, 17, 22, 32, 158
*USS Dacotah*, 23, 26, 30-31, 35, 163-65
*USS Florida*, 54, 77, 143, 194
*USS Fort Donelson*, 175, 190
*USS Frolic*, 180
*USS Fulton*, 35-36
*USS Gemsbok*, 25
*USS Gettysburg*, 204
*USS Howquah*, 30, 35-36

*USS Iron Age*, 17
*USS Iroquois*, 5, 31, 77-79, 158-59
*USS James Adger*, 168-69, 174
*USS Jamestown*, 5, 8
*USS Keystone State*, 35-36, 191
*USS Mahopac*, 188
*USS Malvern*, 199, 203-5
*USS Maratanza*, 23
*USS Minnesota*, 17, 137-38, 189
*USS Monadnock*, 188
*USS Monticello*, 7-8, 34, 50, 91-92, 205
*USS Mount Vernon*, 7, 32-34, 158-60
*USS Mystic*, 18, 91
*USS Nansemond*, 35-36, 48, 49
*USS New Ironsides*, 188-89, 191, 199
*USS Niphon*, 35-36, 60-61, 104-5, 110-11, 167, 169
*USS Penobscot*, 24
*USS Pequot*, 27-29, 182
*USS Peterhoff*, 18, 34
*USS Tristram Shandy*, 204
*USS Quaker State*, 163
*USS Santiago de Cuba*, 179, 182, 191
*USS Sassacus*, 142-43, 193-94
*USS Saugus*, 188
*USS Sonoma*, 71-72
*USS Stars and Stripes*, 157, 161
*USS State of Georgia*, 18, 158
*USS Tioga*, 71-72
*USS Vanderbilt*, 200
*USS Victoria*, 7-8, 13, 77
*USS Wachusett*, 71
*USS Young Rover*, 25

Vance, Zebulon Baird, 149, 170-72, 175-78, 180, 182, 184
*Venus*, 35, 48-49
Virginia, 10, 16, 25, 47, 56, 85, 130, 141, 176

Walker, James, 71
Walker, Norman S., 84, 87, 167
War of 1812, 70
Washington, D. C., 9, 14, 65, 106
Weldon, N. C., 130
Welles, Gideon, 13-14, 16-17, 24-26, 32, 70, 72, 85, 88, 93
West India Squadron, 70, 72
West Indies, 84, 93
West Point, 9
Western Bar, 27, 30, 46, 50, 52, 55, 64, 122
White, John, 171, 176
Whiting, Samuel, 81
Whiting, William Henry Chase, 141, 143, 175; bickers with Confederate navy, 149, 181; builds Cape Fear defenses, 47, 50, 57, 64, 65, 144; participates in defense of Fort Fisher, 187-88, 196-97
Whitworth gun, 38, 48, 53-54, 60-62, 155, 161-62, 194
*Wild Dayrell*, 101, 142-43
Wilkes, Charles, 69-73, 88, 103
Wilkinson, John, 11-12, 76-80, 87, 121, 146-48, 173-75, 199-203, 209
William C. Miller and Sons, 101
Wilmington and Weldon Railroad, 16, 130, 141-42
Wilmington and Manchester Railroad, 130
Wilmington and Rutherford Railroad, 130
*Wilmington Daily Journal*, 136, 139, 162
Wilmington Light Infantry, 45
Wilmington Rifle Guards, 45
Wyllie, Joannes, 178-79